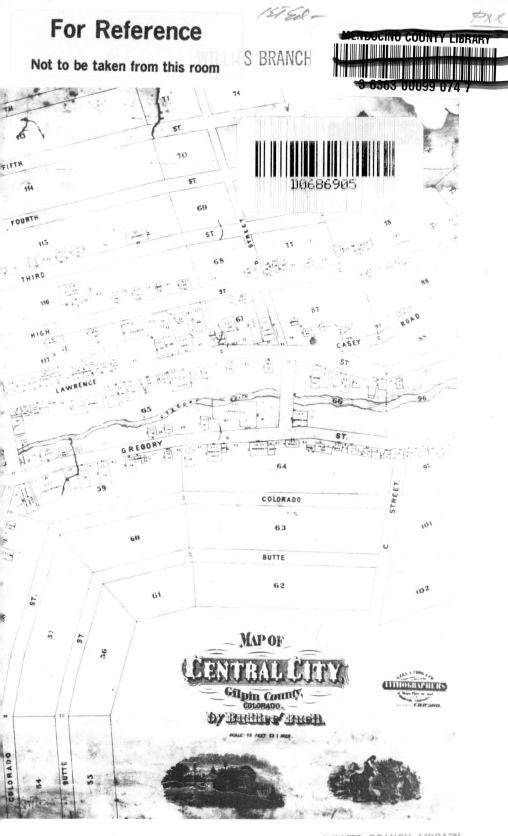

MAP OF

CENTRAL CITY,

Gilpin County,
COLORADO.

GILPIN COUNTY
GOLD

Peter Barclay McFarlane
(1848-1929)

GILPIN COUNTY

GOLD

PETER McFARLANE

1848-1929

Mining Entrepreneur in Central City, Colorado

H. WILLIAM AXFORD

SAGE BOOKS

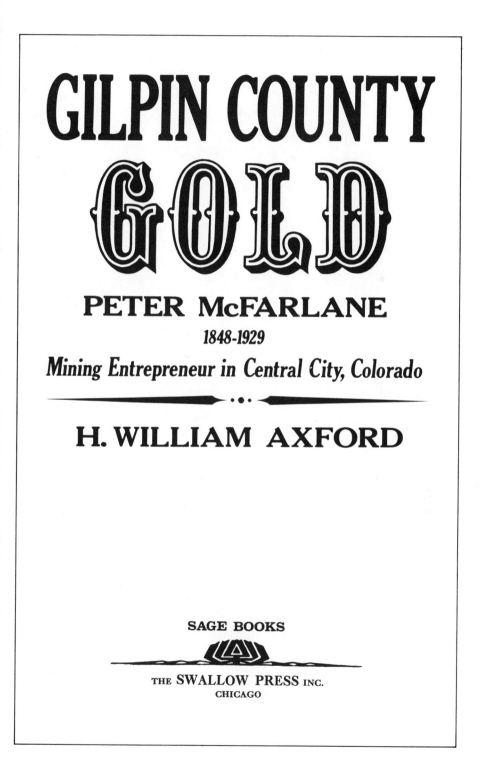

THE SWALLOW PRESS INC.
CHICAGO

First Edition
  First Printing

Sage Books are published by
The Swallow Press Incorporated
811 West Junior Terrace
Chicago, Illinois 60613

This book is printed on recycled paper

ISBN 0-8040-0550-8
Library of Congress Catalog Card Number 76-115034

*To Lavonne
who rekindled the flame
and has
nourished it ever since.*

Contents

Illustrations

Maps

Preface

PETER MCFARLANE came to Central City in 1869. With his brother, William O. McFarlane, he founded one of the most important mine and mill equipment companies in Colorado; at one time they operated foundries and machine shops in Black Hawk and Denver as well as Central City. Peter McFarlane's career was inextricably bound to the mining industry of Gilpin County where he lived for sixty years, and the history of this industry provides the framework for the story of his life.

McFarlane came to Gilpin County at the start of the second stage of the development of its mining industry, when the deposits of placer and oxidized surface gold had been largely exhausted and the industry was faced with the problem of how to extract gold from low-grade sulphide ores. Ore treatment methods brought from California were not applicable in Gilpin County once deep, hard-rock mining had begun. Through several years of experimentation the Gilpin County millmen developed an ore-crushing machine known as the Gilpin County Slow Drop Stamp Mill which could retrieve with auxiliary equipment as much as 75% of the gold in a lode of ore. McFarlane played a significant role in the development of the slow drop stamp mill and a major role in the design of another machine for the treatment of Gilpin County ores, the Gilpin County Gilt Edge Concentrator. The slow drop stamp mill generated an extended and heated controversy among mining engineers on a national level, but McFarlane, despite severe personal criticism, never waivered in his belief that it constituted the only efficient way to treat Gilpin County ores.

In addition to being one of its leading business figures, McFarlane was probably Gilpin County's most civic minded citizen, particularly during the long period of decline in the mining industry after the turn of the century. He sought without success to restore Central City's famous hotel, The Teller House, but earned the gratitude of future generations for his role in establishing the Cold Spring Camp Ground on Highway 119 near Missouri Lake and through his preservation of the Opera House. The McFarlane brothers helped build the Opera House; Peter McFarlane later owned it, repaired it, and filled it with entertainment from the turn of the century until New Year's Day 1927. Through his heirs, the historic old building finally passed into the hands of the Central City Opera House Association, and today it is the home of an internationally acclaimed summer opera and theatre festival.

Before its mines could no longer be profitably worked, Gilpin County poured over $84,000,000 worth of gold into the coffers of the nation and made its own unique contribution to the amalgam of fact, fiction, legend, and romance that surrounds the history of the mining frontier in the West. McFarlane, to the end of his life in 1929, believed that the Gilpin County mining industry could be revived, and his last years were marked by a number of futile attempts to discover a paying lode. Spanning as it did almost the entire history of Gilpin County mining, his career forms a unique and illuminating chapter in the history of the area once known as "the richest square mile on earth." The county was also affectionately referred to by its citizens as the "Little Kingdom of Gilpin." By any measurement, Peter McFarlane was one of its "princes."

CHAPTER I

The Early Years
1848–1869

PETER BARCLAY MCFARLANE was born in Bedeque, Prince Edward Island, on May 9, 1848, one of thirteen children of a Scotch farming family.[1] He came into the world where the strong, clean smell of the sea drifted across an island of rolling fields dispersed among forests of white birch and pine, fir, spruce, maple, and hemlock.[2]

Of his childhood, very little is known. Several references in Peter's diaries and a few cherished anecdotes passed on to his children by his brothers and sisters provide our only primary insights into that period. However, it is possible to sketch in broad strokes the environment in which he grew and some of the influences of his early years.

Life on a farm in the Maritime Provinces of Canada in the middle of the nineteenth century, despite an abundance of physical chores, was not without its own special pleasures for a growing boy.[3] The forest provided the chance for a close communion with nature and served as a majestic playground where the youthful spirit could soar free in games and imaginary adventures. There were also, at that time, practically virgin areas for the young hunter bent on food or sport—a place where a boy could

> set snares for rabbits; hunt partridge with homemade bow and arrow; search for birds' nests, especially the rookeries of crows and the aeries of eagles, and seek out the burrows of foxes.[4]

1

In summer the hillsides and fences along the roads were covered with wild raspberries, strawberries, and gooseberries—all a delight to search out and a greater delight to eat.[5]

Winter brought with it its own distinct pleasures, among them trips to the forest with the men "to fell the big trees for the year's firewood,"[6] and after the first heavy snow, sleigh riding, ice skating, and setting traps for fox, mink, and ermine.[7]

On the other side of the coin, there were cattle to be pastured and milked, firewood to be sawed and split, and water to be hauled for the family and the farm animals. Fences needed building and repairing. Crops had to be planted, hoed, and harvested, and the winter hay had to be cut and stored in the barn. There were also the tedious chores of clearing rocks from the fields and picking potato bugs.[8]

The Scotsmen of Nova Scotia and the other Maritime Provinces steadfastly clung to the customs carried from their ancestral highland homeland across the sea. An important part of childhood was a thorough indoctrination in Gaelic legends expressed in both words and song.

Singing was, in fact, an integral part of the everyday life of the Maritime Scots. "Men would swing an ax or a scythe to the rhythm of a swing song, and women would sing as they rubbed the family wash in a running brook or busied themselves about the house."[9]

Peter McFarlane never lost the love of music and singing which was part of his childhood heritage. His diaries have many references to his fiddle playing; this hobby was one of his chief amusements during the first two or three years he lived in Central City. Note, for instance, the following two entries.

> Not done much of anything today. Playing around the house, reading and playing the fiddle and amusing myself best I can under the circumstances.[10]

> The "Exile of Erin" was the last time I played my fiddle in this year.[11]

In later years, when he had become successful in business, he liked nothing better than to have the men employed in his shops sing at their work. In fact, a family legend holds that every man applying for employment had to sing before he was hired. Among the mechanics and working men of Central City it was said that if a job seeker could sing, he could work for Peter McFarlane. Up Eureka Street from McFarlane's house and foundry at the head of Eureka Gulch was Jacob Mack's Rocky Mountain Brewery. In the summertime, an outside beer garden was a favorite place of resort for the Welsh and Tyrolean miners who followed the Cornish into the Central City area after the 1890s. On warm summer evenings the bleak, scarred hills which cradled Gregory Gulch would ring with the folksongs of the Tyrol and the hills of Wales. When the beer garden closed, the miners would stroll down Eureka Street still singing to the accompaniment of accordions, past McFarlane's house on their way home, and Peter would sit on his front porch till they had faded into the night and the sound of their music had drifted away over the hills.[12]

Religion also played an important role in the daily life of the people of Prince Edward Island. Bedeque, the town where Peter McFarlane spent his boyhood, and the surrounding countryside were settled by Scotch Presbyterians who emigrated from the counties of Argylshire and Morayshire in the early 1770s. These pioneers tenaciously held to and nurtured their Calvinist religion in their lonely settlements in the New World. It was not until twenty years after the first boatload of immigrants arrived in the Richmond Bay area in 1770 that they had a minister to look after their religious needs, but in the absence of a man of God, the men of the households took over. In every family, the Bible was studied constantly. Parents taught it to their children, and

> family worship, consisting of reading from "the Book," exposition by the head of the household, followed by a prayer, often of great length, was conducted in the household. The *Shorter Catechism* was well thumbed by youth. No day was allowed to close without praise and thanksgiving being offered up to Almighty God and his Son.[13]

Consequently, when the Reverend James McGregor arrived from Scotland in 1791, he found

> a people, among whom not only were the forms of their church worship maintained, but among whom, also the same doctrines were taught, that they had learned in Scotland, the same religious customs that they knew in the old land they knew and cherished in Prince Edward Island.[14]

In the little town of Bedeque, the Sabbath was, of course, strictly observed. It was a day devoted to rest, reading, and reflection after the characteristically long church service presided over by the Reverend Robert S. Patterson.[15] As a boy, Peter McFarlane sometimes attempted to forgo these lengthy sermons. On one such occasion, he and his older brother William feigned illness. The family left them at home, but returned somewhat earlier than expected, and caught the young truants enjoying themselves immensely by riding two calves around the farmyard.[16]

The Reverend Patterson's long Sunday sermons apparently had a lasting effect on young Peter McFarlane different from that which the preacher intended. Instead of drawing him into the church, they apparently began a centrifugal reaction which ultimately led to Peter's rejection of the religion of his forefathers. His daughter, for instance, cannot recall that her father ever attended church. Often she asked him the reason for this, and always he replied that his childhood experience of spending every Sunday in church listening to the minister preach interminably about the "consecrated cross-eyed bear" had cured him of any good intentions he may have had in later life.[17]

The town of Bedeque was the center of the temperance movement, which became a serious political issue on Prince Edward Island after 1840, and in the opinion of one local historian was "one of the most prosperous communities on the Island" because of it.[18]

The Scotsmen who settled Prince Edward Island were heavy drinkers, and the taverns which were found in every town and village and at intervals of a few miles along every major road testified to their love of strong liquor.[19] In 1825, the Island imported 54,000 gallons of rum, 2,500 gallons of brandy, 3,000 gallons of gin, and 2,000 gallons of wine.[20] Because of the widespread drunkenness and disorderliness which were the result of the Prince Edward Islander's penchant for hard liquor, and because of the property damage and loss of time from work which stemmed from it, the Legislature as early as 1773 took steps to regulate the liquor traffic. In that year a law was passed requiring the licensing of all retail liquor establishments. The law, however, was ineffective, and soon after the turn of the century clergymen of all faiths and civic leaders began to organize temperance societies for the purpose of bringing the liquor traffic under more positive control.[21]

One of the early leaders of the temperance movement was the

Reverend Robert Stuart Patterson, who established the first temperance society on the Island in Bedeque in 1827, just one year after the American Temperance Society had been founded in Boston.[22] Interestingly, the Reverend Patterson's sermons on the evils of drink apparently had a far more positive impact on Peter McFarlane than sermons with a strictly religious theme. As a young man, Peter joined the Independent Order of Good Templars, a fraternal and social organization which advocated the "importance of life long abstinence from intoxicants,"[23] and except for a few instances very late in life when at his doctor's insistence he took small amounts of whiskey for medicinal purposes, he remained a lifelong teetotaler.[24] The Good Templars lodge hall was a center of social activities in Bedeque. When he left the land of his birth for Colorado Territory, Peter McFarlane carried with him the memories of many happy evenings of fraternal and social conviviality such as the annual oyster supper.[25]

By the time McFarlane had reached school age, a system of free public education had been established on Prince Edward Island. The "Free Education Act" of 1852 provided for up to two hundred free public schools to be placed no more than three miles apart; they were to admit all children over five years of age.[26]

At what age McFarlane began or finished school cannot be determined. His daughter and his cousin, however, recall that he completed the equivalent of an eighth grade education, and from his diary it can be established that he was still in school at age thirteen.[27] Looking back on his school years after his arrival in Central City, McFarlane commented that "those were the happiest years of my life, but human like, I did not know it, and should any person have told me, I would not have believed it."[28] It is probable that he spent a few years working on the family farm when his schooling was finished. In June 1866, however, when he was eighteen years old, McFarlane began to work as a carpenter's apprentice in the shop of John McCallum of Bedeque.[29] He stayed in the trade for approximately two years before emigrating to Gloucester, Massachusetts.[30]

Despite the fact that childhood in Canada's Maritime Provinces seemed to approach the idyllic, in actuality only a small number of those who were born there remained. As they reached their teens, the ambitious and adventurous moved from the farms in large numbers to man the fishing fleets of the Northeast Atlantic coast or to seek their fortunes in the wide expanses of the Canadian or American West. Many young Prince Edward Islanders settled in Boston, which in the Maritime Provinces was "often known as the Boston States, and was the Valhalla of all the ambitious. . .boys and girls who ventured out into the world to better themselves."[31]

A detailed analysis of the motivating factors for this exodus of young people is not necessary here, but two generalizations might be noted in passing. Prince Edward Islanders tended to have large families. Thirteen children, the number that made up the McFarlane family, were by no means uncommon. This meant that in many cases emigration provided the only possibility of independence and economic advancement for younger sons. Secondly, the restricted confines of the Island, its racial homogeneity, and its severely limited economic opportunities tended to increase the normal dissatisfaction which a new generation felt toward the cultural framework into which it was born. The nineteenth century was a great period of population movement. It was an era of adventure and pioneering, and the young found it difficult to resist the attraction of free land, or the get-rich-quick possibilities offered by the gold strikes in the West. Each offered opportunities for the longed-for break with the past and broadened horizons for the future. The following statement by a Prince Edward Islander, who witnessed with obvious regret the exodus of the Island's young people, captures both the conservatism of the older generations and some of the reasons for the discontent of the younger.

> The old people were good, frugal and industrious; they cleared land, built houses and barns, and when they died generally left a good farm free from debt and a good stock of cattle to sons who were not long content to live as their self-denying parents had done, and who would take the first offer of wages to go in a vessel as sailors or fishermen. The number of those who have been lost sight of in that way is as great as those now to be found in the old settlements. Their bones whiten the bottom of the "George's Banks," or they are absorbed in the mixed populations of the fishing towns of New England.[32]

Among those not content to spend their lives amidst the simple, pastoral existence of Prince Edward Island was a group of six young men from the vicinity of Bedeque, "all between the ages of 20 and 30 and all brothers or cousins or the dearest of friends from their youth up who were born within 2 miles of each other."[33] This group consisted of the McFarlane brothers, William and Peter, their cousins, William J. and Peter B. Barclay, William Price, and Eugene Lackey.[34]

The opportunities presented by the revival of gold mining in Colorado after the Civil War seem to have played an important role in the cousins' decision to leave their island homeland.[35] The news from the Colorado gold fields undoubtedly raised much the same excitement on Prince Edward Island as had the gold strikes in California approximately eighteen years earlier. In 1849 a letter arrived in Charlottetown from California describing in vivid terms the fortunes to be had almost for the asking. Immediately, a strong case of gold fever seized the community. Within a short time a company of forty men had been formed, and a ship purchased and outfitted for the long trip around the Horn to San Francisco. It is worth noting that the McFarlane and Barclay brothers spent their childhood amidst tales and legends of a fabulous treasure in gold supposedly buried on Prince Edward Island by the famous English pirate, Captain William Kidd. Among the adult population of the Island, dreams of finding this pirate gold were common, and a superstition grew up that the person who experienced such a vision must carry out his search at night and in absolute silence.[36] Although it cannot be said with any certainty that the legends of buried pirate gold played any significant role in the McFarlane and Barclay brothers' decision to try their luck in Central City, the gold camps of Colorado did offer opportunities to turn childhood dreams of golden treasure into reality.

The cousins apparently left Bedeque separately, with the three oldest, William McFarlane and William and Peter Barclay, departing first and Peter McFarlane following later at their urging.[37] Except for Peter McFarlane, it is impossible to trace with any certainty their steps from Prince Edward Island to Central City, or their dates of arrival. There is, however, some reason to believe that William McFarlane and the Barclay brothers may have lived for a time in Pomeroy, Ohio, before going on to Central City. In October 1871 James B. McFarlane, who had joined the original group in Central City the previous year, left to return to Bedeque. He stopped for a few days on his way in Pomeroy, an incident which generated the following entries in Peter's diary.

> James got into Pomeroy on the 8th current. Took them all by surprise.[38]

Got two letters from Pomeroy tonight. Having quite a glorious time
of it there. Wrote to know about certain jobs in Central City. [39]

From these extracts, it would appear that some sort of a reunion took
place when James arrived in Pomeroy. Whether it involved friends or
family or both, it is impossible to ascertain. What is clear, however, is
that the McFarlanes and the Barclays had close connections in the
town. Further support for this view comes from random jottings in
Peter's diaries. He had a habit of writing the names of people and
places in the blank sheets at the back, and among these are found
several times the name "Pomeroy."

Students of Colorado history do not agree on the year in which
McFarlane bade farewell to his island home and set out on the long
journey to Colorado Territory. [40] His diaries, however, while not as
explicit as one would hope, make it possible to clear up the confusion
on this matter. One diary reference and a newspaper advertisement
make it evident that sometime between May 5 and September 1,
1869, [41] McFarlane climbed aboard a stagecoach in Denver to begin the
last leg of a journey which had carried him more than three thousand
miles. Approximately thirty-five miles ahead, nestled in a rocky ravine
in the high mountains to the west, stood the mining camp which was to
be his home for the next sixty years.

CHAPTER II

An Immigrant Arrives in the "Little Kingdom of Gilpin" 1869

ONE day late in the summer of 1869 a dusty stagecoach, its tired and lathered horses straining at the traces, broke over the crest of Dory Hill, turned left past the little cemetery of the town of Black Hawk, and began the steep descent southward into Dory Gulch, the last lap of a forty-mile journey.[1]

Among its hot, tired, and dusty passengers was twenty-one-year-old, freckle-faced, red-haired Peter McFarlane, his eyes bulging with excitement and his pockets with "fool's gold" which he had picked up at every rest stop on the stage road from Golden City through Golden Gate Canyon.[2] McFarlane was probably unaware of the extent to which his antics amused his fellow passengers as he was undoubtedly preocupied with the panorama of mining operations unrolling before his eyes as the stagecoach lurched down Dory Gulch and with visions of the great adventure about to begin in the famous gold camp that lay but a few miles ahead.

Drawn to Colorado by the urging of his elder brother William, who had arrived in Central City sometime earlier,[3] he was the perfect stereotype of the tenderfoot intoxicated with the "sweet, blind belief that the roads in the West are paved with gold and silver to be had by anybody who will take the trouble of picking them up."[4]

Perhaps more than one of McFarlane's fellow passengers recognized in the bright-eyed youth a reflection of himself at an earlier date. Their enjoyment, therefore, of the tenderfoot's behavior must have been tempered by an awareness of what probably lay ahead for him—not the gleam of gold at every stroke of the pick or blast of the dynamite but rather high hopes and ambitions dissipated in a bone-breaking and futile—but in the end always exciting—effort. The old hand knew that for the masses of men who sought their fortunes along the creeks and gulches, the best that might be expected was a bare living dearly paid for. Henry Villard, a reporter for the Cincinnati *Daily Commercial* who covered the first Colorado gold rush in 1859, succinctly expressed what every old timer knew but tended to ignore. "Of all the human pursuits," he wrote, "gold-hunting seems to possess a peculiar charm in the eyes of a certain class, and this in the face of the fact, that its successful followers are always outnumbered by those whose material and moral wreck it results in."[5] The chance of success in the Gilpin County gold fields, another early observer noted, depended on capital, hard work, and an extraordinary measure of luck. "I tell you," he wrote to a friend, "of all the places I ever saw, this is entirely the worst place for the gentleman of leisure."[6]

McFarlane was only one individual in "a motley procession"[7] that wended its way year after year westward to the Colorado mountains after the first discoveries of gold along Cherry Creek in 1859. Despite their varied backgrounds, the men who swarmed to the gold camps lived more in the "breezy sunshine of hope than in the raw shadow of disappointment."[8] They were, by and large, individuals for whom the game was as important as the winnings—perhaps even more so. Ovando J. Hollister characterized them as men who reveled in the "delightfully painful uncertainties of all descriptions"[9] which gave to the mining camp its aura of buoyant optimism and its vibrant energy. They were, in short, gamblers who consistently courted the fickle goddess of luck and who lived by the creed that next to prospecting and "striking it rich" the next best thing was prospecting and "going broke." Calvin H. Morse, reminiscing in a letter to an old friend on the boom and bust days of Leadville, reflected the spirit which ignored the hard realities of life in the gold fields, preferring instead to remember the exhilaration and excitement dictated by the wheel of chance:

While it turned out unfortunately for me, personally, as I was compelled to leave the camp in the early winter of '95 and '96, and you had been carried out on a stretcher months before. . . . I doubt not that both of us still feel the same interest and share in the hopes of the future of this greatest of all mining camps, and doubtless both of us, were we to live our lives again, would yield to the same temptation to try our luck in Leadville again.[10]

Like a perpetual pendulum swung the mood of the gold hunter. "Chilling disappointment and despondency" could be "succeeded in the next change of the wind by effervescent hopefulness and effervescent delight."[11] A man could write a eulogy on the virtues and rewards of the life of the prospector one moment and then pen something similar to the following the next:

Tell 'em Eastern chaps that all that stuff about the pleasures of prospectin' is. . .rot. Tell 'em that a fellow who has chawed sowbelly and cornbread for four months without a change of diet, and then by way of variety has eaten his old shoes for want of other stuffin' doesn't take much stock in prospectin'. There may be potry in being hungry and cold and ... pecking at a goldurned hole in the ground that ain't got nothin' in it, but blessed if I diskiver it. Tell 'em that a man who is a prospector is a fissure vein of misable jackassery. Tell 'em if any galoot tries to give 'em tally about the bald-headed martyr who dies triumphant in his death just set him down as a two-thousand-ounce fraud.[12]

Nothing could blunt the miner's superstitious faith in the workings of chance. In the end, he believed luck would transcend capital, hard work, and technical knowledge. Sooner or later, its fickle goddess was bound to smile on each of the faithful.[13] This is why when the old hands gathered at night over cups of cheap whiskey in clapboard shacks and saloons to discuss the prospects of the camp, their faces glowed with the same fever of excitement as that which gripped Peter McFarlane as he approached Central City and a rendezvous with his brother.[14]

The stagecoach neared the bottom of Dory Gulch. On every side, the bustle and activity of the mining camp became more and more evident—crews harvesting timbers for the mines and fuel for the smelters from the already partially-denuded hillsides, miners' shacks and cabins hastily slapped together out of roughhewn logs or lumber, shaft houses with belching stacks, and stamp mills spewing out their ugly mountains of tailings.

The tired horses pulled to a stop at the Gregory Toll Gate[15] where

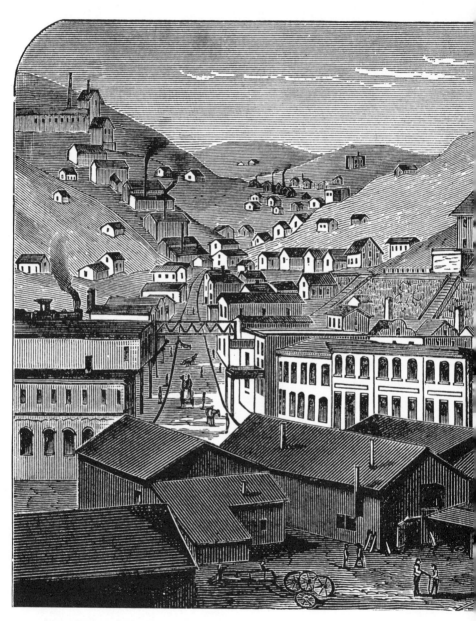

Lower Black Hawk, 1870s. *From Fossett (1879).*

Dory Gulch joins North Clear Creek, and Peter McFarlane caught his first sight of the town of Black Hawk. The driver paid the toll and urged the team on, taking a right turn through the town. He turned left near the sheet metal and boiler works owned by George Stroehle and began the steep climb up Gregory Gulch to Central City, past "houses, mills, drinking saloons and shops, . . .the houses on the left. . .resting on high posts or scaffolding over the deep bank of the stream"[16] which bisected the gulch. Finally, the coach reached the end of the line, the stage office on Eureka Street, where it came to a noisy stop in the midst of the crowd which was awaiting its arrival—

> the daily Concord Coach, with its six horses. . .that arrives on the edge of evening with the Eastern mails. . .and whose coming is the event of the day, bringing the street crowd together, and exciting much speculative gossip. . . .[17]

CHAPTER III

Barclay & Company
1869–1872

WILL McFARLANE's enthusiasm over the opportunities available in Central City, which he had conveyed in letter after letter to his younger brother, had not been ill-founded. As a matter of fact, Peter McFarlane could hardly have chosen a more favorable moment to step into the mainstream of Gilpin County history. The severe depression which struck the mining industry in Gilpin County in 1866 and 1867 and which saw gold production plummet to less than half of the figure for 1864 had come to an end, and the prospects for a steady upward climb in the output of the mines were bright.[1]

The hills surrounding Gregory Gulch reverberated with the pounding of twenty-nine mills working 624 stamps. The Boston and Colorado Smelting Works in Black Hawk, which was started in 1867 by Nathaniel P. Hill, was working to capacity. Before the year was out, gold production would surpass that of any previous year. Just two years ahead lay the most successful twelve-month period in the history of the Gilpin County mining industry when over $3,200,000 worth of gold would be blasted, pounded, and smelted out of its rocky hills.

With the mining industry booming, there was a great demand for skilled workmen such as the Barclay and McFarlane brothers. Wages for good mechanics were at least $6.00 a day and some exceptional individuals managed to command over $10.00.[2]

13

Furthermore, the leasing system, which was introduced early in Gilpin County and through which it was possible for a miner or a group of miners to take a short-term lease on a portion of a mine and pay a royalty to the owners on the gold taken out, offered additional opportunities for those who were willing to gamble for gold. Peter McFarlane had not been in Central City for very long before he was involved in just such an adventure. He and some other men, presumably his brother and his cousins, leased the Wautauga Mine in Russell Gulch. It was a bad investment which ended in failure.[3]

It was one thing to work as day laborers or to commit total resources to one mining pool after another where the chances of success were uncertain to say the least. The McFarlane brothers, however, had bigger things in mind, a fact amply illustrated by the following advertisement which appeared in the "New Today" column of the Central City *Daily Register* on September 1, 1869.

P. F. Barclay	Wm. O. McFarlane
W. J. Barclay	P. B. McFarlane

BARCLAY & Co.

CONTRACTORS

MILLWRIGHTS AND BUILDERS

Would respectfully announce to the people of this place that we have established ourselves here permanently, and are prepared to execute promptly all kinds of work in our kind of business. We keep the very best eastern carpenters for house and store building, and the most experienced workmen in the mountains for setting up machinery and mill work.

PLANS AND SPECIFICATIONS

furnished for every description of work. We also keep for public inspection, drawings of the latest styles of eastern buildings, together with plans and specifications costing from $1,500 to $100,000 furnished by Woodward and Thompson, Architects, New York. Parties contemplating building will do well to call and examine our plans.

SEASONED BEAR CREEK PINE

and all other kinds of mountain lumber kept constantly on hand:
also the best assortment of

HARDWOOD

for wagons & other purposes in the mountains. Shop & office on
Eureka St., Central City, near the mouth of Prosser Gulch.

In addition to this initial advertisement in the *Daily Register*, regular
advertisements appeared in the paper through June 1871. All of these
listed the partners in the company. Furthermore, Barclay & Company
invested in a quarter-page advertisement in the first edition (1871) of
the *Rocky Mountain Directory and Gazetteer*.[4]

Peter McFarlane's diaries provide a fairly comprehensive picture of
the company's varied activities, ranging from making a wheelbarrow or
an ironing board to major construction projects. One of the most
interesting of the latter was roofing and finishing the interior of the St.
James Methodist Church on Eureka Street. This project seems to have
been the largest single contract obtained by the company in the two
short years that the original partnership lasted.[5]

Construction began on the church, the oldest Protestant church still
in use in Colorado, in 1864, but funds for the project were exhausted
long before the building was completed. Only the basement and the
outer shell, not including the roof, were finished before the workmen
had to quit. Thus the building stood for approximately four years, a
skeleton referred to by the residents of Central City as "The Ruins."[6]
Work on the church recommenced in 1868, but due to the deterioration
of the original walls, it was necessary to start over almost from scratch.

It would appear that Barclay & Company obtained a part of the
construction contract in September or October of 1870, as the first
mention in McFarlane's diary of work on the church is dated October
19, 1870: "Worked on the Church doors today mortising and ripping."
For reasons which will be noted later, however, there is a long gap in
the diary from September 5 through October 15, and it is possible that
Barclay & Company were at work on a church contract a month or so
before McFarlane first mentions it.

The church doors were Peter's assignment. It was either a difficult
assignment or a task that, for one reason or another, he particularly
disliked. The job took only six days to complete, but it is evident that he
found it distasteful:

> Working on the church doors today again. Oh dear, am I never going to get them done.

> Still working at those cussed doors and ain't got them done yet.

> Worked on the Methodist Church doors. Got one of them hung into place.

> Glory. Finished the church doors this forenoon. One consolation I have is that if I was six days on them they look first class now that they are done.[7]

The next mention of construction on the church was not made until the middle of August in the following year, when it became apparent that the company had received the contract for closing in the building and finishing the interior. Again, from McFarlane's point of view, it was a particularly demanding task. On August 15 he noted that three of the company were "on the church. . .getting out circles for the pulpit. Cussed hard work anyhow."[8]

It is possible to date the completion of several stages of construction and to determine that all the work was completed by December 1871. The pillars and capitals were set in place and painted by September 1, the shingling of the roof was completed on October 27, and the windows were finished and set in on November 25. Of the work on the pillars McFarlane wrote:

> All day on the church putting on those capitals on the upper part of the pillars. Of all the jobs I ever tried that crowned the rest. It is enough to set a man of ordinary brain topsy turvy.[9]

Shingling the roof was no easier. This was a particularly difficult job because of the steep pitch. Work began on the roof on September 20, 1871, and continued off and on through October 27. Halfway through the project, McFarlane wrote:

> We began to shingle the other side of the church roof. . . .I shall be glad when it is done for we are so high from the ground. Feel very tired and sore from climbing around all day.[10]

Four days later the job was completed, and the sense of relief which he felt was evident in his entry for that day:

> Finished shingling the roof and taking down the staging today. Very [undecipherable] job. Hard work and everything that's bad.

Thank God the job is done and all is well and nobody hurt. Don't
want to work on a similar job anymore. Too much risk for me.[11]

Services and special events were held in the church during the final
stages of completing the interior. McFarlane noted, for instance, an
exhibition and festival,[12] a revival,[13] and on Christmas evening 1871
"about 1000 people in the Methodist Church."[14] The dedication,
however, was not held until July 21, 1872, at which time the building
was mortgaged for approximately one-half the total cost of $35,000.[15]

Approximately one year after Barclay & Company was formed,
construction was started on a dwelling for the partners. On August 19,
1870, McFarlane noted that "Eugene and I worked on our own house
today." That the house referred to was to be shared by members of the
company is confirmed by his entry for August 22: "Eugene Lackey
and myself worked on the Barclay-McFarlane house today." The
Gilpin County Records show that on August 10, 1870, W. O.
McFarlane "preempted" a lot "bounded on the west by a lot owned by
Moses Hall and on the east by a lot owned by Martin Washington,"
upon which was erected "a frame dwelling house."[16]

Construction on the house progressed rapidly, and it was ready for
occupancy on October 15, 1870. In all probability, every effort was
directed to insure that the partners could move in as quickly as
possible. Peter managed to keep his diary going from the day the house
was started until September 4, when the entries temporarily ceased. It
is probable that since much of the work on the house had to be done in
the evening, little time or energy was left for keeping a diary.

If it is true that the six partners were using the shop and office as
living quarters, it does not take much imagination to visualize what
pleasure the six young men must have experienced in moving into their
new home. Measured by modern standards, the "Barclay-McFarlane
house" was probably extremely plain, but to the Prince Edward
Islanders, it must have represented a considerable amelioration of a
rather crude and rough standard of living and a conspicuous example
of their business success. McFarlane's comment on the day they moved
into their house conveys some of the emotion with which the partners
greeted this event, emotions which even six inches of snow could not
dampen.

Moved into our own house today. Eat supper for the first time in
our lives in our own house, and Will Barclay cooked it. Peter

Barclay, William McFarlane, William Barclay, William Price, Eugene Lackey, Peter McFarlane were the ones who partook of the glorious repast.[17]

Soon after the completion of the house, a third McFarlane brother, James, was en route from Prince Edward Island to join the company in Central City. He was expected in Central City on December 16, but the train on which he was traveling from Kansas City to Denver was snowed in at Fort Wallace, and he did not arrive until December 23.[18] Peter recorded the reunion which took place after his arrival:

James B. McFarlane arrived in Central City tonight—and Oh my the token of joy on each one's countenance. Here sits Will Price listening and laughing, eager to catch every bit of news in order to convey it home. Then Will McFarlane deafening his brother with an innumerable host of questions. Here Will Barclay every now and then putting in a word edgewise and receiving no answer. Then Peter Barclay straining his [undecipherable] ears, trying to keep up the run of conversation, laughing with the rest, and sighing or [undecipherable] as the occasion requires. Here sits Jim Mc himself, answering the questions as fast as he can get them off his hands, and always 4 or 5 behind, while ever and anon is presented to the weary stranger a [undecipherable] speaking smile ever repeating welcome, welcome, welcome. So say we all.[19]

For reasons that seem obvious, Peter's diary for December 24 is blank. Christmas Eve that year must been a merry and festive occasion as James McFarlane, arriving like St. Nicholas, brought with him the kind of gift so meaningful to a little group of expatriates: first-hand news of family and friends.

The year 1870 ended on a happy note for Barclay & Company. The fledgling business appeared to be well established and was prospering. A new house had recently been completed, and a third McFarlane brother had joined the original group in Central City.

Beneath the surface, however, all was not well. The acid of dissension had begun to eat away the close family ties which bound the partners together. Not all of the causes of the disagreements which ultimately brought about the dissolution of the original partnership just short of two years after it was formed are clear. One, however, was quite evident, and by itself was enough to explain the split. While the McFarlanes were temperance men, the Barclays liked their share of strong drink. Thus the liquor issue, with all of its intemperate emotions, which had been a center of controversy in the Maritime Provinces since about 1840, was to play a role in the demise of Barclay & Company.

Soon after the formation of the partnership with the McFarlanes, Peter and Will Barclay began to frequent the saloons in Central City—an activity which Peter McFarlane deplored. With the beginning of 1871, diary notations such as "Peter downtown drunk as usual"[20] become fairly frequent, and it was obvious that relationships between the cousins were under a heavy strain.

McFarlane was more distressed by the aftereffects of a night in the saloons than by his cousin's drinking per se. Hangovers meant that the sufferer worked at a low rate of efficiency the next day—if he managed to get on the job at all. In either case, someone else had to assume an additional burden. Although the company was fairly soundly established by 1871, it could not afford any significant amount of absenteeism. Continued success depended on obtaining new construction contracts and carrying them out with a maximum of efficiency. The successful operation of the business was emotionally and physically demanding, and key men regularly debilitated by lack of sleep and overdoses of bad whiskey boded ill for the company's future. It is, therefore, hard not to sympathize with the resentment which McFarlane felt when he wrote that "Peter Barclay did not do much of anything today,"[21] or "Peter Barclay skulking around as usual, very sick, but able to go to town tonight."[22] In McFarlane's eyes, fascination with the dance was in itself bad enough, but being unable to pay the piper ran counter to the strict Protestant ethic in which he had grown up and helped create a situation which would shortly become intolerable. To McFarlane hard work was one of the cardinal virtues and sloth was one of the cardinal sins. One evening after a hot afternoon's work on the roof of Ben Wisebart's O. K. Store on Main Street, during which he laid a thousand shingles, Peter noted in his diary: "I was about the warmest today I ever was in my life. The *Presbyterian* just poured off me."[23] It was partly because there was so little "Presbyterian" pouring off the Barclay brothers that the original partnership in which they apparently played the dominant role in the beginning came to an end on August 3, 1871. Five months later, when Will Barclay was preparing to return to Pomeroy, Ohio, Peter noted that the reason for his leaving and for the frustration of the plans and hopes which had drawn him to Gilpin County was that he was "careless and listless about the things that ought to interest him the most second to none. But I am sorry to state that the saloons seem to be the all prevailing topic with him. . . ."[24]

The courtship and marriage of one of the cousins may have expedited the breaking up of the original partnership.[25] The feminine lead in what appears to have been a lively courtship drama with the Barclay brothers as rivals for the hand of a fair lady was Lizzie Furnald, the daughter of Alonzo Furnald, a druggist in Central City. Lizzie must have been a warm-hearted girl of pleasant disposition, because when she makes her first appearance in Peter's diary it is as a volunteer to help grub out the bachelor abode of the Barclay and McFarlane brothers.[26] For the next few weeks Lizzie appears to have been a constant visitor, sharing the household chores and adding the gentle woman's touch to the simple social activities which livened up the evenings, such as card games and music supplied by one or more fiddlers.[27]

It would have been strange if Lizzie's presence had not generated a spirited rivalry for her favors and attentions among the cousins. Marriageable young women were very scarce in Central City in 1871, so scarce, in fact, that the editors of the *Daily Register* saw fit to publish the following article in the miscellaneous column one day in March.

> Girls are plenty, and men scarce in Maine. At a recent leap year sleighride in a village in that state, it was found there were not enough men to "go round," so they allotted two girls to each young man, and then had to take in several old widowers to make up the necessary number. This is all wrong and if a few hundred of those girls will only come to Colorado, we will promise them at least two beaux each in young, true and sturdy fellows for their next leap year ride. Wake up girls, and come to where you are needed and appreciated.[28]

As spring turned into summer, it is clear from Peter's diary that Will and Peter Barclay were actively competing for Lizzie's hand and that Peter seemed to have the inside track.[29] It is also evident that the possibility of an impending marriage was causing McFarlane some concern. "M.L.F. you'll never be sorry but once if you do," he wrote on May 5. A month later, a note of frustration appeared in his entry for June 5: "Heard someone is going to get married. Don't know what to do about it."

What prompted these feelings is not entirely clear, but Peter Barclay's reputation as a denizen of Central City's gambling halls and saloons stands out as a strong possibility. If he had any feelings of friendship for Lizzie, Peter could hardly have viewed favorably the prospect of her marrying a man whose many bouts with the bottle not only were personally repugnant to him, but also had been a disruptive factor in the Barclay-McFarlane business partnership. In addition, at the time he penned his June 5 entry McFarlane was aware of the fact that Peter Barclay and Lizzie planned to be married while "some of the boys" were "in the valley." The "boys" in this case were Will Barclay, Will McFarlane, and James McFarlane who were apparently working on a construction contract somewhere outside Central City at the time.

As close as the cousins had been since childhood, the timing of the wedding was strange. Strange or not, Peter Barclay and M. L. Furnald were married in the Barclay-McFarlane house on June 7, 1871. In attendance were "Mrs. Hall, Mrs. Murray, Bob Hood," and Peter McFarlane.[30]

Whatever his doubts, once his cousin and Lizzie had been united in matrimony, Peter McFarlane did everything possible to give them a warm sendoff. The next day he looked up Frank Bates and collected a hundred dollars due the company on a contract for a stamp mill; this money he gave to the newlyweds as he saw them off for a short honeymoon in Idaho. That night he noted that "all passed off merry as a marriage will."[31]

Peter and Lizzie were back in Central City by June 16 and settled in the house on Eureka Street.[32] Three days later the housekeeper moved out,[33] and on the twentieth, Will Barclay and Will and James McFarlane arrived home "from the valley below."[34] There must have been an interesting homecoming, with Lizzie now duly installed as the mistress of the house. Peter reported no reactions to this event on the part of his brothers or his cousin. In addition, there is no mention of a celebration of any kind to welcome the new member of the family. As a matter of fact, the results of the new arrangement appear only in a routine entry noting that Peter McFarlane and Will Barclay were sleeping on the floor of what had been the housekeeper's room.[35]

On July 9, 1871, about a month after the wedding, Peter, Will, and James McFarlane and Will Barclay moved into a frame house which was located on the north side of Eureka Street nearer the center of the town, leaving the old residence to the newlyweds.[36] There was a good deal more to this development than the need for more convenient living arrangements following Peter and Lizzie's marriage. Close at hand was the dissolution of the original business partnership and the formation of a new one, McFarlane & Company, which would not include Peter Barclay and in which Will Barclay would play a subordinate role to Will and Peter McFarlane. The new company was legally in existence on August 1, and a public announcement appeared two days later on the front page of the *Daily Register*:

NOTICE

The partnership heretofore existing between the undersigned under the firm name of Barclay and Company is this day dissolved by mutual consent.

> B. F. Barclay[37]
> W. J. Barclay
> W. O. McFarlane
> Peter McFarlane

A partnership is this day entered into between the undersigned for the purpose of carrying on the contracting and building business under the name of McFarlane and Company. All the bills due the old firm will be collected by the new firm, and all the debts of the old firm will be settled by them.

> W. O. McFarlane
> Peter McFarlane
> W. J. Barclay

It seems probable that Peter Barclay received the original Barclay-McFarlane house in return for his interest in Barclay & Company. This would explain why Will Barclay as well as the McFarlane brothers moved into the upper house.

It appears strange that there is absolutely no mention in Peter's diary of the demise of Barclay & Company and the formation of the new company. At the very least, he might have mentioned the fact that McFarlane & Company had replaced the other, an event which Peter could hardly have participated in without some surge of personal pride even while lamenting the circumstances which brought it about. Yet there is no diary reference to McFarlane & Company until the last entry for 1871, some five months after the new concern came into being. This entry is interesting because it reveals for the first time the depth of the antagonism which had built up between Peter and his cousin, Will Barclay—an antagonism which finally eroded away the bonds of family, the attachments rooted in childhood, and those ties forged during their first few months in Central City when pulling together meant the difference between success and failure for the enterprise they had helped launch.

> Before another year shall glide away I hope to see a change even in our own business. One will go to Pomeroy not to come back. I hope if he does, I leave for other parts. One will come to us from Prince Edward Island and be one of the junior partners in this firm, McFarlane and Company. I hope to be in our own shop before long both to work and live in it. The benefits or advantages will be much greater than under the present circumstances. We will be nearer town, near our business. The shop and lot will be our own [free] and clear, and our minds will be at rest.[38]

Bill McCurt —
his foot last night
on the neck of a broken
bottle when he was
getting into bed

Taygun Lackey
is quite up upto
the flying exchange

As for your humble
Servant — he ain't
worth better any
how

Peter McFarland
Central
Colorado

This day the Sun
rose in the morning
something that
very seldom happens
in this Country and
and not only that
but it rose in the
East — or somewhere
towards the Mississippi
river

CHAPTER IV

A Bachelor's Life
1869–1871

Peter McFarlane's diaries show him to have been a man sensitive to the world around him and fully aware of the difficulties of conducting his life in accordance with some scheme of transcendent values. Consequently, here and there among the daily entries, there are references to soul-searching periods in the life of a young man struggling to establish himself in a bustling mining camp in the Colorado Rockies. These references indicate the kind of personal inquisition common in the private papers of particularly sensitive, introspective, or religious individuals—the intimate scene in which the conscience passes judgment on the man.

Since these documents were not intended for anyone's eyes but his own, to be "laid away in the archives . . . toward the final judgement,"[1] they provide some insights into the author's innermost thoughts. Often the reader feels that he has intruded upon what was intended to be a private performance of an autobiographical play in which the author, in addition to writing the script, performs the lead role and writes the critical reviews. Given McFarlane's great love of the works of William Shakespeare, particularly "Hamlet,"[2] the analogy seems singularly appropriate; Hamlet's cry that "the play's the thing wherein I'll catch the conscience of the king" might well have been McFarlane's own.

As the hero passes across the stage in a series of vignettes, we see a young man attempting to maintain the strict religious customs of his childhood in the midst of the rough, iconoclastic atmosphere of a frontier mining camp. The attempt is not wholly successful. Strict observance of the Sabbath, for instance, is violated, and the conscience cries out in horror at what it sees but is unable to prevent. The hero then becomes involved in subjecting the religious beliefs learned in childhood to the scrutiny of a rapidly developing skepticism. Around him all the while swirls the activity of the mining camp. A serious illness raises doubts concerning his ability to carry on. In his reaction to these crises, however, the hero is revealed as a man who in the face of adversity exhibits a spirit not to be easily felled by the "slings and arrows of outrageous fortune," a man capable of thinking for himself and living comfortably with the results.

McFarlane's notes on his early years in Central City reflect a pattern of living which differs markedly from many of the memoirs and accounts of life in the Western mining camps. It falls somewhere in the gray middle ground between the nostalgic eulogies and exaggerated tales of phenomenal wickedness which characterize much of this literature. In his history of California, Josiah Royce noted the tendency of the pioneers to emphasize the extremes of their experiences.

> In one mood, or with one sort of experience, the pioneer can remember little but the ardor, the high aims, the generosity, the honor and the good order of the California community. . . . On the other hand, however, another equally boastful memory revels in scenes of sanguinary freedom, of lawless popular frenzy, of gaming and of murder. According to this memory nothing shall have remained pure: ministers who happened to be present gambled, society was ruled by courtesans, nobody looked twice at a freshly murdered man, everybody gayly joined in lynching any suspected thief, and all alike rejoiced in raptures of vicious liberty.[3]

The western frontier has a peculiar hold on the imagination of Americans. It is a difficult subject to treat with unflagging objectivity because it is altogether too much fun, too full of nostalgia for a past which seems to have no present. Its major themes are Olympian. Consequently, god-like heroes and ungodly villains abound, and the brilliant extremes of human conduct tend to obscure the tens of thousands of ordinary men and women who quietly, stubbornly, and mostly anonymously slowly built the basis for stability and social order in a society that sprang into existence, indelibly marked the American character, and passed into mythology in less than one hundred years.

Peter McFarlane's diaries give us a picture of one of the quiet, stubborn men of Central City's early history. It is a picture considerably different from those of Frank C. Young and Caroline Bancroft, two of Gilpin County's best-known storytellers who reflect exactly the styles described by Royce.

Young's nostalgic reminiscences were compiled some twenty-three years after he had left Central City and were, admittedly, a *tour de force* designed to convince social circles in Denver that something which could be legitimately called "culture" and "society" flourished in the "Little Kingdom of Gilpin" in its heyday. His canvas, therefore, portrayed an idyllic community straddling Gregory Gulch, where under the benign influence of a few aristocrats the arts flourished and the lives of its inhabitants paralleled those of the ancient Arcadians of Greece. The inhabitants of the Gulch were, in Young's view, a people whose "habits were simple," whose "passionate fondness for music" and whose "generous hospitality . . .made them pass among the ancients for favorites of the Gods"—the name of their land a synonym for "peace, simple pleasures and untroubled quiet."[4] Hence, the title of his book, *Echoes from Arcadia*.

In contrast to Young, who chose to emphasize what to him were the elegiac aspects of Central City's early days, Bancroft concentrated on the more flamboyant and violent sides of its pioneer period and illustrated these through the careers of its most picturesque citizens— socialites, financiers, businessmen, public officials, gamblers, whores, and her favorite group of all, the Cornish miners whose customs, folklore, and songs are so deeply imbedded in the history of the mining frontier, and whose brutal wrestling matches provided a popular form of entertainment and the stuff of legends.

Although the Young and Bancroft canvases are valid, they reflect only the extremes of life in Central City during the early 1870s. For the majority of its citizens, the mining camp was neither an intoxicating cultural whirl nor a binge of debauchery. Gilpin County lived on its mines, and the mines conditioned the way of life of its people. Below the glittering surface of the mining camp pulsed the real life and strength of the community which beat in the proud, determined, and stout hearts of the men dedicated to the task of forcing from its deep, hard rock sanctuaries Gilpin County's gold. For these men—the miners, mechanics, laborers, millwrights, wagon drivers, and jacks-of-all trades—grand balls, cotillions, musical recitals, and poetry readings were outside the pale of their lives; and drunkenness, brawling, and gambling were by no means their only form of relaxation from the stringent demands of their occupations. For the small entrepreneur and laborers in the mines, life in Central City was a world not of high culture but of hard days and evenings of backbreaking labor which left little time or energy for more than the simplest of amusements; a world not of gracious living but one of rough clapboard shacks and log cabins, the smell of dirty bodies and dirtier clothes; a world debilitated by intestinal and respiratory illnesses; a world in which brute strength and determination were essential to survival and physical and emotional exhaustion were part of the way of life; and yet a world of some simple pleasures and rewarding experiences.

Central City in the 1870s had a side to its social life which fell between high culture and hedonism. Fraternal lodges such as the Masons, Odd Fellows, and Good Templars were functioning. So were the churches, and the various denominations sponsored throughout the year a wide variety of social and fund-raising events such as dinners, fairs, bazaars, and exhibitions. These events reached a peak as the various holidays approached; the *Daily Register* carried notices of such entertainments as a "grand blow-out" at the Congregational Church featuring a bazaar and an "elegant repast . . . at a fair price," or a "highly entertaining and entirely new exhibition at the Episcopal fair."[5] Itinerant speakers lecturing on controversial topics such as Darwinism or temperance trouped in regularly to Central City along with picture exhibitions, travelogues, and an occasional circus. For those with children there were the plays, recitals, and other events sponsored by the schools. Broadly speaking it could be said that except for the single unique industry on which it existed Central City was not a great deal different from the towns of comparable size from which its citizens had emigrated. Relative to this point, Albert D. Richardson, who travelled widely throughout the West from 1857 to 1867, remarked that

> making governments and building towns are the natural employments of migratory Yankees. He takes to them instinctively as a

duck to water. Congregate a hundred Americans anywhere beyond the settlements, and they immediately lay out a city, frame a State constitution and apply for admission to the Union, while twenty-five of them become candidates for the United States Senate.[6]

The area's single industry, however, governed the tenor and quality of life. Gold could make men rich, but as one astute observer of the first rush to Colorado in 1859 remarked, "Little time is required to learn the great truth, that digging gold is about the hardest way on earth to obtain it . . . "[7] The visions of wealth, the excitement of the search, and the tremendous demands on the body and spirit which characterized life in the mining camp severely tested the men whom it lured to its bosom. Just how severely is revealed by a series of entries in McFarlane's diary for 1871 which document the drudgery and mono-tony of his life, a serious illness, and speculation on the meaning of his own existence which culminated in a profound reorientation of his religious views.

The first indication that McFarlane was feeling the strain of his arduous occupation came near the end of his first year in Central City. "Long ago when I was young and in my teens," he wrote, "I used to have good times. But since then how things are changed. Oh my!"[8] A little later, in what appears to be a mood of resignation, he remarked that he would "soon find the truth in Burns. Man was doomed to hard work."[9] At the time, McFarlane was only twenty-three years old, not really as far from the good times of his teens as it seemed to him. One Saturday night, weary to the point of exhaustion, he picked up his pen and jotted down the following thoughts which clearly indicate the hardships of his profession.

> Glory to God. I am always glad when Saturday night comes along. Let me be ever so tired, the thought of Saturday night renews courage to pursue my work knowing that the blessed Sunday will always bring rest.[10]

Saturdays, however, did not always mean that a day of rest was to follow. Sunday work, although not the rule, was not uncommon despite the fact that McFarlane's religious upbringing forbade it. For instance, the Sunday after the notation above found him working all day on a water tank.[11] The following Sunday, October 15, he spent part of the day in the shop,[12] and a week later he worked another whole day on the water tank.[13] All of this led him to note with some sadness on October 23 that "Sunday work ain't eventually stopped yet."[14] Nor had it a week later, for on Sunday, October 29, he worked in the evening in the interior of St. James Methodist Church,[15] and Sunday, November 19, he spent most of the day at home drafting plans for a house.[16] Finally, it must be noted that even Christmas Day was not sacrosanct, for in 1871, Peter McFarlane worked the entire holiday in the shop, stopping only to attend Christmas services at St. James Methodist Church in the evening.[17]

If McFarlane had limited his interests and energies to the contracting business which he was trying to establish, his life might have been somewhat easier. This was not the case, however. As noted earlier, the Gilpin County system of leasing mines provided special opportunities to gamble in mining ventures, and soon after he arrived in Central City, Peter and his partners were leasing and working a mine. Peter's later description of this enterprise offers interesting insights on the financial condition of the partners during the first six months they were in business.

> It is a full half century since the writer pooled with others to operate under lease the Wautauga mine in the Russell district. It had been idle for some years when we took hold of it. . . . On the one hand we had youth, muscle and vigor to aid in producing results. On the other, little sense, less money, and no experience; surely a trinity of worthless assets. . . . Our first shipment of ore went to the smelter and was delivered in the month of November 1869. For this consignment we received a check from the Boston-Colorado Smelting Co. for $96.00. . . . During the time the ore in this lot was being taken out the leasers by agreement amongst themselves omitted their noon day lunch. This was done in order to reduce the then high cost of living and save a little money to buy black powder and fuse and other mining supplies. . . . The second shipment . . . showed very little gold and the two meals a day were again resorted to. The third and final smelter consignment gave only a "trace." Four cords treated at the stamp mill ran us in debt for hauling and crushing. . . . We shut down and quit, still as poor but wiser than we were six months prior.[18]

Despite the assertation, Peter and his colleagues were not much wiser. The lure of finding a paying mine was too strong, and in the spring of the following year, they were working another lease. This project also ended in failure, and McFarlane later recalled the experience as follows.

> In March, 1870, myself with others discovered what is now known as the "Keystone," and sunk a shaft very near the Gold Cup shaft. We took out some wonderfully rich lead ore, but in those days we were forced to send it to a common stamp mill for treatment as there were no lead smelters in the United States—that is to say, a smelter that was designed to smelt a lead ore carrying gold. No matter how rich in lead the ore might be, there were no smelters then in operation that were after anything but gold, silver and copper, and for a lead ore treated at the smelter to extract the gold, the miner had to pay the smelter $35.00 per ton for treatment and got nothing for the lead. . . . and a lead ore treated in a stamp mill meant the loss of both the gold and the lead. . . . There was nothing for us to do but shut down and abandon the property, . . . which we did.[19]

To say that Peter McFarlane's first years in Central City were all work and no play would be only a slight exaggeration. During the week, the demands of the business left little time or energy for recreation. Not every Sunday was taken up with business work, but in a bachelor household it was a day for catching up with chores that had accumulated during the week, such as housecleaning and washing and mending clothes. When Sunday leisure time was available, it was likely to be spent in quiet, personal ways—resting, letter writing, reading. Peter read as much as possible, and his interests were broad, spanning literature, philosophy, history,[20] and the Bible. He subscribed to three newspapers: the *Scottish American Journal,*[21] the Summerside, Prince Edward Island *Journal,* "certainly the poorest sheet in America,"[22] and, most important of the three, the New York *Herald.*[23] It was for this latter publication and for mail from home that he eagerly awaited the arrival of each stagecoach from Denver.[24]

A bachelor's life in Central City as McFarlane experienced it was relieved by a few other simple pleasures, such as card and checker games, music, walks in the mountains, raspberry picking, pitching rocks at squirrels, target shooting, visits to the local slaughterhouse, and horseback riding.[25] Unlike his Barclay cousins, McFarlane was able to resist the more flamboyant kinds of pleasures available in the town, if indeed he was ever tempted by them at all.[26]

During the two-year period covered by his diary, Peter mentions attending the theatre only three times. The first two occasions, which fell on successive nights, seem to have reflected less an interest in theatre per se and more an attempt to take his mind off his mother's death. His mother died on March 24, 1870, from the effects of a case of measles.[27] About three weeks later, McFarlane received the news of her passing, and on the following night he attended a theatrical performance for the first time in his life.[28] The next evening again found him in the theatre in an attempt to "drive my cares away."[29] The only other theatre attendance mentioned by McFarlane was when he escorted a lady, an event eliciting no further comment from him.[30]

During the years 1870 and 1871, Peter recorded only two other instances of more colorful amusement outside his prosaic pattern of reading or raspberry picking. One was a circus which set up its tents for a week or so in the Central City area in April 1871 and in the best circus tradition ran the following advertisement in the *Daily Register*:

> Bartholomew & Company's Miniature Circus. New, Novel. Astonishing. Wonderful Children, Lilliputian Trick Horses, Equestrian Goats, Educated Bears, Trained Dogs and Monkeys. Astonishing Performances, Leapers, Tumblers, Acrobats and Contortionists, and witty Clowns. The Wonder of the World, the performing elk, Eclypse. Also, the equestrian goat, Sebastian. And a host of other novelties too numerous to mention.[31]

Bartholomew & Company, however, apparently did not live up to its advertising. McFarlane and his brother James attended but "got badly sold on the strength of it," Peter sourly remarked.[32]

The other occasion was a photographic exhibition held in the St. James Methodist Church during the last week of November and the first week of December in 1871.[33] The local newspaper description of this event is worth reproducing in full.

> A few ladies and gentlemen were invited to be present last evening to witness an exhibition of views with camera and calcium light by Mr. J. Collier, the photographer of this city. The purpose of the exhibition was to test the apparatus and the relative volume of oxygen and hydrogen required in this altitude. The views exhibited were taken at random from over 300 in Mr. Collier's collection, all of which were selected in London with great care, and comprise all that is noted in grand scenery, fine old castles, statuary, etc.,—in the old world. Among the most beautiful views shown last evening were three or four of Fingal Cave, three of Abbotsford, exterior

and interior, a view in Edinburgh, and the views of statuary in
Westminster Abbey, and Litchfield Cathedral. . . . One gentleman present who had recently seen a similar exhibition in Boston
declared this to be far superior, both in regard to the views
exhibited and the skill shown by the exhibitor. Those who have
attended the ordinary stereopticon exhibitions only, can have but a
slight idea of the effect produced by these perfect pictures with the
most perfect apparatus. We believe it is Mr. Collier's intention to
give a few public exhibitions at some future time, . . . and from
the universal approbation expressed last evening, we are sure that
they will be among the most popular entertainment of the
season.[34]

If his pleasures were simple, so was McFarlane's standard of living,
as is illustrated by the following inventory of household items and
business equipment:[35]

MCFARLANE & COMPANY INVENTORY

January 1, 1872

1 clock	1 hoister
1 safe	1 lard oil can
2 coal oil drums	1 scale
3 chandeliers	2 desk lamps
2 grocer scales	3 scales
2 show cases	2 fire extinguishers
1 stove	8 pipes, 2 elbows
1 truck	1 skid
1 desk	1 office chair
1 copying press [and] press stand	5 tea caddies
23 candy jars[36]	1 oil pump
1 cheese box	1 tobacco cutter
2 tea chests	5 hatchets
1 saw	2 cracker boxes
2 graf [sic] boards	1 bed stand
1 wast [sic] basin	1 stove and pipe
2 pots	1 wardrobe
1 carpet	1 table
1 fire axe	1 slop pan
1 matress [and] 1 spring	pans, kettles, etc

2 pillows, sheets and cases	1 buggy
1 blanket [and] comforters	1 horse and harness
1 bureau	1 wagon
1 wash stand with basin and soap	1 revolver
3 cane chairs	
1 bath tub	
2 marble slabs	

In the Barclay-McFarlane bachelor household a division of labor for chores was made. To Peter fell most of the cooking, a task he disliked intensely. Why he was assigned a chore he considered so onerous is not clear. Perhaps he had some talent for preparing meals, or maybe it was just because he was the youngest of the group.

Early in October 1871 James McFarlane left Central City to return to Prince Edward Island. In recording his reactions to his brother's departure, it is significant that Peter saw fit to mention that he would miss his help in the kitchen:

> Spent a very lonesome night after James left. Seems as though I would miss him for a year. In fact, I know I will in the cooking line. He was about as much help as all the rest.[37]

There are other instances which show McFarlane's irritation at being saddled with the cooking chores. For example, on September 10, 1871, he noted that since his brother Will and his cousin Will Barclay had succeeded in balancing the company's books, "they won't have any excuse for not cooking now." Even more to the point was his entry on October 20, 1871:

> Will Barclay and I worked all day on Bensal's till 7 o'clock tonight. Finished up all we could do. I have to come and get supper. Never so mad in all my life.

The only real relief that McFarlane experienced was during a two-month period in April, May, and June of 1871, when Mrs. Robert Murray, the wife of a Barclay & Company employee, moved in and apparently assumed all of the housekeeping responsibilities.[38] With obvious joy Peter noted shortly after her arrival: "Such a difference between butchering and cooking one's own dinner and having someone cook for me."[39]

The interlude was brief, however. When Peter Barclay brought his bride Lizzie to live at the Barclay-McFarlane house, Mrs.Murray left. Whether young Mrs. Barclay took over the cooking we do not know, but in a real sense it does not matter, because in about three weeks the McFarlanes and Will Barclay had moved into the other Eureka Street house, and Peter was back at his old task. On the first evening in the new cottage he recorded in his diary: "This is the first evening in our own house. I done all the cooking today. Got roast beef for dinner."[40] And a week later he noted: "Kooked [sic] all the meals since we left the lower house."[41]

For Peter, cleanliness had always been a major problem in the bachelor household. His standards in this respect seemed to be somewhat higher than those of his cousins, the Barclays, particularly Will, who seemed unconcerned over the problems created by a lack of soap and water in close living quarters. It was, therefore, with great disgust that he wrote: "Will B and Jim Mc on their beds. Will B's feet stink so that I cannot go into the bedroom at all."[42] And several nights later he returned to the subject, noting that "Will Mc washed his feet tonight. I wish someone else would follow his example."[43]

By the middle of his second year in Central City, McFarlane had had his fill of a communal bachelor's existence. "I am sorry to say," he wrote, "that this cussed thing of batching is played out and so am I. It is certainly more than God Almighty intended any man to do."[44] Furthermore, there is evidence that the hard physical labor and the monotonous routines of his daily life had begun to have a serious depressing effect on his outlook on life. An attitude of weariness and boredom was indicated by his entry on October 3, 1871: "Time hangs heavy. Would that this cup might pass from me."

It is impossible to know for sure what was running through McFarlane's mind as he wrote these lines, and there is a danger in reading too much into them. Perhaps his depression reflected a certain amount of disillusionment—a feeling that the promise of the Colorado gold fields, so bright two-and-a-half years before when he stepped off the stagecoach in Central City, had become slightly tarnished. To be sure, the company's business was good,[45] but success may have fallen a good deal short of the expectations which brought him to Central City. In any event, it is certain that McFarlane's cup did not "run over" and that the strains of two years of effort were showing. His words stand as testimony to the effects of the hard life of the mining camp on a man of some sensitivity.

In addition to the problems already mentioned, McFarlane's early years in Central City were punctuated by two personal crises. The first was a serious illness and the second a serious revision of his religious practices and beliefs. The circumstances under which he lived likely helped to precipitate both.

As might be expected during a time when water supplies were not necessarily pure and homes left something to be desired in the way of weatherproofing and heating, respiratory and intestinal ailments were commonplace. References to the illnesses of one or more of the men are fairly common in the diary, such as: "James did not work today. Got the concentrated biles or something like them. He has to go to the side hill very often,"[46] or "On the shelf today from the effects of a sore throat, cold and such like. Have not eaten anything since last night at supper. Will McFarlane took my place at Harper's. Peter Barclay laid up too with a cold."[47]

For a period of six weeks or so in the spring of 1870, Peter McFarlane suffered more severely from what appears to have been a serious case of rheumatism. Since he does not report having seen a doctor and the diagnosis apparently was his own, it is necessary to take his word for his affliction.[48] It not only kept him off the job for a considerable length of time but also raised some doubts in his own mind regarding his eventual recovery. Although the first mention of his malady occurred on April 24 when he recorded that his "rheumatism was most awful sore,"[49] it is evident that he had been ill for some time.[50] On May 1, in a long entry spiced with poetic phrases and a confusing comment on the Biblical story of the Garden of Eden, he revealed how badly he was suffering.

> Again the merry month of May has made the hills and valley gay. The birds rejoice in leafy towers. The bees hum round the shady flowers. Blithe morning lifts her rosy eye. The distant hills are looking high. Whilst here I wander oppressed with rheumatism and am not likely to get the better of it for some time to come. Truly the way of transgressors are hard especially in this country—this God forsaken hole. Was there ever the equal of this [?] No, never since old Adam and Eve lived in the Garden of Eden. An

awful pity then he had not have plucked the forbidden fruit instead of her.

At this time, Will McFarlane, Will Barclay, and Eugene Lackey were in Fountain, Colorado, working on a contract for Barclay & Company.[51] Fountain Colony was not far from the famous hot springs called Fountaine-qui-Bouille, and since these springs were

> highly estimated among the settlers . . . for their virtues in the cure of rheumatism, all cutaneous diseases and the special class for which the practicioners sole dependence has hitherto been mercury,[52]

Peter apparently decided to join his brother in Fountain and test their curing powers.

He left Central City for Fountain Colony on the morning of May 3, 1870, went as far as Denver the first day, and there "put up at the California House" for the evening.[53] The next morning he left Denver aboard "A. Jacobs coach" and about 12:30 p. m. arrived at Fountain where he took lodging with Will Barclay and his brother in an establishment with a most uninviting name—the "Terrible Hotel."[54] For the next four days he worked part time on several relatively easy carpenter jobs, "laid around some," and generally felt pretty miserable. "The rheumatism was very, very bad this afternoon. Concluded to go to Soda Springs."[55] The next seven entries in the diary warrant quoting in full as they reveal a good deal of Peter's personality.

May 10, 1870

Eugene Lackey and myself started this morning for Colorado City and the Soda Springs. Got there 12½ P. M. Bathed in them. Drank some of the water. But whether there is any value in it or not for me remains to be revealed. 10 o'clock P. M. Do not feel any sensible difference for the better anyway. Today I begin my 23rd year. Whether it is going to be anymore benefit to me than the one just sealed forever in eternity—good and bad deeds with it—is something I do not know.

May 11, 1870

Rested very bad last night. Have not put in a worse night for two months. Impute it to the journey yesterday and jumping out of the wagon at the station and that cussed seat falling down so often and jerking my back with a sudden fetch up. After breakfast, feel better than I have for some months. Am in hopes that a change has taken place for the better. . . . Did not rest well last night. Only slept an hour or so.

May 12, 1870

Got up out of my bed at 6 o'clock A. M. Felt somewhat better than yesterday although that pain still continues in my kidneys and without any signs of getting well. Walked out to the springs this morning and back. Do not feel much better yet, but am in hope that sun and care[,] combined with soda water, may have the desired effect.

May 13, 1870

My God, Oh my God. Here it is the 13th day of May 1870. 12 months ago I was home and enjoying the best of health. If any person had told me that in 12 months I would be a complete invalid, I should have laughed at him. But by ginger, I am aware of the fact now, aware of it to my own sorrow. 12 o'clock noon report. Consider there is life in the old lion yet. There is sap in the saxton tree and while there is life there is hope, and where there is sap, there ain't much danger, is there?

May 14, 1870

Was just as bad last night as I wanted to be. Was never in much worse pain. I have come to the conclusion that I would go driving to the Fountain Post Office next—stay night. May just as well suffer pain there as here. Am a little easier today. Spend most of my time playing chequers and come off rich.

May 15, 1870

Did not go to the springs today because I got a ride in some fellows wagon and came near getting my back broke. The horses ran away and jolted me considerable which jolting hurt my back most awfully and caused me great pain through the night. Have been a very bad boy today.

May 16, 1870

Feel a little better today than have for 1 week. Have constitutionally and mechanically come to the conclusion that I will linger here no longer. Start for the south in this evening's stage, lay idle for a day or so which will do me more good than all the soda water I can drink when I have to walk 3 miles to and from the spring to get it—and that does me more harm than the water does good.

Therefore, resolved: that considering the above stated fact, I shall leave this place this very night for Fountain in A. Jacobs coach.

Keeping his resolve, Peter returned to Fountain the next day and remained there doing little work until June 1 when he, Eugene Lackey, and Bob Hood headed back toward Central City.[56] By this time, although he was apparently still troubled by his rheumatism, the worst of the attack had passed, and he could note on June 2 that "the rheumatism is getting better fast." Significantly, he mentions it only occasionally hereafter. As a matter of fact, it is probable that McFarlane enjoyed better than average health the remaining fifty-nine years of his life. For instance, at the age of fifty-two he could write: "My own health is good and I am strong and active. I do not think that any two men this side of Penzance could put me on my back the way I feel now."[57]

With his health on the mend, he could enjoy the scenic beauty of the trip back to Central City. The first day out from Colorado City he stopped to visit the Garden of the Gods and "saw something worth seeing."[58] The next day he went into Huntsville via the Plum Creek road, covering forty miles before the day was over and seeing, as he put it, "some of the greatest sights ever was seen on earth by anyone."[59]

On the evening of June 3, while stopping at the Tremont House in Denver, he "went into the club room," the first time in his life he had ever been in one, and "saw the gamblers playing Keno."[60] The next evening he was back in Central City where he found "Barclay & Company all well."[61]

Although he recovered from his bout with rheumatism, it had been a difficult experience for him and one not easily forgotten. As the year drew to a close and he looked back on his first year and a half in Colorado Territory, the most poignant memories seemed to be those which had left the deepest scars and the bitterest taste. On Christmas Day, for instance, he noted in his diary: "12 months ago this day, I rolled and tossed in my bed with the rheumatism and thought my time had come. Here I am a living memorial of God's mercy." His last entry for the year was in the same vein:

1870 was a hard year for me and no wonder if I ain't sorry to hear the death rattles in its throat. Go now and weep and wail for the misery you have brought upon yourself and left for 1871 to blot out. 71 commences tomorrow in the morning and I think he will need all of the help we can render him [undecipherable]. 70 had just sealed up for ever good. By 70, may Heaven have mercy on you and welcome 71. May God grant you grace to fully atone for your [undecipherable] sins and those of your predecessor.[62]

It is obvious that on New Year's Eve 1870 McFarlane was not in the mood for the traditional boisterous welcoming of the new year. His thoughts were fixed on the past, not the future, and they were lugubrious.

In sharp contrast was his mood on December 31 a year later. Although he reminisced about the past, it was the future of McFarlane & Company which dominated his thoughts. He looked forward to the departure of Will Barclay from Central City and an end to the tensions brought on by his cousin's drinking. He had plans for bringing Andrew McFarlane from Prince Edward Island to fill Will Barclay's place in the company, as well as for a new house and shop on Eureka Street which would be closer to the center of town. The fledgling company, founded two-and-one-half years before, seemed destined to survive, and on the last day of 1871, McFarlane was radiating an optimism which had been absent the year before.[63]

Although his business affairs seemed to be improving, there were occasions when McFarlane was bothered by a sense of guilt during late 1871. In a frontier community such as Prince Edward Island where the farm was the basic economic and social institution and where the population was characterized by a high degree of religious, economic, and ethnic homogeneity, it was relatively easy to maintain the customs, traditions, and institutions of the Scottish homeland. This was not the case, however, in the western mining camp with its heterogeneous and fluid population. On the contrary, the mining frontier's atmosphere of self-reliant individualism created an environment conducive to the erosion of traditional patterns of thought and action, a process with which the frontier churches were very familiar. As William Warren Sweet put it: "All frontier churches were united in a common struggle to save the vast new West from sinking into semi-babarism."[64]

Hard on the heels of the pioneers, therefore, came the frontier ministers, mostly Baptists, Congregationalists, and Methodists, bent on sustaining the religious commitment of as many people as possible and reviving it in others. The tasks they set for themselves were difficult and the results often disappointing. Not all western towns were inhospitable to their efforts, but a story from Pueblo, Colorado in 1875 indicated the difficulties faced by the man dedicated to bringing the word of God to the frontier settlements and towns:

> Pueblo's one minister has left. He couldn't stand the racket. He was willing to try most anything, the Fejee Islands, interior Africa, the hottest corner of perdition, if need be, but he couldn't go Pueblo. Hence, the "Heathen rage" as before, and we don't know why.[65]

The situation in Gilpin County differed considerably from that in Pueblo. In 1870 Central City, Black Hawk, and Nevadaville boasted among them a total of eight religious denominations owning seven buildings with over two thousand seats.[66] Central City was noted from its very beginning as one of the less rough and less rowdy Colorado mining camps. The Reverend William Crawford, the first Congregational minister in Central City, and for that matter in Colorado, described life in the settlements straddling Gregory Gulch:

> Perhaps there are those who think our society so rude and wicked that there is no living in comfort. Wicked enough and rough enough it is, but not wholly so. In few places will one meet with more well informed and cultivated people, or with pleasanter families. Our people demand and appreciate good preaching. Many of them have been accustomed to the best.[67]

McFarlane fitted the pattern described by the Reverend Crawford. Sundays found him regularly in church, but the Methodist rather than the Presbyterian.[68] It was not until June 19, 1870, almost ten months after his arrival, that he attended a Presbyterian service, the "first of its kind" since he left Prince Edward Island.[69] In subsequent months, he often joined either the Congregationalists or the Baptists in Sunday services.[70] This shopping around indicated that he brought with him to Colorado Territory some doubts about the religion in which he had been raised, and it hinted of important changes in his religious views.

In January 1871 a series of revival meetings began in Central City and lasted into the following year.[71] The highlights of this prolonged revival were a visit to Central City in June 1871 by the evangelist Dwight L. Moody and a marathon effort in November and December by the Reverend George Balcom, a Baptist minister from New York, who carried the word of God into the saloons as well as the churches. [72]

McFarlane took a keen interest in this effort to rekindle the flame of religion in the three little communities along Gregory Gulch, and his cryptic comments on several of the revival meetings he attended indicated that he was undergoing a significant change in his religious orientation from an unquestioned faith to a thoughtful skepticism. It was the conflicts in emotion which this process generated which accounted for his uneasy conscience toward the end of 1871.

The religious revival in Central City was six months old when Dwight L. Moody arrived to preach in the Congregational Church. On the evening of June 15, 1871, he delivered what a local newspaper termed an "earnest, argumentative and electrifying exhortation, which was received with undivided attention." [73] Two nights later, Peter McFarlane was in the audience, and he noted afterward that he "never had heard such a sermon in his life." Nevertheless, he penned a postscript: "Failed to make a convert of me." [74]

Not long after he heard Moody preach, entries began to appear in McFarlane's diary which indicated his discomfort with some of the simple Sunday pleasures we noted earlier. Certain Sunday activities were not in accordance with what he had been taught regarding the proper observance of the Lord's day. Such things as helping a friend break a mare, target shooting, fiddle playing, and card games caused him to lament: "God forgive me . . . . Truly the spirit is willing but the flesh is weak." [75] The spirit, however, was not willing, and McFarlane continued to pursue "sinful" Sunday pleasures and to record his fits of remorse for having done so. For instance, this entry appears in his diary for November 12, 1871:

> This day, My God, how that word affects my conscience, the sins are many and vile, and altogether to be avoided, but now that they are committed they must be accounted for in the first place. I do not know that I need enumerate them all over again or put them on this sheet. Played cards, My God forgive me. The first time I ever done the like on Sunday, and by the grace of God it will be the last. And I played the fiddle. God forgive me.

McFarlane constantly vowed to mend his ways and just as regularly broke the pledges. [76] That there was something more behind this than simple sloth is shown by an entry for September 14: "I have a morbid feeling in the worthlessness of life, and it is daily strengthening." It seems clear that at this time Peter was searching for something to replace a faith that was fast slipping away.

In December he attended two of the Reverend George Balcom's revival meetings which were held in the St. James Methodist Church. Although Moody had failed to convert McFarlane, he had earned his respect. This was not true of Balcom whose revivalistic thunderbolts not only were ineffective but, as far as McFarlane was concerned, offensive. On December 17, he heard Balcom preach for the first time and that night noted that he was "completely disgusted." Two nights later, he again went to the revival meeting and came away "just as hardened." Perhaps McFarlane's feelings regarding Balcom's performance were, in part, similar to those expressed by an anonymous citizen of Central City in the local newspaper:

> The recent visit and labors of the Reverend Balcom have created a ripple in the affairs of our three mountain communities . . . . The indefatigable labors of this man, untiring efforts to do good, and his singlemindedness of purpose must commend him as perfectly sincere and honest . . . . And yet, it cannot be deemed uncharitable to say, this worthy brother's labors are hardly free from blame and worldliness . . . . Christianity depends for its success upon its divine founder and needs no claptrap or eccentricity to advertise it. [77]

Although the Reverend Balcom's pulpit mannerisms may not have appealed to McFarlane, it was not his method of "advertising" Christianity that produced the strong negative reactions. Rather, Peter was experiencing a growing disillusionment with the basic tenets of Christianity itself. Concrete evidence that this was the direction he was heading is found in one of the books in McFarlane's library—Robert Ingersoll's *The Ghost and Other Lectures.* [78] Peter had underlined several passages in his copy and had made marginal notes. In the chapter "Man, Woman and Child," for example, he had underlined this passage:

> While looking upon these things I was forced to say that man advanced only as he mingled his thought with his labor,—only as he got into partnership with the forces of nature,—only as he learned to take advantage of his surroundings,—only as he freed himself from the bondage of fear,—only as he lost confidence in the gods. [79]

Later in the same essay, McFarlane also underscored these lines:

> I have noticed all my life that many people think they have religion when they are troubled with dyspepsia. If, there could be found an absolute specific for that disease, it would be the hardest blow the church has ever received.[80]

Finally, alongside Ingersoll's interpretation of the "religionist's" basic position: "Do not unsettle my mind. I have it all made up, and I want no infidelity . . . ."[81] McFarlane penciled in the margin his own view: "There lives more faith in honest doubt (believe me) than in half of the creeds."[82]

Although he never agreed with Ingersoll's atheism, Peter sympathized with his dictum: "Let us think."[83] The broad area of "honest doubt" which this process produced was more than a temporary reaction to the fluid society of the mining frontier. Many years later, when writing to an old friend, McFarlane inquired if he were still "entrenched in that imaginary sand castle known as Christianity."[84]

In no sense can it be said that McFarlane slipped into "semi-barbarism" during his early years in Central City. He did, however, become the kind of thinking individual upon whom exhortations to return to the faith of his childhood were wasted, the kind of individual who preferred the intellectual challenge and loneliness of "honest doubt" to the security of unquestioned faith. In this respect, it can be said that as a young man he exhibited an intellectual restlessness and curiosity equal to that which originally drove him from his home on Prince Edward Island to the mining frontier of the West.

CHAPTER V

McFarlane & Company
1872–1882

THE decade covering the years 1872–1882 was an eventful one for Peter McFarlane and for his company. The optimistic plans for the future which had raced through his mind as he closed his diary for the year 1871 were soon realized. Before another year had passed, the new house and shop "nearer the center of town" was under construction, and the decade was still young when Andrew McFarlane joined his brothers in Central City, taking Will Barclay's place as a member of the partnership. On May 21, 1874, fire gutted most of downtown Central City—a catastrophe for those who were burned out, but an opportunity of major proportions for two young, ambitious men whose business was construction. Peter and Will McFarlane, true to the heritage of their Scotch ancestors, were quick to exploit the opportunities which Providence had set before them, and as Central City re-built itself, McFarlane & Company passed from adolescence to maturity, and its owners became citizens of importance. On November 1, 1877, Peter McFarlane was married to Marie Elizabeth Frey. The decade ended with the McFarlane brothers' purchase of the Hendrie and Bolthoff foundry on Eureka Street on August 15, 1882.

The date of Will Barclay's departure from Central City is uncertain. In any event, it probably was not soon enough to suit his cousin Peter. Despite the severely strained relations between the cousins, which McFarlane recorded in some detail in his diary during the latter part of 1871, and the fact that Will Barclay, according to McFarlane, was trying to borrow money to return to the East as the year closed, he was still in Central City on September 19, 1872, and still a partner in the company. On that date, McFarlane & Company purchased a lot on Eureka Street from Aunt Clara Brown, Central City's famous black laundress and businesswoman.[1] But sometime within the next three years William terminated his association with the firm;[2] in his place as partner we find Andrew A. McFarlane, the brother to whom Peter referred in his last diary entry for 1871.

The exact date of Andrew McFarlane's arrival in Central City is as elusive as the date of William Barclay's departure, but we know that he was there much earlier than the middle of 1875, for on July 10 the Central City *Daily Register* noted that Andrew McFarlane had "been elected foreman of the Rough and Ready Hook and Ladder Company."[3] This suggests that Andrew must have been in Central City long enough to become fairly well known in the community. It seems improbable that a relative newcomer would have received this kind of recognition—even a gregarious and politically minded man such as Andrew apparently was.[4]

The fulfillment of McFarlane's plans for a new house and shop further down the gulch on Eureka Street is easier to date. The deed describes the lot purchased from Aunt Clara Brown as:

> That lot or parcel of land situated on the south side of Eureka Street in the city of Central immediately opposite the residence of Morris Thomas on the said street in the City of Central, said lot being the width of twenty-five or more feet front on the south line of the said Eureka Street, and thence extending Southerly one hundred feet of the same width of thirty-five or more feet, and is bounded on the east by a lot known as the Smart property, now owned or occupied as an office by J. Alden Smith Esq., and on the West by a lot owned by Hugh A. Campbell and used as a dwelling for tenants.[5]

In the Gilpin County tax records for 1873, an entry describes Campbell's lot as being "bounded on the east by the shop of McFarlane and

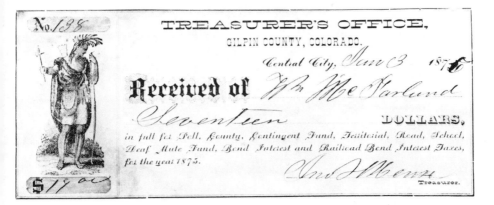

Tax receipts.

Central City, Colo. _____

Mr. J. A. Richmond

McFARLANE & Co., Dr.

CONTRACTORS, AND DEALERS IN

DOORS, SASH, BLINDS & MOULDINGS.

H. I. HALE, PRINTER.

Sept 21st Righting Box 3 x 3 x 4

Peace

M. Queen, Ranch. Mg. Co.,

Bought of McFARLANE & CO.,

Concentrating, Milling and Mine Machinery,

MANUFACTURERS OF AND DEALERS IN MILL AND MINE MACHINERY.

Brass Castings a Specialty.

Eureka Street.

Dec.	1	Balance	1969	1
"	13	To pd. Jo Powers for floor work	50	85
1888				
Jany.	"	" M. Can " "	66	00
"	3	" A. H. Jones for stove	3	00
"	21	" 105# B.B. coal	1	05
Feb.	6	" Pd. M. barrow #	36	66 0
"	14	" food bill at Morrison & Favens	1	00
"	24	" 380# B.S. coal	3	80
			3137	6

Previous page: Central City, 1880s, looking north-northwest. The Teller House (right of center) is clearly advertised. Across Eureka St. and at the end of the block is St. James Methodist Church (cf. photo of church on p. 161). Peter McFarlane's house is down and across Eureka St. in the next block from the church (cf. map opposite page). *William Henry Jackson photo. Courtesy Denver Public Library, Western History Department.*
Above: Eureka St., rebuilt after the 1874 fire, standing at intersection with Main St. looking northwest. The Teller House, unnamed, is the four-story building on left. St. James Methodist Church is across the street. In right foreground is the Hanington and Mellor bank, housed in the new Wells Fargo building. *From Fossett (1879).*
Opposite page: Street map of a section of Central City, redrawn from 1874 endpaper map. Note locations (some post-fire buildings superimposed on this pre-fire map) of Teller House, Opera House, banks, St. James Methodist Church, McFarlane home, and Hendrie and Bolthoff foundry the McFarlanes purchased in 1882.

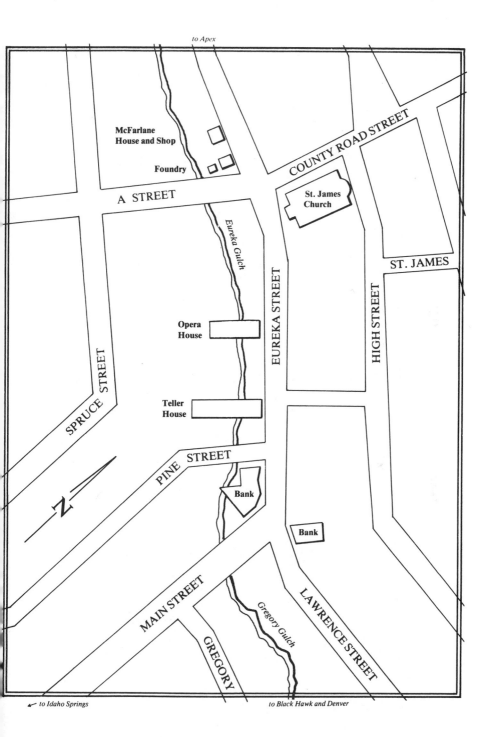

to Apex

McFarlane
House and Shop

Foundry

A STREET

COUNTY ROAD STREET

St. James
Church

Eureka Gulch

EUREKA STREET

ST. JAMES

HIGH STREET

SPRUCE STREET

Opera
House

Teller
House

PINE STREET

N

Bank

Bank

MAIN STREET

GREGORY

Gregory Gulch

LAWRENCE STREET

to Idaho Springs

to Black Hawk and Denver

Peter McFarlane home, Eureka St. *Neinbury photo, 1932. Courtesy Denver Public Library, Western History Department.*

Company."[6] From these documents two facts emerge: one, it was on the lot purchased from Aunt Clara Brown that Peter McFarlane built the white frame house which still stands on Eureka Street and serves as a focus of social activities during the summer Opera Festival; two, this house was finished before the end of 1873.

The new structure reflected a considerable upturn in the fortunes of McFarlane & Company. This, in turn, was related to the overall healthy condition of the mining industry in Gilpin County. While the total of $3,389,240 worth of precious metals produced in the county in 1871 would never again be reached, the two-and-one-half years between then and the fire of May 1874 were years of general prosperity, with the average yearly production of precious metals approaching $1,800,000.[7]

The first major construction project obtained by McFarlane & Company in 1872 was for the erection of a large custom stamp mill,[8] a fifty stamp battery, in Black Hawk for George Randolph, manager of the Ophir and Narragansett mines and a prominent figure in Gilpin County mining and social circles. This contract probably represented the first in which McFarlane & Company was responsible for the planning and erection of an entire stamp mill, and as such marks a milestone in the company's history. The McFarlane brothers had worked on stamp mills previously. Peter's diary mentions work involving stamp mills for Joseph Harper, W. B. Rockwell, and Bela Buell; but in all probability these contracts were for building construction, building repair, or the installation of machinery rather than for the construction of an entire mill. The Randolph contract, on the other hand, even included the designing of the stamps:

> The lightest slow drop [mill] we ever built is the Randolph 50 stamps in Black Hawk. They weigh 450# each and [were erected] in 1872 for a custom mill, and the mill is yet in operation.... We yet have the patterns and could easily duplicate this mill.[9]

The fact that McFarlane & Company made the patterns for the Randolph mill stamps indicates that by 1872 the McFarlane brothers had a foundry of some size, as well as a carpenter shop. This is confirmed by a list of Central City businesses which appeared in the local newspaper the previous year, and in which Barclay & Company was listed as a "foundry" equipped with one engine capable of producing twelve horsepower.[10]

The original Randolph mill, besides the fifty stamp battery already noted, had ten apron plates and ten bumping tables, and it was run by water power,[11] a fact that may have helped the McFarlane brothers secure the contract. In 1869 they had built and installed the water wheel for the New York Mill in Black Hawk. This mill was located on North Clear Creek just south of the Randolph site.[12] The dollar amount of the contract is not known, but an estimate can be arrived at by comparing the costs of similar contracts.

In 1909 Peter McFarlane quoted a figure of $1,018 to manufacture and erect in Idaho Springs an experimental five stamp mill based on the Randolph patterns. Because it was to be an experimental mill, the bid did not include any concrete foundations. Six years previously, McFarlane & Company had submitted a bid of $16,135 to manufacture and erect for Robert L. Martin a forty-five stamp rapid drop battery in the Gregory-Buell Building in Central City. This mill was to utilize both battery and apron plate amalgamation. Auxiliary equipment included one Blake jaw crusher, ten Gilpin County concentrators, and four Wilfley concentrators.[13] Again, no building or machinery to power the mill was involved in the bid. The cost of manufacturing and erecting a thirty stamp mill, including a mill building and power to run the mill, quoted by Fraser and Chalmers, a Chicago firm, in 1885 was as follows:[14]

Plant at foundry	$5,850
Freight	2,718
Lumber	1,800
Cost of setting up	4,000
Building	1,500
Engine and boilers	1,250
	$17,118

Labor costs, as a fiscal variable, are difficult to ascertain. It seems fairly clear, however, that between 1872 and 1909 wages for skilled labor in Central City did not climb substantially. In 1879 carpenters were earning $3.50 to $3.75 a day, and in 1880 skilled mechanics $3.00 to $4.00 a day in the old established mining camps.[15] By 1907 McFarlane & Company was paying $3.00 a day for apprentices in its Central City shops.[16] Presumably, the going wage for skilled labor at that time was $1.00 to $2.00 a day higher. Thus, over approximately a twenty-five year period, wages in the Central City area rose only fractionally. From these statistics and calculations it can be stated that the Randolph contract was probably not less than $15,000, although it might have been higher. In any case, it represented, as previously noted, the largest project yet attempted by the McFarlane brothers.[17]

For Peter McFarlane, the contract had ramifications beyond its obvious impact on the prosperity of his business. Without doubt it marked the beginning of his personal involvement in the controversy of how to extract the value from the low grade ores of Gilpin County. In mining circles this question took on national importance soon after the surface ores were exhausted and deep rock mining began, and it continued to be debated until large-scale mining operations ended. The question involves technical matters, but because of its national importance and because it played such a central role in Peter McFarlane's career, it is essential that its major elements be understood.

The initial success of the early miners in Gilpin County was due to the fact that they were able to work the outcroppings of veins of ore where long exposure of the matrix to the elements had caused it to decompose, freeing the fine gold and re-depositing it in a coarser form. In this coarse state it was rather easily extracted by the usual primitive methods of the prospector and the first crude stamp mills. The stamp mills made their appearance in Gilpin County as early as 1859 and were of a type used successfully in the California gold fields. As long as there was decomposed quartz to work, these mills were efficient, retrieving as much as 75% of the gold content. As the miners went deeper, however, the efficiency of the stamp mills dropped to as low as 30%.[18]

The problem stemmed from the fact that the low-grade ores which the miners encountered as they drove their shafts deeper differed markedly from those of California. Instead of being coarse and easily freed as was the case in California, the gold in most Colorado ores was very finely distributed throughout the ore.[19] Colorado ores also contained a far larger percentage of sulphurets (undecomposed ore).[20]

In addition, the Colorado miners encountered a phenomenon called "rusty gold": instead of being bright yellow the gold had a "grayish, brown, dull tint."[21] Experiments with rusty gold showed it to be almost impervious to the action of quicksilver; that is, it would not combine or amalgamate with it as is normally the case. In one such experiment a

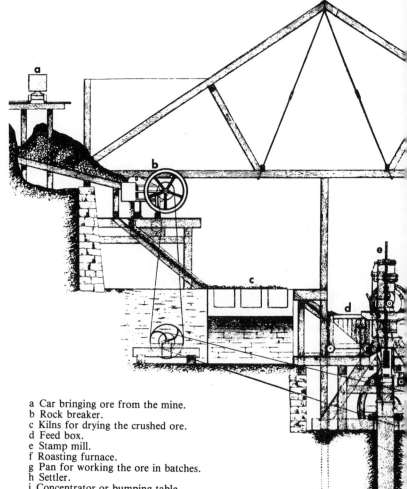

a Car bringing ore from the mine.
b Rock breaker.
c Kilns for drying the crushed ore.
d Feed box.
e Stamp mill.
f Roasting furnace.
g Pan for working the ore in batches.
h Settler.
i Concentrator or bumping table.
j Retort for the amalgam.

Typical ore mill (cross section).

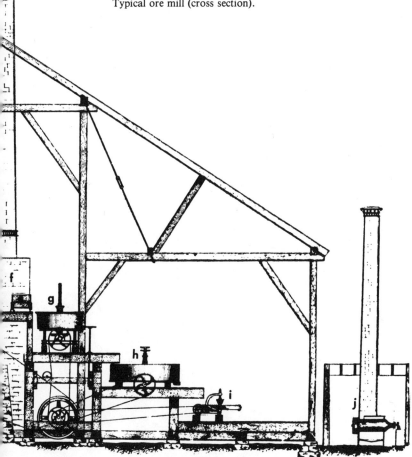

A five stamp
Gilpin County
Slow Drop Mill
manufactured in
Peter McFarlane's
Denver foundry.
Now on exhibit
in Black Hawk.

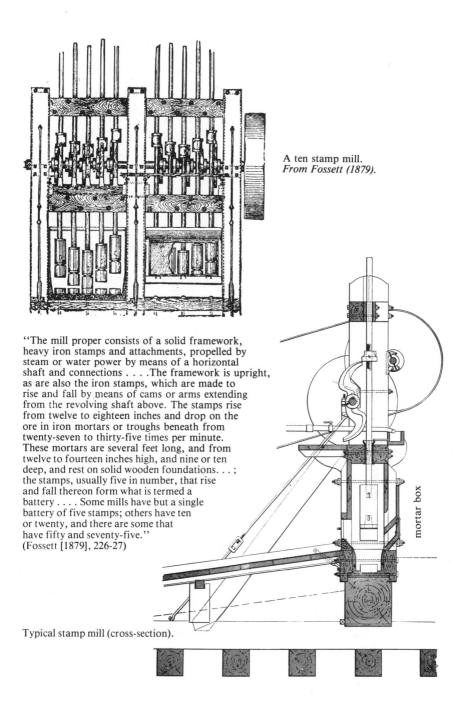

A ten stamp mill.
From Fossett (1879).

"The mill proper consists of a solid framework, heavy iron stamps and attachments, propelled by steam or water power by means of a horizontal shaft and connections . . . .The framework is upright, as are also the iron stamps, which are made to rise and fall by means of cams or arms extending from the revolving shaft above. The stamps rise from twelve to eighteen inches and drop on the ore in iron mortars or troughs beneath from twenty-seven to thirty-five times per minute. These mortars are several feet long, and from twelve to fourteen inches high, and nine or ten deep, and rest on solid wooden foundations. . . ; the stamps, usually five in number, that rise and fall thereon form what is termed a battery . . . . Some mills have but a single battery of five stamps; others have ten or twenty, and there are some that have fifty and seventy-five."
(Fossett [1879], 226-27)

mortar box

Typical stamp mill (cross-section).

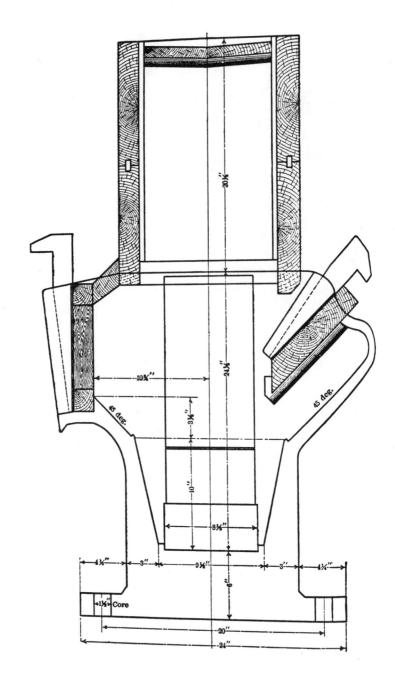

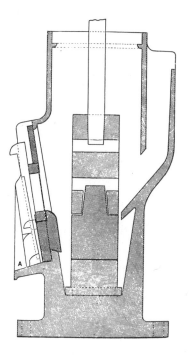

Page opposite: Mortar box (cross-section) of a typical
Gilpin County Slow Drop Stamp Mill. The two slanted areas
on either side, labeled "45 deg.," are the amalgamation plates.
Above: California type mortar box (cross-section).
Note no amalgamation plates and low point of issue (A) of stamped ore.

Comparison of Typical Mills Mine	Width at issue in inches.	Depth of discharge in inches.	Weight of stamps in pounds.	Number of drops per minute.	Height of drop in inches.	Crushing capacity per stamp per 24 hours in tons.
Golden Star, Deadwood, S.D.	12½	10	850	85	9½	4
Hidden Treasure, Black Hawk	24	18	550	30	17	1
North Star, Grass Valley, Calif.	17½	4	850	90	7	1½
Pearl, Bendigo, Australia	15	3½	840	74	7¼	2¼

large needle of gold from the Bates Mine was immersed in mercury for an extended period of time without the least change of weight.[22]

Tests showed that rusty gold had a thin film of iron oxide which prevented amalgamation unless the gold was thoroughly scrubbed with some kind of abrasive.[23] Gold of this nature could not be efficiently processed with a simple stamp mill since the retrieval process depended upon amalgamation after the ore was crushed.

As they bored deeper, therefore, the Gilpin County miners were faced with a technological problem of considerable magnitude and one for which their previous experience proved of little help. It was this technological problem which lay behind the prolonged depression of the mining industry in 1866, 1867, and 1868 and which produced what one expert labelled the "process mania" that accompanied it—frantic experimentation by both professional engineers and practical millmen to find some way to unlock the wealth of Gilpin County's mountains. The end product was the Gilpin County Slow Drop Stamp Mill, the pride of its creators, but the object of severe criticism from mining experts on both coasts. The slow drop mill made its appearance around 1868. It was a feature in the Gregory Gulch area by 1870. Later models differed in some respects from the earliest, but the basic design remained unchanged, and the slow drop stamp mill continued to be the basic machine for processing ores as long as there was a mining industry in Gilpin County.

The stamp mills used in California were designed exclusively to crush ore. They utilized a shallow mortar box with a low issue (the point where the crushed ore, mixed with water, left the mortar box). The stamps generally weighed 750–850 pounds. The height of fall was 4 to 6 inches and the rate of fall was 90–105 drops per minute per stamp. No attempt was made to retrieve any of the gold in the mortar box. This was the function of a variety of equipment outside of the stamp mill proper through which the crushed ore was processed after it was crushed.

Starting with an analysis of the ores they had to work with, the Gilpin County millmen concluded that because the gold was so finely intermixed and so tightly wedded to the ore, it would have to be crushed considerably finer than was the practice in California. To achieve this the mortar box would have to be deeper and have a higher issue. These requirements in turn dictated that the stamps had to be lighter and fall from a greater height at a slower rate of drop. In its final configuration, the typical Gilpin County slow drop mill would employ stamps weighing 550-600 pounds which fell 18 to 20 inches at a rate of 30 drops per minute per stamp. Finally, the Gilpin County process called for trapping the bulk of the gold in the mortar box itself by adding quicksilver to the ore as it was being worked. The quicksilver would amalgamate with the free gold and by the action of the stamps would be thrown against amalgamated copper plates mounted in the mortar box where it would adhere. This feature was called battery amalgamation, and it was the core of the controversy between the Gilpin County millmen and their critics. Simply stated, the Gilpin County slow drop mill was a dual- instead of a single-purpose machine, designed for extremely fine crushing and battery amalgamation where- as the California fast drop mill was designed for crushing only.

Significantly, with the development of the slow drop mill, the amount of gold which an efficiently run operation was able to extract from the Gilpin County ores rose again to 75%, a figure that compares very favorably with the 70% achieved in California at that time.[24] By the end of 1875 the Central City *Register* could boast with justifiable pride:

> The mining outlook in all sections is ... highly encouraging. We have solved the problem of "how to do it," and are gradually bringing the world to our way of thinking. ... The principles which have guided our actions to this end, steadily adhered to for the next five years, will place Colorado where she rightly belongs— at the very head of the bullion producers of the world.[25]

Despite their success in developing methods and equipment to treat Colorado ores, the Gilpin County millmen were unable to silence their many critics, the most prominent of whom was Dr. Rossiter W. Raymond, noted mining engineer and for many years the U. S. Commissioner of Mining Statistics. In 1870 Dr. Raymond opened what was to be a long, unresolved controversy in his report to the Congress on the condition of the mining industry west of the Rocky Mountains. After reviewing the causes of the depression of 1866, 1867, and 1868, he summarized his views of the Colorado mining industry as follows:

> The strong ... reaction in Colorado against new processes, from which the Territory has suffered so much, has gone so far as to make the mill-men obstinately refuse to adopt even the well-

proven apparatus of other regions. In the matter of speed of stamps, there is a singular prejudice in favor of very low rates. I have frequently seen steam-batteries geared to run at 18 drops per minute, and the average speed is not greater than 25 to 30. In other districts of the West, stamps of equal weight are run generally at 60, and frequently as high as 100 drops per minute. The reasons given by the Colorado mill-men are plausible, but they do not, in my opinion, meet the case fully.[26]

Not content with having attributed the Colorado practices to obstinacy rather than proven results on the ores with which the Colorado millmen had to work, Dr. Raymond proceeded to lecture them further in the manner of a stern father talking to a lazy and wayward son.

To the important questions: "How came those mines that once were profitable to fail? What is the secret of the present success of others?..." There are no general or universal replies.... If we consider, however,... that bad management will ruin any mine, however valuable it may be, we may say with confidence that bad management has done more to injure mining in Colorado than all the other causes together. And this bad management has been fourfold—in laws, in the extraction of ores, in the reduction of ores and in general finance.... Scientific men, so called, have made stupendous mistakes in judgment, but these have been surpassed by the blunders of practical men, so called.... This year marks the new era in mining in Colorado. The old spirit of *idleness* and speculation has passed away. The new spirit of labor and economy has sprung into power. It is beginning to recognize that the men to develop the resources of a country are the men who live in it; that the foundation of wealth is labor; that capital is only the hoarded labor of the past loaned to the labor of the future; and that, under all, before all, above all, if there is to be progress, there must be work![27]

Having gotten their mines producing again after a long struggle, the Gilpin County millmen could hardly have taken kindly to a lecture such as this, particularly the charge of being lazy. Their published replies were, on the whole, temperate under the circumstances. "We often hear how milling is done in California and Nevada," said the *Daily Register,*

as if their modes must necessarily produce the same results here. First and last, we have had a host of Pacific coast men here to instruct us; and formerly each coming man was hailed as another Moses to lead us out of the wilderness.... We see no disposition among our mill men to be self-opinionated or old-fogyish. Experience has taught them to hasten very slowly in taking the advice of those whose experience has been in another field.[28]

In a paper read before the American Institute of Mining Engineers in 1871, Dr. Raymond vented his ire against Gilpin County's technique of fine crushing and battery amalgamation which necessitated a slow rate of drop of the stamps:

> Stamp batteries should be built and run to secure the highest efficiency and economy in crushing only, without reference to amalgamation. The amalgamation process should be adopted to the batteries, not the latter to the former.[29]

He concluded his paper with the opinion that his views were "coming more and more to be those of American millmen, even those in Colorado."[30] On this score, Dr. Raymond was far too optimistic. In spite of the criticism, the Colorado millmen believed that they had found their own way out of the wilderness, and they continued to rely on the slow drop mill, fine crushing, and battery amalgamation.

A dozen years after Dr. Raymond opened the controversy, it reached its climax in Colorado itself. The American Institute of Mining Engineers convened in Denver in conjunction with the great National Mining and Industrial Exposition (August 1–September 30, 1882), the first of its kind in the world. Four thousand five hundred and fifty-one mines were represented. Six hundred and seventy-eight tons of ore valued at $718,850 were on exhibit.[31]

The opening session of the Mining Engineers' convention was at the University of Denver on Saturday, August 19. On Monday the delegates journeyed to Central City for an inspection of the mills and mines in Gregory Gulch and the surrounding area, convening that evening in the Opera House to hear a paper prepared by Andrews N. Rogers, superintendent of the consolidated Bobtail Mining Company. The meeting was an historic occasion, since it brought face to face the most influential and severe critic of the Gilpin County mining industry, Dr. Rossiter W. Raymond, and the man who had brought the milling techniques developed in Gilpin County to their highest state of efficiency, Andrews N. Rogers, who fittingly had been elected a full member of the Institute earlier that evening.[32]

After conceding Raymond's charge that the Gilpin County lodes had been badly handled in the early days and were still suffering the effects of 100-foot claims which often prevented proper exploitation, Rogers struck to the heart of the issue:

Exhibits at National Mining and Industrial Exposition, Denver, 1882.
From Harper's Weekly, *September 16, 1882.*

The milling practice here is somewhat different from the methods employed on the Pacific slope. This has led to much unfavorable comment respecting the construction of our mills and the mode of operating them. It is claimed that the millmen of this section are slow, bound to old prejudices, and that the mills do neither good work nor much of it. This is a grave charge which having received the sanction of high authority, claims attention at this time because of the opportunity furnished for a candid discussion of the subject.... While the customs of this section have been tenaciously held to in the face of adverse criticism, it has not been from lack of understanding the points at issue, but from convictions, based on long experience, that the practice of other sections is not applicable to the circumstances of this section. It is held that the milling ores of this district contain a larger percentage of sulphurets than those of the Pacific slope, and that the sulphurets, as a rule, are of less value. In order to mill to any high percentage of the contained value, very fine crushing and good battery amalgamation are essential. This, the underlying proposition, followed out, has after the usual changes, mishaps and waste of money in experimenting, built up the present stamp mill system, which is but little modified from an ancient custom, except in the matter of better construction and more attention to detail.[33]

For Rogers the crucial issue was not the efficient disposal of rock, but the efficient retrieval of gold. In defense of battery amalgamation, he asked the question, "If 75% of the gold, which a good mill will save, can be caught in the battery without other attention than is given by a feeder, why should it be permitted to escape for the purpose of making a race for its recovery with a multiplication of expensive devices beyond?"[34]

In answer to those critics who held that extremely fine crushing would produce a battered and laminated amalgam which would be difficult to handle, Rogers produced the results of experiments carried out at the Bobtail Mill which showed that ore crushed to a fineness of 700,000 particles to the cubic inch when magnified 600 times under the microscope clearly showed that the grains of gold were neither battered nor laminated.[35] "The gold," he stated, "was granular in structure with the appearance of crystalline formation tending to clusters." In fact, in some instances the gold and quartz were "still wedded to each other in bonds so intimate as to defy both stamps and quicksilver." In the light of these experiments, Rogers concluded, it could not be claimed that the Gilpin County stamp mills were overworking the ore with "dead stamping." "Rugged as the stamp mill may appear as a machine," he said, "it has to do with a most delicate problem, and, if we are to believe our senses, must work to a degree of fineness almost beyond human comprehension."[36]

On the subject of the rate of drop of the stamps, Rogers pointed out that all attempts to increase the speed of the stamps in a mill designed for battery amalgamation had failed due to the fact that the increased action did not let the dirt settle evenly in between beats. Rather, it was churned to one end of the mortar where it piled up with the result that some stamps beat directly on the mortar shoes while others stopped on a too-thick pile of dirt to be effective. This not only prevented amalgamation, but resulted in broken stamp stems as well. At this point, Rogers drove home his final argument. Gold and quicksilver, both having high specific gravities, settled to the bottom of the mortar in a slow drop mill where they became intermixed with the finely crushed sands. The action of the stamps and the water tended to scrub or polish the grains of gold, making efficient amalgamation possible. It was in this manner that the slow drop stamp mill overcame the problem of "rusty gold" noted earlier.

As proof for his arguments, Rogers produced the results of a study carried on at the Bobtail Mill during a twenty-six-month period between 1876 and 1878: the mill crushed 57,371 tons of ore and retrieved 73.57% of the assay value.[37] It is here worth re-emphasizing that efficiently run fast drop mills in California, where all retrieval was outside of the mortar box, retrieved approximately 70% of the gold in the ore.

It was, of course, incumbent on Dr. Raymond to reply to Rogers' paper. And a most interesting reply it was, revealing as much about the personality of the man as his professional views. "I am deeply impressed by the arguments in this paper," he said. "It is difficult to dispute or even to question its facts.... This paper is a proof that the work here has not been done ignorantly and out of a blind and positive belief in slow running."[38]

On the face of it, it would appear that Dr. Raymond's capitualtion was complete. This, however, was not the case. Even though he could not refute Rogers' arguments, nor the documented proof of the efficiency of the Bobtail Mill, he nevertheless told the convention that he still felt it a "strange phenomenon" that "some of the best mills in the country—those run with the greatest economy—are running at over a hundred drops per minute."[39] On this point his own obstinacy was clearly evident. Despite Rogers' presentation, Dr. Raymond's mind was closed to the necessity of fine crushing and battery amalgamation in processing Colorado ores. "If the necessity of battery amalgamation," he said, "is the only reason you crush less per unit of power or per unit of fixed capital and general expense and labor, there is room for a discussion in which I do not now undertake to engage."[40]

In his reply to Rogers, Dr. Raymond exhibited a strong streak of arrogance as well as obstinacy. His original criticisms of the Colorado millmen, he said, were directed at a rate of fall in some mills which did not exceed 15 or 18 drops per minute, not the 30 drops per minute that Rogers was using in the Bobtail. "Now," he went on, "I call atention to the fact that Mr. Rogers has got from 30 drops a minute much better results than would be got from 15, and, in view of this, *I think I may claim to have contributed in a humble way to a great public bene-faction.*"[41]

It is difficult to explain Dr. Raymond's attitude even while noting that he was hardly a humble man. One can certainly sympathize with any professional man who has his ideas refuted at a meeting of his professional society. The shock to the ego is not pleasant, but the mark of a true professional is how gracefully he can handle such a situation. In Dr. Raymond's case there seemed to be lurking somewhere in the background a strongly held prejudice against the "practical" man, or more accurately the man without formal professional training.

Among his publications, Dr. Raymond had a pot boiler novel with a western theme. In one scene the author recounts an anecdotal tale involving a bet between a wise old prospector living high up in the Sierras and a group of flatlanders over how fast ice will melt. The old prospector claims that up where he lives the ice is "colder" than that found in the stream after it reaches the desert. The experiment is set up and the money put down. The old prospector, of course, wins the bet. The author then comments that during the discussion on thermometric theory which follows, the old prospector's simplistic explanation is rejected by the losers and onlookers. Dr. Raymond concludes: "it is thus that the simplicity of science usually fares among the unscientific. There are no theorists so wild as your 'practical men.'"[42]

Dr. Raymond was not, however, entirely consistent in this view.

Toward the end of the novel, his hero manipulates a dislocated shoulder back into place and sets a compound fracture of the leg for a man who has fallen off a horse. In the course of these ministrations he puts the patient's mind at ease by noting that "doctors are alright when you don't know what ails you; when you do, you don't want 'em."[43] To this, the Gilpin County millmen would probably have answered "Amen!" They knew what had ailed them, had found a remedy, and in their opinion, had no need for further gratuitous advice. Curiously, this point had been well documented by Dr. Raymond himself in an earlier report to Congress:

> In view of the limited extent of the productive gold-district of Gilpin County, the number of stamps which it keeps in operation is unequalled, except by the Comstock Silver district, in the history of American mining.[44]

Peter McFarlane was a staunch defender of Gilpin County milling methods. In a letter to an old friend, Philip Mixsell, superintendent of the M. X. Mining and Milling Company in Idaho Springs many years later, he succinctly expressed the views which he championed throughout his career. "In the matter of milling," he wrote, "Calif 'ain't in it.' Is way behind Gilpin County in my opinion."[45] Replying to a request for information regarding the Gilpin County slow drop process, he articulated some of his reasons for this opinion:

> The advantage of battery amalgamation is apparent when one considers how gold particles may be thrown upon the plates many times—perhaps thousands of times before finding lodgement. But without battery plates, and only an apron plate outside the battery over which the gold passes only once, the chances of recovery are comparatively slim. The ore in this county is base and refractory and hard to amalgamate, and only by a perfect system of battery amalgamation can it be fairly well saved.... Another advantage of the slow drop mill is there is double or treble the copper surface to the ton of ore treated than is usually found in the rapid drop mills.[46]

Three years later McFarlane had modified his views somewhat regarding the efficiency of the old slow drop mill. Writing to George E. Collins of Denver, he expressed the opinion that this piece of equipment was "happily a thing of the past." "It was," he said, "*the* mill for many years, or until the more rapid drop was perfected."[47] Taken by itself and at face value, it would appear that McFarlane had abandoned the position so strongly defended by the Gilpin County millmen for over thirty years and had finally admitted that the critics of Colorado milling practices were, in the end, correct. This, however, was not quite the case.

It will be remembered that it was the Gilpin County millmen's insistence on the fine crushing of the ore and the battery amalgamation that drew Raymond's and other experts' criticism. In their opinion the stamp mill should be designed for crushing only. As A. N. Rogers noted, it was the question of battery amalgamation that occasioned all of the points of difference between the California and Colorado practices. Despite the fact that he now believed that the old slow drop mill was "happily a thing of the past," McFarlane had not really abandoned the faith. True, he was now recommending a mill with heavier stamps (750 pounds as compared with 500–600), a shorter fall (8–10 inches as compared with 16–20), and a faster rate of drop (60–65 per minute as compared with 30), but the purpose of these modifications was to achieve better battery amalgamation. At no time did he advocate using the stamp mill for crushing only.[48]

McFarlane's letter to Collins is interesting for reasons other than his views on milling processes. In a long passage in which he compares the old slow drop mill to his pet horse, he reveals the depth and breadth of his self-education and a delightful sense of humor. For this reason, the passage is worth quoting in full:

> The old slow drop mill reminds me of an old horse I drive in my dog cart, who I shall introduce to you as Paddy. His real name though is Arthur William Patrick Albert. But I call him Paddy for short. Well, I have worked with that animal for many years (as I have with slow drop stamps) in an endeavor to improve him (that is make him of more use to me as a horse). But no matter how much grain I fed him; no matter how much I curry him, urge, coax, cajole, sympathize, sooth, flatter, praise, exhort, exposticate, entreat, beseech, invoice, importune—nay on bended knees with tears in my eyes, despair on my countenance and distraction in my very soul have I supplicated that dumb brute. Yea, and I have gone further than that in the hope born of desperation that he still had some goodness in him, but that I had not the ability to bring it to the surface.
>
> I have increased my efforts, have quoted to him from Shakespere and Shelley and dilated and if possible enlarged on their

trancendental beauty, and have told him a lot about Tennyson, Pope, Byron, Burns and Bunyan's *Pilgrim's Progress:* have read to him Baxter's *Saints' Everlasting Rest* (that seemed to tickle him a little bit), and Darwin's *Descent of Man* (he acted here as if he wanted to say 'yes a h[ell] of a descent'), Scott's *Lady of the Lake, David Copperfield,* and Beecher's *Life of Jesus the Christ.*

Here I changed my tactics and tried an application of vocal music. For instance, I sang "Rocked in the cradle of the deep," "Nancy Lee," "Dearie," "Abide with me," "Hot time in the old town," "Yankee Doodle," "Home sweet Home," and a thousand others of like tenor, yet diversified enough, but all calculated to touch his sympathetic nature and yield good results.

Nor was that all. For fear that my singing might not be captivating to him, I bought one of those phonograph machines (a good one. Paid $275.00 for it), and led the poor bewildered creature up to the house, having raised the window so he could hear better, and started the thing up. To this, as likewise to all, he paid no attention.

As a last resort, I trotted out the violin and piano accompaniment, but all to no avail. He still had only one step to every time. While other horses could travel 6 miles an hour, 3 was his utmost limit. And it cost me just as much to have him perambulate 3 miles as it cost other horses to travel 6. If anyone doubts this story, I have and yet own the patient quadruped whose acquaintance you have hereby made, and he is on exhibition daily ... and I think is open to interviewers. And I am sure will corroborate and substantiate too the tale I have just unfolded to you. Paddy stands in the same relationship to other animals of his type as do long drop stamps to the more rapid.

The controversy over the best way to treat Gilpin County ores continued beyond the time when it no longer mattered. Through it all, McFarlane stood firm in his belief that the old methods, that is, slow or medium-rapid drop stamps and battery amalgamation, provided the only answer. For this belief he was subjected to a good deal of harsh criticism, but in his own mind he was convinced that he had followed the Apostle Paul's advice to "Prove all things, and hold fast to that which is good."[49]

In addition to establishing McFarlane & Company on a sound footing, the Randolph mill contract of 1872 was also instrumental in the emergence of the McFarlane brothers as civic as well as business leaders in Central City. In the municipal election of April 1873, William ran for alderman on the Republican ticket in the first ward and was elected. For the next ten years, Central City's first ward was almost the private property of the McFarlanes. William was re-elected in 1874. Peter took his seat on the city council in 1876, and was re-elected in 1877. In 1878, Peter was elected mayor; following his term in this office he was returned to the city council in the elections of 1880 and 1881. In the latter year, Mayor John Best resigned before his term was up, and Peter replaced him as mayor *pro tem.* [50]

The McFarlanes' business connections with Colonel George E. Randolph, Civil War hero and one of Gregory Gulch's most colorful and influential pioneer citizens, certainly did not hinder their successful venture into local politics. [51] Randolph had come to Colorado in November 1864 as manager of the Boston Milling Company in Black Hawk. In July 1868 he was chosen as a Gilpin County representative to the territorial Republican convention in Denver. By 1872 he had survived the many crises that had plagued the mining industry of the county as the surface ores were worked out, and his Ophir and Narragansett mines were operating at a profit, largely owing to his ingenuity and talent. In the fall of the year he moved his socially ambitious wife out of Pat Casey's remodeled log cabin in Nevadaville, which had been their home for a number of years, into a fashionable house on Casey Street in Central City. [52] Eight years of hard work had paid off, and George and Hattie Randolph had become members of the inner circle that dominated the economic and social life of the four communities straddling Gregory Gulch. An extended business association with a man of his stature was valuable to the McFarlanes, two ambitious young men.

Useful as their political connections were for business purposes, the McFarlanes' business success did not depend upon these connections. Basically, their "industry ... integrity ... persistent effort and close application to legitimate business" [53] lay at the root of their success. In short, they were excellent businessmen who eventually built a substantial company through hard work. These characteristics were to be demonstrated in the months following Central City's catastrophic fire.

About midday on May 21, 1874, a fire broke out in a shack housing a Chinese laundry in Dostal Alley. Whipped by the wind, it raged for six hours before it was finally brought under control. One hundred fifty buildings in the center of town were destroyed at a loss of approximately $230,000. [54]

The McFarlane brothers were fortunate. The fire was brought under control as it reached the Teller House, and their combined shop and home some three blocks farther up Eureka Street was untouched. Consequently, what was for many residents of Central City a major disaster was for the McFarlanes an opportunity. Central City would have to rebuild, and they were prepared to make the most of the situation.

The task of raising the city from the ashes began as soon as the first shock had worn off. Two days after the fire occurred, the *Daily Register* echoed the determination and spirit of the town:

> We are going to have a new, and, if properly directed, much more substantial and better city than that which disappeared on Thursday. At no previous period has there been manifested such enthusiasm on the present and future prospects.[55]

In the same issue the editor observed that if anything the disaster had fed rather than dampened the irrepressible optimism of the mining camp:

> The air is full of smoke and dust and flying debris. The universal activity reminds us of old times when the city was founded, and everyone is expecting to make a fortune in 30 days.

No doubt some did. There were others, like the McFarlane brothers, who, while not making great fortunes, nevertheless profited handsomely in the rush to re-create the capital city of the "Little Kingdom of Gilpin."

By the end of 1874 scores of new brick and stone buildings graced the main streets of the town. Leveled and graded streets, sidewalks, and here and there handsome store fronts of ironwork provided a touch of elegance missing in the old clapboard and log cabin town perched precariously on both sides of the gulch. In appearance, as well as by the product of her only industry, the "Golden Queen" began to live up to her name. As the new year began, the town was described as follows:

> The business wants of the city require about one hundred business houses. These occupy compactly, both sides of Main Street, and the adjacent portions of Eureka, Lawrence, Gregory, Spring and Nevada streets. The Teller House up Eureka, forms the fitting capitol of new Central. The banks cluster around the corner of Eureka and Main streets, now the best business point. The cost of

these new buildings aggregate about $150,000. Those underway
and projected will increase it not far from $300,000. . . . Home
capital is doing all this.[56]

During the following year, another eighty-eight buildings were completed, valued at $125,000,[57] and the work of reconstruction was
largely over. The town pulsed with life and the *Daily Register* was led to
observe with some puzzlement:

> The cry of hard times is general, yet numerous inquiries among
> the Central merchants yesterday elicited the fact that all were
> doing far better trade this year than last, or at any previous time
> since '66. Something wrong somewhere.[58]

Nevertheless, as the holiday season approached with its abundance of
gay spirits of several varieties, the editor saw fit to issue the following
word of caution to the young ladies of the town:

> If you are awakened by the Central glee club with the beautiful
> ditty, "Come where my nose lies bleeding," with catarrh accom-
> paniment, it is not proper for maids to go out "into the garden,"
> and pick a bouquet for the serenaders.[59]

Prosperous and as spirited as ever, Central City entered the nation's
centennial year full of hope and pride of accomplishment.

The extent to which Peter and Will McFarlane were able to profit
from the building bonanza that followed the fire was considerable,
although hard to document in terms of dollars. While other building
firms are frequently mentioned in the "gossip column" of the *Daily
Register* in connection with construction projects, McFarlane &
Company's name is conspicuously absent during the first year of the
city's rebuilding. The most probable explanation is that due to the
limited space given local news in the paper, only prime contractors on
any project rated mention.

Another factor may have been that because the McFarlanes were so
deeply committed to the Randolph mill project, they ceased to advertise
in the *Daily Register* during 1872; and because of this, the editor may
have doubted that their efforts were newsworthy or that he should
supply any free advertising.

That they did succeed in improving their business and financial
position considerably during the community's reconstruction there is
no doubt, for by the summer of 1875 they were involved with John
Mellor of the banking firm of Hanington and Mellor in the construc-

tion of "two handsome brick structures occupying ground from Hannington and Mellor's bank seventy-two feet down Lawrence street."[60] John Mellor and Henry Hanington, who had settled in Gilpin County the same year as Peter McFarlane,[61] formed a partnership on January 1, 1875,[62] and opened for business in the new Wells Fargo building on Lawrence Street. Mellor owned the old Concert Hall west of the original Wells Fargo building, which was destroyed in the fire.[63] In the spring of 1875 he began negotiations to purchase the site of the old Montana Theatre, which was contiguous to his Concert Hall property. Rumors of these negotiations reached the *Daily Register,* which noted on May 8:

> We are informed that John Mellor Esq. will build an elegant block on the site of the old Concert Hall and Montana Theatre buildings as soon as the title to a portion of the ground is arranged.

Mellor was successful in his efforts, and by June 1, 1875, workmen were clearing away the debris on the two pieces of property and leveling the ground preparatory to construction.[64] Two weeks later the *Daily Register* reported that the "work of grading the Mellor and McFarlane lots on Lawrence street goes briskly forward,"[65] revealing that the McFarlane brothers were involved in a major real estate deal with one of the partners in Central City's newest banking firm. Construction of the two buildings began near the end of July, after some unforeseen difficulties in getting the ground ready for the foundations. These difficulties caused the *Daily Register* to remark that the owners should not be discouraged as "they will have the consolation of knowing ... when once their buildings are in place, they will add more to the improvement of the city than anything done thus far this season."[66] By the first week in November, workmen were putting the finishing touches on the two-story buildings, which sported "handsome iron fronts."[67] On November 17, John Mellor, his partner Henry Hanington, and Robert A. Campbell, agent for the Kansas City Express, moved in as the new block's first tenants.[68] The total cost of the project was $17,000, a sum which represented almost 14% of all new construction completed in Central City in 1875.[69]

For the McFarlane brothers, therefore, the new buildings on Lawrence Street represented a sizable investment and one with an excellent income potential. Of equal importance was their business association with Hanington and Mellor, for it gave them access to loan capital to expand further their real estate holdings. They were quick to exploit the possibilities which their new business association presented. Work had barely begun on grading the ground for the new Lawrence Street buildings when they borrowed $2,500 from Mellor and Hanington's bank to purchase another piece of property in the heart of the city at the juncture of Main and Eureka Streets. This lot extended twenty-five feet east of the old Wells Fargo building on the north side of Eureka Street and north to High Street. The loan was repaid in full on February 2, 1876.[70] On the same day the McFarlane brothers borrowed another $6,000, in two equal shares from each of two private parties, securing these loans with a trust deed held by John Mellor on the same piece of property.[71] As can be seen, they were not inclined to let any assets which could be put to work lie idle. Consequently, as the new Central City rose from the ashes of the old, the McFarlane brothers emerged as two of its more substantial citizens. They were the owners of a thriving construction business, they held important real estate interests in the business center of the town, and they had begun their significant political career. Five-and-one-half years of effort had been crowned by success. The future of McFarlane & Company was dependent upon the continued prosperity of the Gilpin County mining industry. As the year 1876 opened, the prospects looked bright; the economic situation was summarized by the local press as follows:

> We lay before our readers today a complete and accurate statement of the mining product of Gilpin County for 1875. Much cause for congratulation will be found in the large bullion increase and steady progress and advancement of the past year. It is generally admitted that the leading, and, in fact, the only industry of the county, was never on such a successful and encouraging basis as now, and an air of permanent and lasting prosperity is everywhere evident.[72]

For Peter McFarlane, the next six years were prosperous and happy. Indeed, there is reason to believe that these may have been the most satisfying of all of his sixty years in Central City. There is nothing in his extant correspondence which evinces this happiness in any direct way, but much other evidence points to this conclusion. The mining industry, as the *Daily Register* predicted, prospered, and consequently so did McFarlane & Company. Furthermore, in contrast to the period following 1882 when he was forced to spend extended periods of time

William Orr McFarlane
(1843-1924).
In 1874 married "Libbie" Hale.

Mary Elizabeth Hale McFarlane
(1850-1925).
School, music, and
Sunday School teacher.

Mrs. Peter McFarlane,
nee Marie Elizabeth Frey.

Mrs. Peter McFarlane

away from home supervising the construction of mills not only in other parts of the state but throughout the West, for a half dozen years McFarlane seems to have been able to enjoy a normal home life. On November 1, 1877, that "cussed thing of batching" finally came to an end with his marriage to Marie Elizabeth Frey of Central City, and the following year George McFarlane, the first of his three children, was born.

In addition to a flourishing business and a happy marriage, the years 1876-1882 saw McFarlane rise to a position of importance in the affairs of the community, a situation reflected in his election to the city council in 1876, 1877, 1880, and 1881. It was his election as mayor, in 1878, however, that clearly showed the esteem in which he was held by the citizens of Central City.

As the election approached, many along Gregory Gulch supported the suggestion that it ought to be conducted on a nonpartisan basis rather than by the traditional nomination of candidates in party caucus.[73] Consequently, in both Black Hawk and Central City "citizens conventions" were held to nominate a nonpartisan slate of officers, much to the displeasure of the *Daily Register,* which was resolutely Republican and stoutly in favor of partisan elections.[74] The citizens convention in Central City took place on the evening of March 27, and its transactions were reported as follows:

> The convention called by "many citizens," met last evening at the County Court House and was called to order promptly at 8 o'clock by W. H. Bush Esq., who nominated Col. Geo. E. Randolph, Chairman. . . . Peter McFarlane being the only person in nomination received the unanimous vote for nomination as mayor.[75]

The next evening the Republican regulars gathered in Turner Hall to nominate their slate. The *Daily Register* enthusiastically reported the results:

> The Republican Convention at Turner Hall last evening was of that character as to dispel illusions in regard to a mixed or mongrel ticket. Long before the meeting was called to order, the hall was crowded, and the sound judgement of the Central Committee in the selecting of a different place than the County Court House, was apparent. No other place would have been adequate to have held the vast throng that assembled to dispel all thoughts or intimations which might have been formed that the

citizens of Central desired other than a ticket composed of pure Republicanism.[76]

The ticket, however, was not one which represented "pure Republicanism," as the *Register* itself was forced to admit, for three of those nominated for office at the Republican convention had also been nominated at the citizens convention the night before. And while all were Republicans, they were not the staunch party adherents so admired by the editor of Central City's leading newspaper. The three "mongrels" named to the ticket were Peter McFarlane, nominated by acclamation for mayor, Ed Salisbury, chosen as the candidate for police magistrate, and Thomas H. Walter, nominated for alderman from the second ward.[77] The *Daily Register* consoled itself in the fact that the other seven nominees were "pure, unadulterated Republicans, and should receive the support of all the Republicans in the City."[78] Peter McFarlane was thus the unanimous choice for mayor at both conventions, a fact that made his election a mere formality, since the Democrats did not put up a candidate.

McFarlane's term as mayor was an exciting one, for it coincided with the opening year of Central City's opera house, the town's proof to the rest of the world that culture as well as mining flourished in Gregory Gulch. McFarlane had a personal interest in this project, which attracted nation-wide attention, because McFarlane & Company had executed its splendid interior. (A later chapter shows in detail that this project had a sentimental meaning for him that lingered long after the obvious financial benefits to the company had been forgotten.)

When he assumed the reins of the town government in 1878, McFarlane probably did not suspect that before his one-year term of office was over, the reign of the "Golden Queen" as the mining capital of the state would come to an abrupt end. The construction and opening of the Opera House coincided with the discovery of rich deposits of silver in the vicinity of Leadville. Beginning in June 1877, the rush to Lake County was on, creating once again in the months that followed the spectacle of thousands of exuberant, boisterous, incurably optimistic men frantically scrambling toward the spot where new veins of mineral were being exposed—thousands of men driven by visions of overnight wealth, impatient to start the search.[79] When the year was over, the inhabitants of Gilpin County were shocked to learn the extent of Leadville's success, for the dollar value of Lake County silver had exceeded that of Gilpin County gold by over $170,000.

The burgeoning town created an enormous demand for supplies and equipment best obtained in Denver. For the first three years, all of the traffic between Leadville and Denver was handled by mule and ox trains. The railroads, however, were acutely aware of the profits to be made in supplying the new mining camp, and by the summer of 1878, the Atchison, Topeka and Santa Fe, the Denver South Park and Pacific, and the Rio Grande were all pushing rails into the upper Arkansas Valley as fast as their resources permitted.[80] The Rio Grande finally completed the first rail link with Denver on July 20, 1880.

Because of this strategic location with rail connections to the East and to the mining camps of the mountains, Denver became the chief source of supplies for the mining industry and the prime benefactor of not only the Leadville boom but those which followed in other areas.

> The chief city of the State, stagnant and inert before, now began to assume the appearance of an active, bustling community. Real estate, for which there had been neither inquiry nor sale of consequence during the preceding four or five years, suddenly rose into unwonted prominence for safe and profitable investment. The increase of population became so great it was impossible to provide shelter for the multitudes, notwithstanding the enormous and wholly unprecedented advance of building that followed. . . . Commerce and manufactures were strained to their utmost to meet the volume of orders that poured in upon them.[81]

Millions of dollars came to Denver. Also, those firms serving the mining industry began to concentrate in Denver, in order to enjoy the advantages that railroad transportation afforded in the competition for business coming out of Leadville and other mountain communities.

One such firm was the pioneer company of Hendrie and Bolthoff, which had introduced the first California fast drop stamp mill at Black Hawk soon after the initial gold strikes in Gregory Gulch and which had subsequently constructed most of the early stamp mills in Gilpin County.[82] They moved to Denver in 1882, and Peter and William McFarlane purchased their machine shop and foundry, a landmark on Eureka Street since 1861.[83]

The ruins of the machine shop and foundry still stand on the south side of Eureka Street, appropriately located between two other monuments to Central City's past, the Opera House and Peter McFarlane's lovely Victorian house, which at one time quartered the shop and offices of McFarlane & Company, but which is now maintained in pristine condition as a well-to-do home of the 1880s and 1890s. In 1964 I visited the foundry where Peter McFarlane conducted business for almost forty-seven years. The floor was littered with hundreds of canceled checks, a few dozen old books, and several battered pieces of furniture, the most interesting of which was a wooden desk in the corner of the room. This desk, with its six-inch footrest almost worn through, could well have been the one listed in the January 1, 1872 inventory of McFarlane & Company assets.[84] Next to the desk was a safe. The door of the safe stood crookedly open, probably jimmied by vandals, who, fortunately, passed by the only items of historic value left in the office—a large portion of private and business correspondence, which in one way or another has now found its way into this book.

With the purchase of the Hendrie and Bolthoff foundry and machine shop, a chapter in the life of Peter McFarlane and in the history of McFarlane & Company came to an end. It had been a decade marked by unbroken business success, political recognition, and, topping it all, a happy marriage. All of these combined into a manner of life contrasting starkly with experiences ten years earlier. The large house on Eureka Street was a mansion compared to the building further up the street, the small frame house that had served as office, shop, and crowded bachelor quarters for Peter, his two brothers, and his cousin, where when a visitor stayed overnight, there were, as Peter noted, "three of us in bed like boys."[85]

Ten years after the January 1, 1872 inventory was taken, McFarlane & Company was doing a gross yearly business of over $60,000, and had investments in real estate, mining and other stocks valued at over $24,000.[86] Ironically, at just the time when other businessmen were moving to Denver, Peter McFarlane pushed his roots deeper into the hard rock of Gregory Gulch. Although it may not have been evident at the time, with the purchase of the foundry and machine shop on Eureka Street he tied his fate to that of Central City.

CHAPTER VI

Men to Match
the Mineral Mountains
1882-1892

T HE purchase of the Hendrie and Bolthoff foundry by the McFarlane brothers climaxed a decade of effort that, in many respects, was the kind of raw material out of which Horatio Alger fashioned his popular didactic romances. Strict adherence to the Alger formula of hard work, honesty, thrift, luck, perseverance in the face of all obstacles, faith in the future, and a willingness to sacrifice on its behalf paid good dividends for Peter and Will McFarlane. Just over a decade after their arrival in Central City with no capital other than strong bodies, trained hands, a set of personal and business ethics deeply rooted in Scotch Presbyterianism, and the buoyant optimism characteristic of those who rushed to the gold camps, the McFarlane brothers had become solid, respected citizens of Colorado's oldest mining camp. True, they did not rank with Gilpin County's more flamboyant figures, but their achievements placed them among the Little Kingdom's aristocracy. In its year-end business report for 1880, the local newspaper noted that the

> McFarlane brothers are the heavy contractors of the mountains. Many of the handsome buildings which adorn our streets are their work. They do a large business of building mules [hoists], shaft houses and building generally. Their business will equal any similar in the mountains.[1]

69

The Spartan virtues which had led to success in the decade just ended were to be put to an even more severe test in the following decade, as mining along the gulch declined in importance. The mining industry of the *state* was sound and expanding. In fact, throughout the entire decade, Colorado would lead the nation in the production of precious metals. But the end of Gilpin County's long reign as queen of the Colorado mining camps was at hand. Its mines would continue to produce over $1,000,000 worth of gold and silver each year for the next two-and-one-half decades, but by 1880 Gilpin County was no longer the mining capital of the state. In 1877 its mines accounted for one-third of the gold and silver blasted out of the Colorado mountains. Four years later this figure had tumbled to one-tenth. The attention of the mining industry, as mentioned earlier, had become focused on Lake County and its bustling, booming, and bawdy capital, Leadville, which was producing over 40% of the gold and silver mined in the state. There another mining boom had begun.

> Across the broad prairies, the track marked by white, and bleaching skeletons, through the silent valleys, over flowing rivers, up precipitous mountains, came the wagons of the madly anxious miners. . . . Every moments delay may cost a million—every hour on the road means a fortune lost forever.[2]

Central City was still a good mining camp and would continue to be so for another twenty-five years. Leadville, however, was a spectacular camp, and the allegiance of the men who moiled for gold on the mining frontier of the great American West was first and always with the spectacular. Consequently, it was the already established mining camps, particularly Central City, that furnished the hard core of the boomers heading for Leadville—sinewy, hard-handed, experienced hard rock miners and prospectors, eager as always to blast into a virgin lode, eager for yet another game of poker with Lady Luck.

The capitalist was no less eager than the miner or the prospector to join the game and toss his assets into the pot. On the heels of the prospectors and miners who rushed into the Leadville area in 1878 came a wave of investment capital to develop and work the lodes below the surface outcroppings and to build the mills and smelters necessary to extract the precious metals from the ores. The result was that not only men but capital was drained away from Gilpin County; this resulted in the closing of some of its marginal mines and a serious contraction of further exploration and development of its mineral resources. In the face of these hard economic facts, the wisdom of the McFarlane brothers' decision to purchase the Eureka Street foundry at the height of the Leadville boom would seem to be open to question, but subsequent events would prove it to be less ill-conceived than it might appear at first glance.

The vitality of Central City is shown by the fact that of the twenty mills with 800 stamps which were in operation in Gilpin County in 1880, the majority worked steadily through the next decade. In addition, Clear Creek County (to the south) had seven mills with 106 stamps and four crushing mills, and Boulder County (to the north) had nine mills with 185 stamps. Taken together, these installations represented a sizable market just for stamp-mill replacement parts, such as mortars, shoes, stamps, stems, and cams. When the equipment needs of the mines are added to those of the mills—for instance, such items as hoists, boilers, pumps, pulleys, ore buckets, and ore wagons—it can be seen that the opportunities for an aggressive, well-run company whose business was the manufacture, installation, and repair of such equipment were considerable. The market for mining and milling supplies and equipment for just Clear Creek County alone was estimated to be approximately $300,000 in 1880.[3] Since the dollar values of gold and silver produced in Gilpin County and Clear Creek County in 1880 were roughly equal, it can be assumed that the Gilpin County miners and millmen ordered an equal amount of supplies and equipment.

Because of their talent for grasping business opportunities, it is hard to escape the conclusion that Peter and Will McFarlane's decision to buy the Hendrie and Bolthoff foundry was the result of a fairly careful analysis of the mining industry of Gilpin County and the surrounding area, an analysis which revealed not only an expanding market for the products they had in mind but rising prices as well. A business note in the *Weekly Register-Call* on January 21, 1881, reported a situation that the brothers undoubtedly were following closely when considering the purchase of the Eureka Street foundry from Hendrie and Bolthoff. The paper noted that "mining machinery of all kind is coming into demand in Gilpin County, and the prices for the same are correspondingly higher than formerly." The impetus behind this growing market was the conviction of the Gilpin County miners that the mines would have to be pushed deeper than anyone had first imagined if the prosperity of the county was to be maintained. As the newspaper put it:

> As the years pass by, the theory that the true success in this region lies in deep mining is becoming more and more demonstrated. It is becoming a notable fact that the mines which produced the largest, are those which are explored the deepest.[4]

The growing market for mine and milling machinery of all kinds was the direct result of putting this theory into practice.

With the mining industry of Gilpin County prospering, the McFarlane brothers were assured of at least a modest level of prosperity. Peter and Will, however, intended to profit from the mining boom spreading over the state. Although they were essentially conservative businessmen, they were by no means reluctant to invest in business ventures which had a reasonable chance of success. In the fall of 1878, for instance, they joined with Hendrie and Bolthoff to reopen and operate the Golden Flint Mine, near the head of Gamble Gulch, which had been idle for a long time. This project included the building of a fifteen stamp mill to process the ore.[5] It apparently was a total failure, for by the fall of the succeeding year the Golden Flint was again idle.[6]

The shift from an essentially local to a state-oriented business, which the McFarlane brothers accomplished early in the 1880s, was no mean achievement. Their location put them at serious competitive disadvantage with respect to the mine and milling equipment manufacturers who were located in Denver at the hub of the railroad network which supplied the mining camps of the Colorado mountains.

Firmly established in Denver by 1885 and ready to take full advantage of the Leadville boom were the new Denver Foundry and Machine Works at 1734 Fifteenth Street operated by James W. Jackson; the plant of the Colorado Iron Works at Eighth and Larimer; the Excelsior Foundry and Machine Shop on Sixteenth Street; the Kennedy-Pierce Company at Seventeenth and Blake; the Stearns-Rogers Company; and of course, Hendrie and Bolthoff.[7] In addition to these locally owned manufacturing establishments, the competition included the distributors of eastern companies such as Fraser and Chalmers of Chicago. It was a formidable line-up, and the fact that McFarlane & Company not only survived but within ten years was operating foundries in Denver and Black Hawk as well as Central City is testimony to the business acumen and driving energy of Peter and Will McFarlane.

The decision to purchase the Eureka Street foundry and bid for a share of the business stemming from the state-wide mining boom resulted in a considerable upheaval in the private lives of Peter and Will McFarlane. The fairly comfortable routine, which was the reward of their efforts following the fire of May 1874, and which had allowed them time to participate in local politics, came to an abrupt end. For the next ten years, the pressures of business left no time for politics and precious little even for their families. One of the brothers had to oversee the operation of the foundry and machine shop in Central City and make sure that the company's position in the local market was secure, while the other had to spend most of his time out in the areas where the prospectors and miners were discovering and developing new lodes. There he was in a position to submit bids for buildings and equipment and serve as the on-site foreman once a contract had been secured. The responsibility for the Central City operation fell to Will, the field work to Peter. For neither was the arrangement easy. Constant communication covering the details of bids, contracts, delivery problems, bills, and money owed the company was an absolute necessity. Consequently, the end of each day usually meant a tiring session with pen and paper, and at no time was this as efficient as when the brothers could sit down and discuss face to face the details of their business.

The *McFarlane Papers,* unfortunately, do not contain any of this correspondence until several years after the purchase of the Eureka Street foundry, and then only scattered and unrelated pieces. Much of the correspondence, however, relative to the construction of a 120 stamp mill in Telluride in 1892 and 1893 has been preserved, and from this material it is possible to obtain an accurate picture of the conditions under which Peter and Will operated after 1882.

The Telluride contract was for a mill to process ore from the Gold King Mine[8] which was operated by the San Miguel Consolidated Mining Company. This company was headed by William Story and Lucien L. Nunn, president and vice president, respectively, of the First National Bank of Telluride. At $800,000,[9] it was probably the largest single contract to date for McFarlane & Company and probably the most lucrative. Terms were agreed to soon after April 1892;[10] with construction several months along, Peter estimated that they would clear $25,000.[11]

Around the middle of April, Peter left Central City for Telluride to survey the mill site preparatory to completing the detailed drawings.[12] By June construction was underway, and he was at the site until it was completed approximately seven months later.[13]

The contract had called for the mill to be running by September 1,[14] but there were many delays in construction. Getting equipment and supplies as he needed them was a particularly vexing problem for Peter. He could not keep his construction crew together unless he had a steady flow of material from the Central City shops and from the subcontractors. His letters to Will that summer and fall are full of passages such as the following:

> Roofing has not arrived. . . . I am afraid there was some mistake about H. B.[15] telephoning you that it had been taken out of Denver two days before you wrote, nor yet has the chain to raise the crushers come. You will see from this that I am pretty nearly ashore from want of material. Nobody working today for fear that I'd get out of work tomorrow.[16]

> We are very much hindered for want of material of all kinds, except lumber. Hendrie/B have delayed us more than anyone else —than all the rest together. 27 days they have had the order for the roofing and they have been all summer trying to get a chain. The result is that I am going to try and raise the crushers with rope blocks after paying $120 to them for their chain blocks. They could not understand why I could not raise 30 feet by lengthening out the hand chain, when they knew the blocks would only pull apart 12 feet. . . . Such stupidity is hard to account for.[17]

If Will were loath to open his mail while the Gold King mill was going up, it would not be hard to understand why. Almost every delivery contained communications such as those quoted above. Some of the problems he could do something about, some he could not, and there is no reason to believe that the pressure on him in Central City was any less than on his brother in Telluride, except for the fact that it was Peter who had the impatient owners constantly looking over his shoulder.

As frustrating as the problems involved with construction were, they were not nearly as vexing as those involved in obtaining payment while the construction progressed. Mining promoters seldom entered into a venture with all of the capital needed to bring a mine or mill into production, and the contractors often did not know from one moment to the next whether or not they would even get paid. Often the bright promise of a particular lode became extremely tarnished after an initial success. The result was another hole in the ground or a silent stamp mill marking the burial plot of frustrated hopes. In such cases, the bankrupt owners deeded the mine with its shaft house and maybe a stamp mill to the company which built them, and the new owners in turn leased them to someone else for whom these monuments to proven failure had no meaning.

Fortunately for the McFarlane brothers this classic story of the mining frontier was not to be repeated in connection with the San Miguel company's huge mill. There were, nevertheless, problems with respect to meeting the monthly payments as specified by the contract, and these caused Peter constant worry because he and Will could not afford to underwrite the entire project and so needed regular payments as they went along.

The contract called for $25,000 to be paid before the end of June.[18] No payment had been made by July 19, and Peter wrote to Will of his plans for obtaining the money:

> Gov. Story[19] went to Ouray on Saturday and I have not seen him since, and, therefore, do not know what about the money, but he'll be home tomorrow.... I'll get after him as soon as he does return, and you may bet I'll make him fork over $15,000 p. d. q.... I have it put up this way. Story is in politics and a misstep in this business would be fatal to him because of Muldoon.[20] He knows he must pay for the mill.... Nunn is in Europe for the purpose of raising more money. To sum it up, I think there is money to pay us, and Story knows if we ain't paid we'll raise a howl, and if Muldoon gets ahold of it, it will cook Story's political goose. Therefore, Story is determined we'll be paid.[21]

Gold mining was a risky game for all who chose to play it, and after twenty-three years of playing, Peter knew full well that to survive he could not hold back any aces that came his way. That he had analyzed the situation correctly is evident from the fact that at the time he was penning the above letter, a check for $10,000 was already in the mail from Story.[22]

This sum, however, still left $15,000 due on the June payment, and Story was quick to see that it was forthcoming, together with an appeal for support for his candidacy for governor.

> Your brother has just sent me your recent letter to him in regard to my candidacy for the nomination of Governor on the Republican ticket. I suppose from what I hear that it will be impossible to get an instruction at the present time, but an instruction from you will be of the greatest value to me; for the reason, that all of the larger counties which have no candidates, and Arapahoe County especially, is intensely interested in electing a Republican Governor, and it will go for any person who it thinks the people somewhat generally wish. An instruction from your county would add greatly to my chances.
>
> In regard to Judge [J. B.] Belford, I wish you would say to him that I only went into the canvass at the earnest request of a number of friends. I have made no active effort to secure the nomination, for I think it is always unwise for a person to urge himself forward for an office, farther than to ask assistance from his friends, because if the nomination should be foisted upon the party, one would of necessity have a much harder fight to make for the election; but you may say to him that any assistance he renders in the way of securing the nomination will be gratefully appreciated by me, and if I am nominated, that I shall certainly desire his services in the canvass and be willing to arrange liberally with him for his services.
>
> This, of course, is confidential to you.
>
> Very sincerely yours,
> William Story[23]

Peter had been quite correct in his opinion that Story would take great care to see that his "political goose" was not roasted over a fire of unpaid bills.

Peter's long stay in Telluride on the San Miguel company contract was not unusual. For instance, he spent the last four months of 1888 and at least the first six months of 1889 in the Breckenridge area. In addition, it was in the period following the purchase of the Eureka Street foundry that the company began to expand its operations outside of Colorado, particularly in Arizona, New Mexico, and Montana, and it was Peter who packed his tools and blue prints and went out to supervise the erection of a shaft house or a mill. His frequent absences from Central City after 1882 were long enough to evoke comment in the local newspaper when he finally arrived back in town:

McFarlane and Co. have completed all their work on the Plutus Company's smelter above Idaho Springs, and Mr. Peter is once again the pious citizen of yore.[24]

Despite the fact that the company and the mining industry were really his first loves, it is hard not to believe that the long weeks and months away from home were difficult times for Peter, and that the conflicting loyalties of home and hearth and business were not distressing. Life in a boarding house in a raw mining camp could hardly have been pleasant for a man who was used to something considerably better. Furthermore, it was during this decade that two more McFarlane children were born, Frederick in 1884, and Yetta in 1889. On at least one of these occasions Peter was able to be home, as shown by the fact of a letter from him to Minnie Frey of Idaho Springs, his wife's sister, notifying her of the birth of a niece. The letter is extremely interesting because of the sober wit in place of Peter's normally cheerful humor:

> Lizzie gave birth at six o'clock this morning to a daughter, and is quite anxious that you shall hear of it as early as possible.
>   It has black hair and eyes and from the deep corrugations on its forehead, looks as though it were scowling defiance at its new surroundings, and not yet quite satisfied with the world. It also has a look of melancholy as though there were something "over which it sits and broods," but unless it is the original sin of its various aunts, I can offer no cause. I know it has no actual transgressions of its own to be sorry for.[25]

The letter also illustrates Peter's intellectual development over the years. Gone is the crude English of his diaries; in its place appears a manner of expression which is that of a man who has read widely and thought deeply. Unfortunately, documents such as this are very rare in the *McFarlane Papers.* Almost everything Peter left among them deals entirely with the business, and it is only occasionally that even in these the inner man shines through.

By 1890, through hard work and astute business management, Peter and Will McFarlane had securely established themselves as major figures in the mine and milling machinery industry of the state and had accumulated approximately $100,000 worth of mining properties and other real estate holdings in the process.[26] Immediately ahead, however, were two difficult years marked by a depression in the mining industry in Gilpin County, during which the production of gold dropped below $1,000,000 for two consecutive years, the first time the county had failed to produce over $1,000,000 in gold since 1867.[27] The root of the trouble was the difficulty in obtaining development capital following the discovery in 1891 of rich silver deposits at Creede and on Breece Hill in Leadville and new gold deposits at Cripple Creek and Victor the following year.

The depression, unfortunately, struck at a time when the McFarlane brothers were badly in need of large amounts of ready cash. In 1891 Silas Bertenshaw of Black Hawk succeeded in obtaining a patent on the "Gilpin County Gilt Edge Concentrator." Peter and Will McFarlane for a number of years had been manufacturing a similar piece of equipment known as the "Gilpin County Bumping Table." Now they were in the awkward position of having to cease making this type of concentrator, paying Bertenshaw royalties, buying him out, or continuing to manufacture and risk a suit. In addition, it was at about this time that James W. Jackson of Denver offered to sell his foundry and shops in Denver, an opportunity desired by the McFarlane brothers for more than a year.

As the depression continued, McFarlane & Company's creditors began to press for their money. Particularly worrisome was a $5,000 note held by the Rocky Mountain National Bank of Central City. Some years previously, Peter and Will had secured this loan to purchase a three-quarters interest in the Baxter Mine on Quartz Hill in Central City. The mine was idled by the depression, and the interest on the loan and the taxes on the mine were, as Will put it, "eating us out of our boots."[28]

Every attempt to sell the mine during this period in order to pay off the note was unsuccessful.[29] In a letter to Will a number of years later, Peter admitted that it had been a bad investment from the very beginning. "You know very well," he wrote, "that neither you or I will live to see a profit extracted therefrom ... unless we catch a sucker."[30]

With their creditors demanding money, Peter and Will had to bend every effort to collect what was owed them, but everyone else in the county was in the same situation. Money was scarce, and for those owing it, it was a difficult period. The extent of their difficulties can be judged from a letter Will wrote to Bela Buell attempting to collect a debt almost twenty years old:

I write to you to see if you can do anything for us on this
$600.00 that we hold of yours. I suppose you are hard up, but
Bela we are worse off than hard up, for if we do not get help
from somewhere, we will loose [sic] everything we have, for we can
neither sell anything, nor can we collect anything, nor can we
borrow anymore.... We are all about as usual, although our
troubles are killing Libbie. But I hope this can't last long which-
ever way things go.[31]

On top of everything else, in the fall of 1890, McFarlane & Company
put up a mill in Prescott, Arizona, for which the firm never was paid. It
is possible that had business been better in Colorado, they would not
have bid on the contract, for Peter was skeptical of their prospects of
payment from the moment of his arrival in Prescott to start construction. Writing to Will on his impressions of the man who represented
the combine operating the mine, he reported:

I am decidedly afraid of that man. He don't seem to have either
native sense or business sense. I hardly credit him with ordinary
intelligence. He is a very inferior looking man, and it is going to
require fine management to get any money out of them.[32]

The brothers suffered a loss of close to $2,500.[33] When business was
good, this would not have been too serious a matter, but in the midst of
a depression the company could ill afford it.

It was in the midst of all these financial troubles that Peter and Will
had to contend with the patent problem which further complicated
their business affairs. Both Silas Bertenshaw and the McFarlanes had
developed similar machines known as concentrators or bumping tables.
But it was Bertenshaw who obtained a patent.[34] The machines, like
the slow drop stamp mill, were the result of the Gilpin County miners'
constant experimentation to find ways of increasing the yield from the
county's low-grade ore deposits.

Only a portion of the gold in any batch of ore was ever trapped on the
amalgam plates inside the mortars of a slow drop stamp mill. The rest
flowed out of the mortar with the pulp, and if it were not retrieved at
this point, it was lost. The deeper the miners went, the less gold there
was per ton of ore. Consequently, successful treatment of the pulps and
slimes became an absolute necessity if the Gilpin County mines were to
be worked profitably.

One widely tried device was a belt-driven jig. The pulp flowed from the mortar into a wooden receptacle where paddles set up a pulsating motion. The theory behind the jig was that ore particles of approximately the same size, but having different specific gravities, would arrange themselves in layers through the movement of the water; the gold-bearing particles, because of their high specific gravity, would settle to the bottom layer.

Also tried extensively in the early days was the Frue Vanner manufactured by the Frue Vanning Company of New York City. This machine consisted of an endless belt of India rubber cloth 6 feet wide and 27 feet long. The belt traveled within an inclined frame and had a horizontal vibrating motion. The gold concentrates, being heavier than the rest of the pulp, clung to the belt, while the lighter material was washed down and off the machine by a constant and carefully regulated flow of water. Neither of these devices proved satisfactory in treating Gilpin County pulps and slimes.

Sometime near the end of 1886 or the beginning of 1887, the McFarlane brothers in Central City and Silas Bertenshaw in Black Hawk, apparently working independently, developed a machine

> in which concentration is effected by distributing the crushed ore upon a horizontal, or inclined table or trough, the separation of the heavier and metal bearing particles from the lighter . . . being accomplished by means of continuous oscillations or reciprocations with sudden jarring or bumping movements imparted mechanically to the table, the ore being mixed with water being fed thereon and the concentrates discharged therefrom at the upper end, . . . while the refuse . . . passes off over the other end. [35]

The early bumping tables manufactured by Bertenshaw and the McFarlane brothers were identical except for one detail: Bertenshaw's had a sheet iron table set in a wooden frame; the McFarlanes' utilized a copper table. [36]

The new device was quite successful in treating the Gilpin County pulps, although it did not always live up to its advertised standards of performance. The brochures distributed by McFarlane & Company stated that the Gilpin County Bumping Table would save twice the value in concentrates as would the ordinary jig, and what is more, McFarlane & Company offered a guarantee to that effect if the buyer would pay an extra $25.00. This kind of overenthusiastic advertising was bound to result in some complaints. One customer noted that the "table was a fair success, but not doing anything up to your warrant. It saves about ⅓ more than a jig." Because the machine fell short of the manufacturer's claims, he quite naturally wanted a refund of $25.00.[37] The machine was enough of a success, however, that in the summer of 1887 Peter began to explore the possibilities of obtaining a patent,[38] but he never filed an application with the U. S. Patent Office. This was to prove a serious oversight. What discouraged him from doing so appears to have been a letter from the Frue Vanning Company in New York answering his inquiry as to whether or not the Gilpin County Bumping Table infringed in any way on the Frue Vanning Company patents. "I cannot understand," the New York man replied, "how a Patent can be obtained for an end bumping table at the present day except on some mere detail of construction which could easily be avoided by anyone wishing to infringe the patent."[39] Evidently this letter was enough to convince Peter and Will that attempting to patent their bumping table would be a waste of time.

Sometime in 1888 Silas Bertenshaw began to manufacture a bumping table with both the table and frame made of cast iron (rather than sheet iron table and wooden frame). An advertisement for this machine in the November 18, 1888 issue of *Mining Industries* carried the notation that a patent was pending. Bertenshaw called this new bumping table the "Gilpin County Gilt Edge Concentrator." He based his claim for a patent on the following argument:

> When the tables are of wood, or of copper, or wood lined with copper, and the table is oscillated, receiving a blow at each oscillation, the only movement given the material is the throw from such a blow. When, however, a table of cast iron strikes the bumper, there is not only this throw from the bumper, but all the particles, the units of the mass of iron of the table itself are thrown into vibration, the mass being given a tremulousness continuing from blow to blow, and this is communicated to the material thereon as the vibrations of the glass plate are communicated to sand upon it, and this I have found aided materially in the separation desired; hence my use of cast iron for such tables.

Contrary to the opinion McFarlane had obtained from the Frue Vanning Company, Silas Bertenshaw had, in the opinion of the U. S. Patent Office, developed a "better mouse trap," and it therefore issued him a patent on the Gilpin County Gilt Edge Concentrator on January 21, 1891.

UNITED STATES AMERICA

To all to whom these presents shall come:

Whereas Silas Bertenshaw of Black Hawk, Colorado has presented to the Commissioner of Patents a petition praying for the grant of Letters Patent for an alleged new and useful improvement in

Concentrators

a description of which invention is contained in the Specification of which a copy is hereunto annexed and made a part hereof, and has complied with the various requirements of Law in such cases made and provided, and Whereas upon due examination made the said claimant is adjudged to be justly entitled to a Patent under the Law.

Now therefore these Letters Patent are to grant unto the said Silas Bertenshaw his heirs or assigns for the term of seventeen years from the _____ day of _____ one thousand eight hundred and ninety one the exclusive right to make, use and vend the said invention throughout the United States and the Territories thereof.

In testimony whereof I have hereunto set my hand and caused the seal of the Patent Office to be affixed at the City of Washington this _____ day of _____ in the year of our Lord one thousand eight hundred and ninety ____ and of the Independence of the United States of America the one hundred and fifteenth.

Countersigned _____
O. E. Mitchell
Commissioner of Patents
Assistant Secretary of the Interior

Patent issued to Silas Bertenshaw for the Gilpin County Gilt Edge Concentrator.

S. BERTENSHAW.

CONCENTRATOR.

No. 445,154. Patented Jan. 27, 1891.

Fig. 13

Fig. 14.

Fig. 15.

Witnesses
Ira R. Stewart.
Alfred T. Gage

Inventor
Silas Bertenshaw
by W. Henderson,
his Attorney.

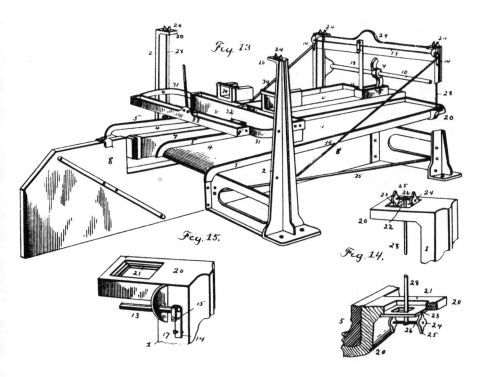

McFarlane & Co.
PROPRIETORS OF
CENTRAL = CITY = AND = BLACK = HAWK
Foundries and Machine Shops,

Sole Manufacturers of the Gilt Edge Concentrators.
Builders of Stamp Mills, Concentrating
and Mining Machinery.

The GILPIN COUNTY CONCENTRATOR is used in all the stamp mills in the
county and is giving the best satisfaction.

Central City, Colo., 7 21 — 1892

C. A. Tripp Esq.
Missouri Pacific Agt. Denver.

Dear Sir,

Yours of 19th rec'd. We expect to
ship shafting & pulleys from Medart Pulley Co.
in about two weeks. Please write us and
state what your rate will be after the
cut goes into effect on freight from River to
Colorado.

Yours &c
McFarlane & Co.

S H to Pueblo or Denver

1st	2d	3d	4th	5th	a	B
180	135	112	90	70	77½	67½

Kansas City to Pueblo or Denver

1/	2/	3/	4/	5/	a/	B/
125	95	80	65	50	55	45

Route via Missouri Pacific

7/21/92 & oblige yours C. A. Tripp

Upper Black Hawk, on north fork of Clear Creek, showing unloading platform of Gilpin Tramway and, alongside it, the foundry McFarlane & Co. purchased from Silas Bertenshaw. *Courtesy Denver Public Library, Western History Department.*

Bertenshaw's claim that the cast iron table was superior to either the copper or the sheet iron variety was substantiated in practice. Writing to Will from Breckenridge in the summer of 1889, Peter complained that the copper tables that had been shipped to him were of inferior quality. "I very seriously question," he wrote, "whether the uneven bottom can be remedied unless we use a cast iron table. . . . Our table reputation is considerably run down in this camp and I would like to show that we can put in good ones."[41]

Apparently convinced that Bertenshaw's improvements were no more patentable than the original copper and sheet iron tables, McFarlane & Company began to manufacture bumping tables with cast iron troughs. Consequently, when Bertenshaw received his patent a year and a half later, they were in an awkward position, for if they continued to make cast iron tables, they were liable to be sued for patent infringement. Three alternatives were now open to them. They could quit manufacturing bumping tables, they could try to work out a royalty arrangement with Bertenshaw, or they could try to buy him out. The first course was ruled out because the Gilpin County Gilt Edge Concentrator was proving to be a popular piece of milling equipment with a potential overseas market.[42]

Therefore, on April 6, 1891 overtures were made to Bertenshaw, and McFarlane & Company purchased the patent rights to the Gilpin County Gilt Edge Concentrator for $5,000.[43] For an additional $5,000, they purchased Bertenshaw's foundry and machine shop in Black Hawk. All of this required an increase in price for the bumping machine, as explained in a letter to an Idaho firm later that year:

> Yes, some two years ago, we sent out circulars with the price at $100.00, and at that time we could make them for that. But since that time, things have changed, for Bertenshaw got a patent on the machine and to save ourselves and our customers from damage we paid Bertenshaw $10,000 and had to take his contracts.[44]

Bertenshaw's willingness to sell was undoubtedly related to the depressed condition of the Gilpin County mining industry at that time. He subsequently moved to Denver where sometime later he and W. S. Parkinson were engaged in the manufacture and distribution of "Dr. S. J. Dickinson's Patented Health Bed Rest."[45] This new business marks a curious shift in the career of one of the great pioneers in the Colorado mine and milling machinery industry.

For some time previous to the Bertenshaw affair, Peter and Will had been probing the possibilities of setting up a Denver branch of the business. The first opportunity for such a move came in the fall of 1889 in the form of an offer from Arthur Hendey, H.H. Meyer, and Henry R. Wolcott to have the McFarlanes buy into the Excelsior Foundry and Machine Shop.

This company had been organized on April 1, 1878,[46] but despite the fact that Hendey and Meyer were both inventors of note, it was not very successful. In approaching the McFarlane brothers, the owners were not only interested in obtaining capital. They also had their eyes on the excellent reputation and host of business contacts that Peter and Will had built up within the mining community over the past twenty years.

The first overture was made sometime late in September. On October 1, Will, who was supervising a number of contracts in the Aspen-Glenwood Springs area, took the train to Denver, and that evening met with Hendey, Meyer, and Wolcott. On the following day he wrote to Peter:

> They want us to go in with them, and we are to have one third and get the same pay that Hendy gets.... So I told them it was just a matter of how cheap they let us in. Henry said the property was worth about $200,000 ... but that we ought to get in for $110,000 to $120,000, and we would have to get $35,000 to $40,000.... He could get us about $15,000 at 8% for our stock, and we would have to get $25,000 more.[47]

The next day, Will sent off another letter to Peter outlining how they might raise the money if they decided to accept the Denver group's offer:

> When I got here [Aspen] last night I asked Dave[48] about money. He thinks after a while he could let me have about $10,000.... We can get $5,000 on the Hawley Mdse. stock,[49] and we can sell our interest in the half block in Denver for say $8,000. So I can see where the money can be had, but the interest will take over $3,000 a year.[50]

Although it was Will's opinion that "they want us in as bad as we want to get in,"[51] the deal fell through, and the extant correspondence provides only a hint as to why.

While Will was in Denver to meet with Hendey, Meyer, and Wolcott, he also paid a visit to James W. Jackson, owner of the Denver Foundry and Machine Shop and a pioneer figure in the mine and milling machinery business. Jackson had come to Denver in 1870 and opened a machine shop on Ninth Street between Lawrence and Larimer. He was quite successful, and in 1880 moved into larger quarters at 1734 Fifteenth Street.[52]

In the course of his conversation with Jackson, Will learned that he was planning to sell his business and move to the east coast for reasons of health. Jackson set a price of $60,000 for his tools, stock, and the company's good will.[53] Undoubtedly Jackson's offer influenced the negotiations with Hendie, Meyer, and Wolcott. James W. Jackson had an excellent reputation, and outright ownership of his business probably looked like a considerably better proposition than a one-third or one-fourth interest that the Excelsior group was offering.[54]

Although the initial contact with Jackson resulted in further conversations, nothing developed until almost three years later when Jackson made it known through a third party that he would sell everything— tools, patterns, and stock—for $50,000.[55] McFarlane & Company countered with the following offer:

> We will pay you $45,000 as follows: $5,000 on signing contract of sale; $10,000 on receiving possession; $5,000 on or before July 1, 1893; $5,000 on or before July 1, 1894; $10,000 on or before January 1, 1895; $10,000 on or before January 1, 1896. Interest at 6% due every 12 months from the date of notes. Notes to be secured on tools and C and we agree to keep same insured for not less than $20,000. We will take the building and ground for three or five years at $250.00 per month and keep the same insured and repaired.[56]

Because Peter was in Telluride at the time supervising the construction of the big mill at the Gold Kind Mine, all of the negotiations with Jackson were conducted by Will. Peters's reply to Will's letter notifying him that they had reached the stage where Jackson wanted an offer reveals how eager he was for the company to have a base of operations in Denver. "I just got your letter about Jackson," he wrote. "*AT LAST* it has the ring of business. Well, I am glad of it. Hit or miss, it's all right, and I feel sure it's a hit."[57]

Sometime prior to September 29, 1892, the terms of the sale were agreed upon, for on that day, McFarlane & Company ordered a satin banner from a Fort Worth Company bearing the following legend:

HOISTING ENGINES,
FURNACE CASTINGS,
CONCENTRATION
MACHINERY,
ENGINES, BOILERS,
IRON STACKS.

CORLISS ENGINES.
MINING MACHINERY.

STAMP MILLS,
CORNISH ROLLS,
AMALGAMATING PANS,
ROASTING CLYINDERS,
CRUSHERS,
HOISTING MACHINERY.

James W. Jackson
Iron Founder and Machinist
Cor. 15th and Newalta Sts.

TERMS CASH.   ESTABLISHED 1870.   P. O. BOX 2171

Denver, Colo., Aug 3 1889

Mess. McFarlane & Co
Central Cy Colo.

I rec'd
your favor of 8/1/89 relating to the difference
in our accounts of $2⁶⁰ for which you
claim you sent me an Invoice. Not doubting
but what you sent me this bill, I regret to
say I never received it & therefore did not
credit your account with same. Trusting
this will fully explain my sending you
this last statement, I remain

Yours Resp'y

James W Jackson

CORLISS ENGINES. MINING MACHINERY. HOISTING ENGINES. STAMP MILLS BUILT AND ERECTED,
CORNISH ROLLS,
AMALGAMATING PANS,

McFARLANE & CO.

ROASTING CYLINDERS,
CRUSHERS,

SUCCESSORS TO

HOISTING MACHINERY,

JAMES W. JACKSON,

FURNACE CASTINGS,
ENGINES, BOILERS,

Iron Founders and Machinists

CONCENTRATING MACHINERY.

SOLE MANUFACTURERS OF
THE
GILPIN COUNTY
GILT EDGE
CONCENTRATOR.

1734 Fifteenth Street.

JOHN RASMUSSEN, MECHANICAL ENGINEER.

ESTABLISHED 1870.

WORKS AT
CENTRAL CITY, BLACK HAWK AND DENVER, COLO.

Denver, Colorado, June 22 1893

Peter McFarlane Dear Sir

I enclose you Blueprints of the changes we spoke about
and find I could get 45° of drop between Crusher &
Rolls. I did not leave out the mud sills as I could
not see any good way of securing the sides
from caving. You will notice I have two cross
girts one in each end of Pit which will tie
the Posts together but none in the center
as the stringers for Rolls & crusher will act
as such and can have a brace or a support
to carry the upper Posts Hoping these changes
will suit you I enclose the Letters & instructions
I had from Mr Collins Thinking you may
put them with the other Papers in regard to
Concentrator, I also send you a small Blueprint
of the 7½X11 Dodge 14X30 Patt Rolls & Feeder &
11X16 Engine Truly Yours John Rasmussen

McFarlane & Company

Successor to James W. Jackson

Manufacturers of Corliss engines; mining machinery; stamp mills; Cornish rolls; crushers; boilers; smelters; owners of the patent and sole manufacturers of the Gilt Edged Concentrator. Corner of 15th and Newatta streets, Denver, Colorado, U.S.A.[58]

About one month later, on October 20, the banner was unfurled across the front of the building at Fifteenth and Newatta Streets proclaiming the fact that the McFarlane brothers of Central City and Black Hawk had moved into Denver.

Twenty-three years had elapsed since Peter McFarlane climbed off the stagecoach in Black Hawk. The enchanting visions of gulches of gold which had filled his head with thoughts of vast riches just for the asking and filled his pockets with fool's gold on the trip up Golden Gate Canyon from Denver had long since vanished, replaced by the knowledge that success in the business of mining for gold was more often than not the result of hard, sustained effort. True, a few lucky ones had "struck it rich," but many more of those who rushed to the gold fields became part of that army of derelicts that hovered around every mining camp in the West, sustaining itself and shattered dreams on cheap whiskey.

In the summer of 1892, while working on the Gold King mill at Telluride, Peter took time out from his work to look up one such derelict—his cousin Will Barclay whom he had not seen for many years. Peter's letter to his brother about this meeting is worth quoting at length, as it incapsulates a part of the history of the mining frontier that is all too often forgotten in the rush to recount and relive the stories of success:

> I went to Grant Lake yesterday and found Will Barclay, and to all appearances I found him a total wreck. He had no idea I was coming and I took him completely by surprise. He was sitting on a window sill in front of a saloon (there are only ½ dozen houses there and they are so scattered in the brush that one would think nobody was living there) but he saw me before I ... was yet 100 feet from him, and knew me in a second. He trembled all over, his hands shook so that he did not know what to do with them ... and the perspiration rolled off his face. He was dressed just [in] wornout boots, overalls in bootlegs, and old dirty, white

(once) slouch hat, vest and no coat. I was afraid he was going into the brush and give me the slip as he left me several times unceremoniously, but I found out that the poor fellow had gotten to that stage where he has to answer frequent calls, about once an hour. His beard is quite gray.... He wears a mustache. To sum him up at a distance of 20 feet he looks like a great, husky, strong, rugged man, heavier than I ever saw him. Weighs 185 lbs. But surely whiskey has got the best of him. He came to the hotel and had dinner with me.... After dinner we went fishing on the lake.... He never once referred to his wife or boys.... Said he was prospecting up on a certain mountain ... but a man told me while I was waiting at the track for the train to come along that he has not prospected any this summer, but is tending bar at the saloon where I first found him. Said he was known by the name of "Whiskey Bill" and had not drawn a sober breath since he came to Grant Lake 2 months ago. The saloon keeper runs the hotel and Will gets what little he eats there.... I do not think he wanted to see me nor do I think he wants to see anybody. He has just got in that quiet little place where he can get all the liquor he wants and see nobody, or very few at most, and live and die there where no one will chide him, or care when he goes.[59]

Peter and Will McFarlane, however, were the kind of people who cared. Somehow they later managed to entice Will Barclay out of his saloon at Grant Lake and into a job in their newly acquired foundry and machine shop in Denver.[60] Unlike Will Barclay, they had proved themselves men to match Colorado's mineral mountains.

CHAPTER VII

The Prosperous Years
1893–1906

THE McFarlane brothers' decision to establish a branch of their business in Denver coincided rather closely with the election of Grover Cleveland as President of the United States, the first rumblings in the economy which culminated in the "Panic of 1893," and the repeal of the Sherman Silver Purchase Act. On the face of it, it was not a propitious time for expansion, but a deeper look at the situation seems to prove the contrary.

The causes of the panic which began in May 1893, as in all such cases of severe economic dislocation, were complex. The major factors were prolonged agricultural depression following a wild land boom in the West, eight consecutive years of an adverse balance of payments due in part to business conditions in Europe and to the liquidation of American securities by European investors, overspeculation in railroads, and the speculation in the formation of trusts and other business combines which affected overall price stability.

Further complicating an already complex situation was the money question, which had agitated the nation since the end of the Civil War. For over twenty years the emotional and moralistic arguments of those who advocated a gold-backed currency and those who backed silver had served as grist for the mills of politicians, bankers, financiers, newspaper editors, and demagogues. One of the results was that as the economy came under a severe strain, as it did at the beginning of the 1890s, confidence in the basic soundness of the nation's monetary system had been undermined, and to all of the other causes pressing toward a serious economic crisis was added the factor of fear. At best, fear paralyzes men's capabilities for positive, rational action at the time such action is most needed; and at its worst, frightens them into steps that only accentuate the conditions that need to be alleviated. Thus, when a series of business failures, beginning with that of the National Cordage Company in May 1893, signaled dangerous times ahead, a "cloud of apprehension seemed to settle over the country" and "blind uncertainty paralyzed action."[1]

This initial response, however, soon evaporated. As the economic crisis deepened in the summer of 1893, the American tendency to seek a simple solution to a complex problem made itself felt, and when Congress convened in special session, many powerful leaders of the country were clamoring for the repeal of the Sherman Silver Purchase Act of 1890. In this act, which obligated the Secretary of the Treasury to purchase 4,500,000 ounces of silver each month, the country found the devil which many people believed had to be exorcised before a return to "normalcy" could be achieved.[2] In the midst of the public clamor for the mystic rites to begin, John Hay wrote sarcastically to Henry Adams:

> All men of virtue and intelligence know that all the ills of life—scarcity of money, baldness, the common bacillus, Home Rule, Jimmy Van Alen, and the potato bug—are due to the Sherman bill. If it is repealed, sin and death will vanish from the world, ... the skies will fall, and we shall all catch larks.[3]

Despite the fact that silver had been created on a par with gold "by fiat of the Almighty,"[4] Congress repealed the Sherman Act in October 1893. The impact on the mining industry of Colorado, which produced 58% of the nation's silver,[5] was, as will be seen, considerably less severe than usually depicted. Repeal certainly did not drive the silver mining industry into the "valley and the shadow of death" as Senator Henry M. Teller mournfully and dramatically predicted during the weeks the issue was before Congress.[6] Furthermore, the facts clearly indicate that the shutdown of the mines in the summer of 1893, three months before the repeal of the Sherman Act, was due as much to the political campaign which the silver interests were waging in Congress and around the country as it was to economic factors related to the drop in the price of silver. As events subsequent to the repeal of the Sherman Act were to prove, the major producers of silver in Colorado could, and did, operate profitably even after the price of silver dropped to 59 cents an ounce.

The closing of the silver mines in the summer of 1893 was precipitated by a series of events which led to a drastic drop in the world-wide price of silver, the climax of which was the closing of its mints to the free coinage of silver by the Government of India on June 26. The price of silver which had been $1.05 an ounce in 1890 and 83 cents an ounce on the first of June 1893, plummeted to 63 cents immediately after India's decision was announced.[7] Nevertheless, in spite of this turn of events and the repeal of the Sherman Silver Purchase Act in October, the production of silver in Colorado continued at a high level, as the following production figures for the years 1893-1900 clearly show:

	Fine Ounces	Dollar Value
1893	25,838,600	$20,154,107
1894	23,281,398	14,667,281
1895	23,398,500	15,209,024
1896	23,513,000	15,349,642
1897	21,278,202	12,766,919
1898	23,502,601	13,866,532
1899	23,114,699	13,868,811
1900	20,336,512	12,608,637[8]

From the above statistics it can be seen that, under the circumstances, the annual production of silver remained amazingly high between 1894 and 1899. Except for 1897, the figure was in excess of 23,000,000 ounces a year, or only approximately 10% below the year of highest production, 1893. The average price of an ounce of silver during this period was 62.5 cents, or 41% below the figure for 1890. The paradox of a drastic fall in the price of silver and only a moderate downturn in production calls for an explanation.

Stripped to its bare essentials, the answer lies in the fact that the major mining operations in Colorado were extremely profitable concerns working gold- and silver-bearing ores which also contained rich by-products of lead and copper in combinations amenable to "cheap and effective smelting."[9] Just how profitable the mining industry as a whole was is shown by the production statistics for 1889. In that year the state produced $33,131,117 worth of gold, silver, copper, lead, and zinc. Total expenses of production were $13,834,332. In other words, the cost of producing a dollar's worth of metal, exclusive of depreciation, was 41 cents.[10]

Within the industry there were mines which had an even larger margin of profit. Two excellent examples were the Last Chance Mine at Creede and the Mollie Gibson in the Aspen District. The average cost to produce an ounce of metal at the Last Chance was 24.5 cents per ounce, and this figure covered the total costs of development including boarding houses and wagon roads. An idea of the profitability of the Company can be gathered from the fact that between January 1 and August 31, 1892, it paid out $750,000 in dividends. At the Mollie Gibson, the average cost to produce an ounce of metal up to 1892 was 26.6 cents, and in the summer of 1892 the Company reported that it was shipping 218,000 ounces of silver a month at an average cost of 13.3 cents an ounce.[11] With a market price of 83 cents an ounce at the time, the owners of the Mollie Gibson could boast of a profit margin exceeding 600%. When the price of silver fell to 63 cents an ounce near the end of June 1893, their margin of profit still was close to 373%. These facts go a long way toward explaining why production rose in Pitkin County by over 900,000 ounces in 1894 in spite of the drop in the price of silver. They also provide an insight into a neglected aspect of the Colorado mining industry in its later stages of development: its concentration of ownership. This in turn opens up a fresh perspective on the closing of the mines in the summer of 1893.

Thirty years after the first discovery of gold in Colorado the mining industry had developed to the extent where there were only sixty-nine companies producing over $100,000 worth of metal a year. This group represented less than 10% of the 773 mines reported in the 11th census of the U.S. Two hundred and seventy-nine mines, or more than 36%, produced less than $1,000 worth of metal a year, while 425 fell into the category of producing $1,000 to $100,000 worth.[12] In the Aspen District three mines accounted for 63% of the total production of the District between 1879 and 1893, and in 1893 there were only ten paying claims in the entire District. In the Leadville District there were only eighteen. Between them, the two Districts accounted for 40% of the silver production of the state, and Colorado accounted for 58% of the nation's total. The profile of the industry as of 1890 showed a small number of exceedingly profitable operations at the top and a very large number of operations which were marginal. It was this latter group which bore the brunt of the fall in the price of silver and whose demise largely accounts for the 10% drop in silver production in Colorado after 1893.

The high level of silver production following the reopening of the mines in September demonstrates that the accepted explanation for the shutdown, i.e., that silver could not be produced profitably in Colorado for 60 cents an ounce, must be rejected. The closing of the mines was, in fact, a *tour de force* by the men who controlled the silver industry to counteract the swelling national demand for the repeal of the Sherman Silver Purchase Act, force marginal operators out of business, and ram through a reduction in the daily wages of the men employed by the mines and smelters. The ultimate goal was to reverse the downward trend in the price of silver and to increase profit margins which were already high.

The attempt to prevent the repeal of the Sherman Silver Purchase Act failed, and the price of silver never rose above 68 cents an ounce for the remainder of the decade, but the goal of reducing wages in the industry was achieved. When the mines began to reopen in September, approximately a month before the repeal of the Sherman Silver Purchase Act, miners and smelter men across the state were forced to accept a 16.6% reduction in wages. In the Aspen and Leadville Districts, the most productive and profitable in the state, the reduction was approximately 33%.[13]

A fascinating clue to the silver industry's strategy appeared in the form of an interview with Nathaniel Witherell, vice president of the Consolidated Kansas City Smelting and Refining Company, published by the New York *Times* during the shutdown of the mines in Colorado. "The future of the smelting industry is more promising," Witherell said, "than it has been in ten years." He then proceeded to explain why:

> In the early days it was so profitable that strong competition sprang up. This has resulted in reducing profits to a very narrow margin. The present depression will weed out the weak concerns leaving the stronger in possession of a broad field. While this will naturally result in higher prices charged producers for smelting it

will benefit them by weeding out the mines that cannot produce silver at less than, say, 80 cents an ounce. This, in turn, will have a tendency to reduce the exorbitantly high wages which now rule. Labor at Kansas City which is worth $1.50 per day costs $3.00 in Denver, where living expenses are not more than 10 to 15 percent higher. Values of all kinds, except labor, have been sacrificed. Labor must bear its share of the burden.[14]

Despite the fact that individual mining camps were hard hit by a drop in the price of silver and the repeal of the Sherman Silver Purchase Act,[15] it is obvious that neither of these events drove the Colorado silver industry "to the dogs" as the silver interests were wont to claim. The men toiling in the bowels of the earth for less than $3.00 a day, however, or the marginal operators forced out of business might well have voiced this opinion with considerable justification, but not the men who controlled the industry. In a parody on this mournful cry, the New York *Times* of January 1, 1894, carried the following headline in reporting a meeting of mining industry leaders in the Manufacturers' Exchange Building in Denver:

WON'T GO TO THE BOW WOWS. COLORADO DECIDES
TO OUTLIVE THE SILVER PURCHASE REPEAL.

This meeting not only demonstrated that the Colorado mining industry was resigned to its defeat on the issue of repeal but it also produced a tacit admission that the closing of the mines during the summer had not been an economic necessity. The keynote speaker was Jesse B. Grant, owner of the largest smelter in Colorado, who assured the assembled delegates that silver mining would not be abandoned in Colorado, for the simple reason that it could be produced cheaper in Colorado "than at any other point."

Behind this confident statement lay not only the cheapness of processing the first-class Colorado gold and silver ores and their rich by-products of lead and copper, but the fact that since 1880 labor costs in the mining industry had been declining due largely to the railroads' penetration into the major mining camps, resulting in a rapid decline in the cost of living and an increase in the labor force.[16] An added factor, of course, was the severe wage cuts forced on the miners by the closing of the mines in the summer of 1893. Herein lie the seeds of the bitterness and violence of the labor disputes which racked the Colorado mining industry for several decades after 1890. It is hard to believe that the wage cuts forced on a proud and productive breed of men in 1893 by an industry whose profits were unusually high did not play a major role in the subsequent violence which plagued the industry from that time on.

With silver production holding steady at above 23,000,000 ounces a year, the discovery of vast new gold deposits at Cripple Creek and Victor, and the flow of capital to the older gold mining districts after the fall in the price of silver, the total production of precious metals in Colorado rose by almost 50% between 1893 and 1900:

	Gold	Silver	Total
1893	$ 7,527,000	$20,154,107	$27,681,107
1894	9,491,514	$14,667,281	24,158,795
1895	13,305,100	15,209,024	28,514,124
1896	14,911,000	15,349,642	30,260,642
1897	19,579,433	12,766,919	32,346,352
1898	23,534,532	13,866,532	37,401,064
1899	26,508,675	13,868,811	40,377,486
1900	28,684,070	12,608,637	41,292,707[17]

With its new facilities in Denver, McFarlane & Company was in an excellent position to take advantage of the most productive period in the history of the Colorado gold and silver mining industry.

The purchase of Jackson's shops raised the question of what to do with those in Central City and Black Hawk. Will was apparently of the opinion that they should be sold, and he suggested to Peter that since sale to an outside buyer would probably be difficult, they make some kind of arrangement to sell them to the employees. In replying to Will's letter, Peter exhibited a notable lack of enthusiasm, although he did not offer an alternative:

> I have noted all you have said about disposing of foundries at Central and Black Hawk, but have not said anything because I do not know what to say. But it seems to me that it's a good opportunity for Walter. . . . I also agree with you in letting Henry run the B. H. I suppose it's almost impossible to find anyone to purchase outright either of the places and we'll have to do the next best thing.[18]

As it turned out, Will was unable to sell to anyone outside the company, or even to any of the employees. Two offers were made, the first on December 14, 1892, and the second, five days later.[19] Neither was successful, a development probably very much to Peter's relief. Soon after, Will moved to Denver to take over the management of the shops on Fifteenth Street, and Peter returned from Telluride to manage the Central City and Black Hawk facilities. For the next fourteen years, the Denver and the Central City branches of McFarlane & Company operated as autonomous units. The brothers cooperated in every way possible, but in effect each was master of his own house.

Although the prospects for the mining industry in Colorado were excellent, business conditions at the time Jackson was bought out were far from good, and the McFarlane brothers needed all of their talents and energies to survive in the interim. Of first importance at the moment was the establishing of the Denver branch of the company on a firm basis.

Shortly after he arrived in Denver, Will managed to secure two large contracts which helped considerably toward this end. Late in March 1894, he bid on a one hundred ton concentrating mill for the Alice Mine on Yankee Hill, and won the contract worth $25,000.[20] The following month, he outbid the Colorado Iron Works on a contract for $16,445 to erect a forty stamp mill in Prescott, Arizona, and it was not without a certain amount of pride that he reported to Peter that the Colorado Iron Works people "were very sore about it."[21]

Competition for business was stiff, but Will's aggressiveness brought in enough of it to keep the Denver shops operating on a full schedule. Such was not the case with the Colorado Iron Works, which at that time had been running only two days a week for over a month, and the Denver Foundry and Machine Company, which had even less work.[22]

Despite the fact that he was doing far better than some of his major competitors, Will was not able to meet all of the payments to James W. Jackson as they came due. The problem, however, was not lack of business, but difficulties in collecting payment for work done. Writing to Peter in May 1894, Will noted that he could pay all of Jackson's notes and the $1,000 arrears in rent as soon as $7,100 owed the company could be collected.[23]

While Will was more than holding his own in Denver, Peter was not idle in Central City. Among the larger orders he received during the year were a ten stamp mill for the Jack Pot Manufacturing Company of Nederland,[24] a ten stamp mill for E. E. Hill of Denver,[25] and a contract to rebuild the Hidden Treasure Mill in Central City, a mill owned by the California Milling and Mining Company.[26] By 1894 the mining industry of Gilpin County had fully recovered from the slump it suffered as the decade opened, and gold production had risen to almost $2,000,000 before the year was out. For the ten-year period 1893-1902 gold production in the county averaged close to $1,700,000 annually, making this the most productive period in the county's history.[27] The renewed vitality of the mining industry in Gilpin County, of course, augured well for Peter. In response to an inquiry from a business contact in Wisconsin, he expressed optimism regarding the outlook for the future:

> Times look a little better here than for some time past. The Sleepy Hollow and Americus and Fisk and Bobtail [mines] a report says have arranged to jointly unwater their property, and in fact, are doing so now. And that means better times for the whole county.[28]

By the end of 1895, business had improved to the point where Peter was hard pressed to meet all of his commitments for construction. In a letter to Edward Mayhew, his chief millwright, who was supervising the construction of a twenty stamp mill at Gates, Oregon, for Lawler Gold Mines Limited, a British-backed company,[29] Peter noted that he had recently obtained a contract for a fifteen stamp mill in New Mexico,[30] a twenty-five stamp mill in Empire, and a twenty-five-ton concentrating mill. He added that he would like to write at more length regarding the problems of getting the Lawler mill ready to go but he was "so busy that it is hard to get the time."[31]

The prosperous times which McFarlane & Company enjoyed following the purchase of the Jackson works in Denver are reflected through the brothers' correspondence for these years. The only major problem, and it was a persistent one, was that of collecting what was owed the firm. On more than one occasion the failure to meet his commitments of an individual who had gambled for gold and lost aroused Peter's short-fused Scotch temper. A pertinent example is found in Peter's letter to E. E. Hill of Denver demanding payment for a mill which McFarlane & Company had built for him in the spring of 1894. At the time the letter was written, the bill owed by Hill was over a year old. He had apparently informed Peter that he was unable to pay because the mine for which the mill had been built had been an utter failure. He received little sympathy from Peter McFarlane:

We have your tale of woe of the 18th instant. We regret very much the outcome of your unfortunate enterprise. It baffles my understanding to comprehend how railroad men (officers I mean) always selected for the position and continue to occupy their places on account of their sagacity and superior fitness can be such D——d fools outside their official capacity. That poor, old, simpleminded, well meaning Roberts led all you fellows where a ten year old boy could have safely predicted the consequences.... It seems to me that all you had to do in order to get a true appreciation of the worth of your mine was to look at your expert.... A pass would have taken your man to your office and a little of the common shrewdness you manifest in everyday life applied in the case would have delivered your company of an expenditure of 6 or 7 thousand dollars. Such unaccountable stupidity deserves to be severely punished, and the sentence of this court is that you pay the full amount of our claim against you, principal and interest.[32]

Although it took almost four years, "Judge" McFarlane's sentence was carried out. By the end of 1898, Hill and his associates had reduced their indebtedness to McFarlane & Company to $105.80,[33] and this amount presumably was liquidated soon after, for the long correspondence with Hill ceases at this point.

As is the case with most self-made men, Peter was not immune to recommending his own tried and proven formula for business success to others, particularly those who owed money to McFarlane & Company, and whose seemingly slovenly and slothful ways were the chief cause of their inability to pay legally contracted debts. Such was the case with W. E. Renshaw, the manager of the Consolidated Gem Mining and Milling Company of Idaho Springs, who received the following bit of gratuitous, and probably unwanted, advice:

There is only one way to work that property if you hope to make it a success.... Give the matter your personal attention. Be on the job at 7:30 A. M., and stay there all day. Eat lunch with your miners. Know what you are doing. Remain at home at night and work on your books. Don't be cavorting in pleasure trips in automobiles being bought and paid for with other people's money, but attend strictly to your own personal mining business.[34]

Although he could hardly have welcomed this outburst, Renshaw probably deserved it, as Peter was making one of many attempts to collect a debt a large part of which had been on the company's books for almost twenty-eight years, and which he eventually had to go to court to collect.[35]

In addition to his mining interests in the Idaho Springs area, Renshaw was a director of the Continental Bank of Denver and a member of the state legislature, serving on the Senate Banking and Finance Committees. With no little sarcasm, McFarlane expressed his feelings regarding a man in Renshaw's position who would not pay his debts:

> What a blessing it is to the state of Colorado that it has a man like Renshaw on its legislative Banking and also its Finance Committee. God surely was in the midst of the last session of the state Legislature. Anybody can see that.[36]

Peter was far more lenient when it came to collecting bills from a miner working a small lease than he was with businessmen who speculated in gold properties. For the capitalist who chose to speculate, Peter had little sympathy if his luck turned bad. He could make up his losses from other sources of income. In the case of the miner who lived by the sweat of his brow, it was a different story. He, too, in a sense, was a gambler, but unlike the capitalist, he had to live off his winnings, and most of the time these were small. His experiences were too similar to Peter's own to prevent sentiment from occasionally entering into business.

A good example of how a miner could play upon Peter's sympathies is the Russell Gulch miner who came into the Eureka Street foundry one day complaining that the frictions for his hoist which he had purchased from Will in Denver did not fit properly. This man owed McFarlane & Company a bill for certain work done three years previously. Like E. E. Hill and W. E. Renshaw, he had made no payments, and, furthermore, he refused to answer any letters requesting him to do so. In spite of this, before the man left the shop, Peter had given him a new set of frictions for his hoist.[37]

As the celebrated "Gay Nineties" came to an end, Peter's shops and foundries in Central City and Black Hawk were humming with activity. He employed on the average thirty-three men and dispensed an annual payroll in excess of $25,000.[38] Accounts receivable records, unfortunately, have not survived. Cash intake, however, was more than $60,000 a year,[39] with equipment sales alone averaging $3,600 a

Peter McFarlane belonged to two lodges,
the Good Templars and the Knights of Pythias.
Pictured here are three Knights of Pythias badges worn by Peter.
The emblem above denotes that he had been head of his local lodge,
i.e., served as its Chancellor Commander.
Shown on opposite page is (left) his Past Chancellor's badge
worn as Representative to a Grand Lodge convention.
The other badge (opposite page, right) was worn when attending
the funeral of a fellow lodge member.

month.[40] At this time business was, in fact, so good that Peter enjoyed a virtual monopoly in the mill and mining equipment business and was on occasion forced to turn down contracts.[41] For instance, in the fall of 1897 he refused a request that he manufacture and erect a five stamp mill, stating that "we are so awfully busy that it would be almost impossible for us to undertake its erection." At this time, Peter had every millwright on his payroll working on a twenty-five stamp mill at Perrigo in Gamble Gulch, and the contract included a penalty clause of $50.00 a day for each day that construction went beyond the agreed-upon date for completion.[42]

Peter McFarlane's operations in Denver, Central City, and Black Hawk made him, without doubt, a man of considerable status in mining circles and something in the nature of a "legend in his own time" among the some 7,000 inhabitants of Gilpin County at the turn of the century who often referred to him as "Lord McFarlane."[43] And it was Gilpin County which had the strongest claim on him, superseding both business and family. As will be seen, neither the entreaties of his brother, who needed his help in Denver, nor those of his wife were to budge him from the "Little Kingdom of Gilpin," an entity which at that time existed only in the minds, hearts, and memories of an ever-shrinking band of pioneers who had found in Gregory Gulch the stuff of legends and had proceeded to make new ones.

As the new century approached, Peter had lived for almost thirty years with both the harsh realities and the exuberant hopes of the mining camps sprawled across Gregory Gulch, and he was one of the few pioneer figures still searching with unabated enthusiasm the depths of Gilpin County's bleak and devastated hills for evidence of the Golden Goddess first seen by John Gregory in 1859. If at this point in its history the "Little Kingdom of Gilpin" had a titular ruler, it was Peter McFarlane, who even after three decades still suffered from the thirst "which gold only quickened but never quenched."[44]

Although his business was in excellent shape, Peter was not to be permitted the luxury of just running his shops and foundries, enjoying the delightful madness of gold fever which causes men to "meet together, stare stupidly at each other, and talk incoherent nonsense,"[45] and relishing the camaraderie of his cronies and his men.[46] In 1899 the subject of his moving to Denver raised its ugly head again, and this time it was a two-headed serpent. Will began to sound the possibility of

Peter's selling out his Gilpin County interest in the spring of the year and moving to Denver. At about the same time, his wife Marie, who had apparently been pressuring for a move to Denver for some months, decided that the time had come to take matters into her own hands. Very probably her major concern was her desire to give their daughter Yetta the high quality education available only in Denver. The Central City Public Schools were all right for their sons Fred and George, but for Yetta, Marie had in mind something special, Miss Anna Wolcott's School for Girls. Nevertheless, it is also probable that Marie was fed up with Central City and its mining-camp way of life and longed for the heady atmosphere of Denver society. Her determination on this score eventually strapped Peter with a loan which he was unable to liquidate until three years after her death in 1922, and only after considerable hardship.

In July 1899 Marie decided to bring to an end what in all probability had been a marital impasse by buying for $8,500 four lots and a partially completed house on Capitol Hill in Denver at the southwest corner of Gilpin and Colfax Streets. She made the purchase from John Best, a Central City pioneer and druggist, and engaged an architect to draw up plans for a house to her liking.[47] The Denver *Times* carried the following headline.

McFARLANE OF BLACK HAWK INTENDS TO COMPLETE HOUSE
BEGUN BY BEST. TRANSFER ANNOUNCED YESTERDAY. WILL
RESULT IN ANOTHER HANDSOME HILL RESIDENCE.[48]

Handsome, indeed! When completed in 1901, Marie's new home had "21 rooms ... completely furnished from basement to attic. Every room had a closet ... [There were] 90 electric lights, two baths, two water closets, [and a] hot water heating plant. Cost, $38,000,"[49] An idea of what an elegant residence it was can be gathered by noting that in terms of 1976 prices, it would have cost approximately $230,000.

Although the records are silent on this point, it seems probable that the house was a considerable source of disagreement between Peter and Marie not just because of its cost but because it brought into the open Peter's stubborn determination to stay in Central City no matter what his wife did. Capitol Hill society had no attraction for him. His heart was where it had been since he stepped off a dusty stagecoach in the summer of 1869 and took his first walk up Eureka Street. And, unlike

Leadville Johnny Brown, no woman was going to tear him away from the mining camp for a foray against the formidable bastions of Denver's "400." Proud, perhaps even to the point of arrogance, Peter remained to the end true to himself, and in so doing avoided the hilarious but nevertheless degrading attempts at culturization which Egbert Floud was forced to endure in Harry Leon Wilson's classic novel of the American West, *Ruggles of Red Gap.*

A few months prior to Marie's purchase of the Capitol Hill property, Will began making overtures toward Peter about his selling out and joining him in Denver. Will wanted and needed his brother's help in running the Denver operation, and it is even possible that he and Marie were working together to dislodge Peter from Central City. In February 1899 he sent a pleading letter asking, "Can you not arrange to come down here? There is plenty of work for both of us."[50] Peter's response, at least on the surface, seemed positive. "I do want to go to Denver," he replied, "and I don't want to remain here." However, he brought up once again the problem of disposing of the shops in Central City and Black Hawk, noting that he had been "trying for six years to find a purchaser," but that it was beginning to look hopeless.[51]

Will continued to press his brother, and the more he did, the more evasive Peter seemed to become, though he did make an attempt to sell out to Stroehle and Sons of Black Hawk.[52] Replying to one of Will's many attempts to convince him to come into the Denver operation he said:

> In regard ... to our business in Denver, I hardly know what to say. I do not see that I can say anything. I guess what you say is true, that there is not a lot of money in it.... As to what to do under the circumstances, I am at a loss to know. It may be that it is best to sell and go out of business entirely. It may be that it's best to build on the Blake Street lots, or it may be that it's best to stay right where we are.[53]

The tone of this letter was identical to one that Peter wrote to Will almost ten years previously when the subject of selling the Eureka Street and Black Hawk foundries first came up: "I have not said anything, because I haven't anything to say."[54] In each case, Peter actually was saying something, namely, that he did not want to sell if he could find a way of avoiding it.

As 1902 drew to a close, the situation remained unchanged—Will urging a consolidation of the business interests and Peter remaining as noncommittal as possible.[55] In the course of these drawn-out discussions, Peter had suggested that the time was ripe for a "proper separation or adjustment or distribution" of their property. His reasoning was that if either of them died, the result would be an "endless amount of trouble for the survivors to straighten things out,... [as] we have mining property and other property scattered all over."[56] This suggestion apparently turned the discussion regarding a consolidation of their businesses down an entirely different road, for sometime between January 1903 and January 1906, the McFarlane brothers decided not only to work out a distribution of their real estate and mining properties but to dissolve their partnership as well. In a letter to Will dated January 1, 1906, urging that they "keep at this division of property till we get it fixed up," Peter offered to sell his interest in the old Jackson works and the Blake Street lots for $25,000 and a quit claim on the "Gilpin County property not including our mines."[57] The negotiations dragged through the month of February. Will countered Peter's offer with one of his own for $22,800. Peter, however, stuck to his original figure.[58] Finally, early the following month the brothers reached an agreement,[59] and a partnership which had become famous throughout the mining industry of the West came to an end.

Will soon began construction on a large foundry and machine shop on the property at Thirty-third and Blake Streets. Between 1906 and 1910, seven buildings housing the W. O. McFarlane Manufacturing Company were erected on this plot, which was 400 feet long and 180 feet deep.[60] Will continued in business until 1910, when he retired and sold out to the William A. Box Iron Works Company. The original structures later housed the Silver Engineering Company until the late 1960s, and subsequently the Colorado Fuel and Iron Corporation.

During the final stages of negotiations with Will, Peter himself was attempting to purchase a site in Denver for a foundry and machine shop.[61] Finally, by July 1906 he closed a deal for a building at Twenty-eighth and Blake Streets, just five blocks west of where Will was putting up his new shops.[62] Soon after this date, the Peter McFarlane & Sons Iron Works Company came into existence, with Peter McFarlane as president, George McFarlane as vice president, Fred McFarlane as secretary and treasurer, and John Rassmussen as manager.[63]

John Rassmussen had been the chief engineer for McFarlane & Company's Denver shops, and in order to obtain his services for the new enterprise, Peter had offered him a salary of $100.00 a month for five years, a quarter interest in the company, and a quarter of all profits. The agreement further stated that at the end of five years Rassmussen could come into the company as a partner or sell his one-quarter interest to Peter.[64]

Bringing Rassmussen into the company was a shrewd move. He was a capable and experienced engineer who had worked with Peter and Will for many years and was fully qualified to assume a major role in the management of the company. Because of Rassmussen's qualification, Peter was freed of any real pressure and able to choose either to sell or close his foundries and shops in Central City and Black Hawk and take an active part in the affairs of the new company. This freedom and the fact that he and Will had finally settled their affairs seemed to have had an exhilarating effect on Peter. Writing to an old friend in Montana, he reported: "My health is good, and I am strong and active. I do not think that any two men this side of Penzeance could put me on my back the way I feel now."[65]

It is probable that part of his good spirits was related to the fact that he had weathered yet another crisis which might have pulled him away from his beloved Central City. Peter was at this time fifty-eight years old, and thirty-seven of these years had been spent in the "Little Kingdom of Gilpin." It was here that not only his principal business interests but his sentiments were, and not even his wife's displeasure could dampen his interest in Gilpin County's future. Writing to H. M. Teller in September, he clearly revealed a stubborn intention to concentrate his efforts in the area where he had lived for almost four decades:

> Replying to yours of 22nd will say that my ardor for the purchase of the property you refer to has been seriously blighted by my wife's determined and unyielding opposition to me having anything to do with the ownership. I will say, however, that I am still quietly arranging matters and will try and have a talk with you when in Denver.[66]

By the middle of 1906, his wife, his daughter, and two sons had moved from Central City to Denver, but Peter McFarlane had by then made it quite obvious that it was his intention to spend his remaining days in his Eureka Street home surrounded by the reminders of a once great mining camp. The prosperous years of the company which he helped found thirty-seven years earlier were over.

Central City, from German Hill, looking west. Teller House is large rectangular building left of center in near background. Gilpin Tramway in distance. *Courtesy Denver Public Library, Western History Department.*

CHAPTER VIII

The "Little Kingdom's" Most Loyal Citizen 1906-1924

Two years after Peter McFarlane established his sons in business in Denver, the mining industry in Gilpin County began its slow slide into extinction. One after another its mines were abandoned, and slowly the silent waters filled the mines and covered the retreating footprints of a pitiful remnant of a once mighty army of miners which for almost fifty years had shaken the bowels of Gilpin County's mineral mountains with hammer, drill, powder, and dynamite. The production of gold, which had averaged more than $1,700,000 worth a year between 1893 and 1902, fell to an average of just over $700,000 for the years 1909 through 1915, and two years later the figure fell below $400,000. If there was any further proof needed to demonstrate that the Gilpin County mining industry was moribund by 1917, the scrapping of the Gilpin Tramway in that year provided it.

The Tramway was a little railroad approximately twenty-four miles long which ran between the railheads at Black Hawk and Central City to the mines on Quartz Hill, Nevadaville, and Russell Gulch. It carried the ore from the mines to local mills and to the ore cars of the Colorado and Central Railroad for delivery to smelters in Golden and Denver. Turned into scrap in 1917, its locomotives, ore cars, and rails helped support the country's war effort.[1]

105

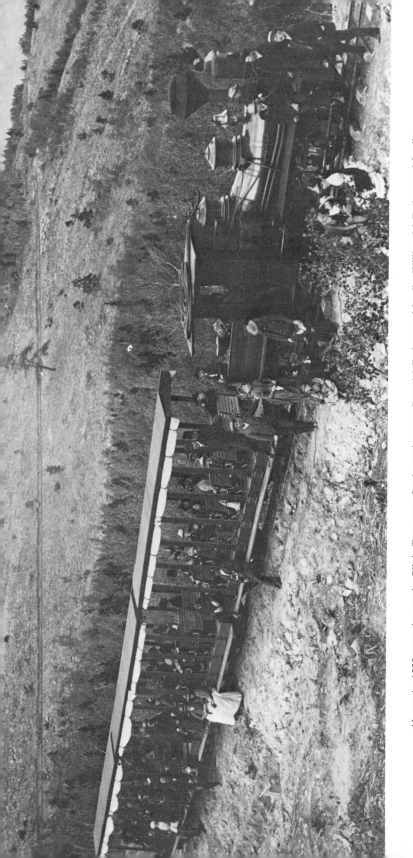

Above: An 1889 excursion on the Gilpin Tramway. On the outing were Peter McFarlane and family; William McFarlane and family; Minnie Frey, Peter's sister-in-law; Ida Kruse of Black Hawk, who later married Fred McFarlane; Henry M. Teller and family; Robert A. Campbell and family.

Page opposite: Another outing on the Tramway. *Courtesy Denver Public Library, Western History Department.*

The decline of the Gilpin County mining industry came at a time when Peter was heavily in debt. Consequently, the years following the dissolution of his partnership with Will were difficult ones. In order to finance the Denver operation, he had had to borrow heavily. In a letter to his old friend Phil Mixsell in Idaho Springs, written in the spring of 1908, Peter reported that "we have borrowed every penny we could get from Jo Thatcher[2] in Denver and both our local banks."[3] The total amount of these loans appears to have been $20,000.[4]

Even this sum was not enough to keep the Peter McFarlane & Sons Iron Works Company afloat in the early years of its existence, and, in the fall of 1908, Peter borrowed an additional $15,000 from John Ross of Golden.[5] He secured this loan with a mortgage on the house that Marie owned on Capitol Hill.

Due to the adverse business conditions which set in after 1906, Peter had to ask for extension after extension on the repayment of these loans. As the years passed by and he was able to meet only the interest due and nibble away at the principal, the matter weighed heavily on his mind. Repayment of a debt was for him a matter of intense personal pride and honor, and it was probably this fact which, more than anything else, led to his decision to sell out his interest in the Denver operation.

Negotiations with his son Fred and with Henry Eggers began in the spring of 1916,[6] and an agreement was reached on July 23. It called for Peter to receive "$45,000, less a ¼ interest owned by Fred McFarlane"; $15,000 of this sum was to be paid before October 10, 1916, and the balance in five years. In the meantime, promissory notes at 5% interest were to be secured by 18,000 shares of stock in the new company which Fred McFarlane and Henry Eggers would organize.[7] On September 1, the new partnership of McFarlane and Eggers was announced. Two days previously, Peter, as part of the agreement, had bought out John Rassmussen's interest in the old company for $3,000.[8]

Peter's determination to remain in Central City instead of moving to Denver and assuming an active role in the management of Peter McFarlane & Sons marked the beginning of his gradual transformation from a dynamic figure in the mining industry of the state to an elder statesman; he had not yet retired, but he was no longer in the thick of the competition. His business declined after 1906, and more and more of his time became occupied with projects not directly related to running it.

Not long after the turn of the century he had acquired a majority of the stock of the Gilpin County Opera House Association. At his own expense, he undertook to arrest the progressive deterioration of the Opera House, one of the great monuments of Central City's better days. In 1910 he installed motion picture equipment in the building, and the heroes and heroines of the early days of movie making flashed across the silent screen every Wednesday, Saturday, and Sunday night.

By 1914 another great structure dating back to the halcyon days of the "Little Kingdom of Gilpin," the Teller House, stood dilapidated and deserted on Eureka Street. Once the social and business center of a proud mining community, the old hotel had become silent, its halls no longer echoing the animated conversation of the booming mining camp coming from "the Elevator"[9] and the Assay Office.

To Peter McFarlane the sorry condition of the Teller House was a painful reminder that Central City was well on its way toward becoming a ghost town. As one of Central City's pioneer citizens, it hurt his pride to think that the town which had once been the mining capital of the state could no longer provide hotel accommodations for the traveler. Consequently, he made an effort to provide a remedy. In a long letter to H. M. Teller, McFarlane outlined his plans for renovating the Teller House and requested his cooperation in the project:

> As you know, "Central City has gone all abroad," and we have no hotel accommodations. The sojourner in our midst, like the true son of the gospel, has nowhere to lay his head. The Teller House is a large, nicely built structure but going to wreck and ruin—principally on account of a lack of patronage ... and in any way it's viewed it presents a disheartening spectacle. It is not my purpose to depreciate its value to its owners. But we have a scheme by which we hope to increase its value to its owners and not loose any money ourselves.... This is our plan. Let the owners put the lowest price on the house that they can with a view of making it a joint stock company.... Here ends act 1. The people of Central to come forward and put in a 80 h. boiler and hot water heating ... with necessary bath tubs, toilets, wash sinks; wash and paint where needed; restore dining room in the old place where it surely belongs; tear down those worthless and dilapedated sheds and outhouses, and otherwise prepare it for decent habitation. This would mean an expense of $10,000 to $15,000. We hope to meet this expense amongst our home people.... What we really want is a hotel that won't drive people away, and we are willing to do something to provide such a place.[10]

McFarlane was willing to do everything except provide the guests with the amenities of a bar, for he added an emphatic postscript to the above letter: "We do *not* want an Elevator!" As far as can be determined, this is the only instance where McFarlane's views on alcoholic beverages moved from temperance to prohibition.

Teller replied to McFarlane's proposal two days later, congratulating him on his plan and offering to sell the hotel to a Central City group for $16,000, with only $1,000 down.[11] McFarlane apparently had some hopes of interesting enough local people in the project to meet Teller's terms, for on March 16 he asked the Denver Dry Goods Company to submit an estimate of the cost of furnishing fifty double rooms. In his letter he stated that "a lot of us here are thinking of taking ahold of the old Teller House and fixing it up."[12]

Thinking and talking, however, were easy; actually raising the money was another matter. McFarlane's project, predictably, never went farther than good intentions. Central City had no hotel because at that time it no longer needed one, and no amount of nostalgia or civic pride on the part of the old-timers still living there could change this fact. Although he never lived to see the restoration of the Teller House in 1932, McFarlane played a key role in making it possible. Had he not rescued the old Opera House from sure destruction, there could have been no later annual Central City Opera and Drama Festival. And it was this festival, started in 1932, which made the restoration of the Teller House a necessity. McFarlane's role in preserving the Opera House, however, is the subject of the next chapter.

At about the same time that he was attempting to restore the Teller House, McFarlane became interested in what was to be one of the largest engineering and construction projects in the history of the state, the Moffat Tunnel. This 6.2-mile bore through the Continental Divide, beginning about fifty miles west of Denver, was the dream of David H. Moffat, a pioneer Colorado mining, railroad, and banking figure. Work began on the tunnel in 1923, and the project was completed in 1928. Its actual construction, however, was only the last act of a drama stretching over more than two decades which were marked by one failure after another to obtain enough private or public financing for the enormous project. Moffat, who died in New York on March 18, 1911, did not live to see his dream become a reality.

The failure of the Moffat Railroad to obtain sufficient capital to finance the project led to several attempts, beginning in 1913, to obtain public funds, and it was at this stage that Peter McFarlane began to take an active interest in bidding on the contract. Will had retired three years previously, but Peter, at sixty-five, had no intention of following suit. From the latter part of 1913 until the actual letting of the contract ten years later, he kept up an active correspondence with the Moffat Tunnel Commissioners in Denver.

Nothing more clearly illustrates the intellectual and physical vitality of the man than the correspondence covering this episode in his life. He seriously believed that he could muster the resources to plan and carry this huge project through to completion, and while an impartial analysis of the situation separates the dream from the reality, the spirit which motivated him must be admired.

Peter McFarlane was partly the product of the western frontier, and as such he reflected all of the frontier's optimism, its eager response to challenge, and its reliance on will and determination to overcome shortages of other resources. If, as in the case of the Moffat Tunnel, he was a visionary, so also was Moffat. He, too, proved unable to muster the resources to drive a railroad line under the Continental Divide. But his example inspired others to complete the task which he started. Although Peter McFarlane and David H. Moffat can hardly be compared in any other way, they stand together as equals in illustrating the heights to which the individual spirit could soar on the western frontier.

McFarlane's Moffat Tunnel correspondence began with a letter to D. W. Brunton, a Denver mining engineer and a member of the Moffat Tunnel Commission. In this letter McFarlane pointed out that he had had "many years of experience in the mining, breaking and hauling of rock," and that he was "eager and anxious" to study the specifications for the tunnel with a view toward making a bid.[13]

Brunton's reply two days later noted that the Commission was not prepared at the time to issue detailed specifications, but that he was glad to learn that "one firm in the state was prepared to submit a bid."[14] Thus encouraged, McFarlane immediately sent inquiries to the Scientific American Publishing Company and the Ingersoll Rand Company, requesting up-to-date material on tunnel construction.[15] At the same time, he wrote to Lucien L. Nunn in Telluride and D. R. C. Brown in Aspen, asking them to take part in the project.[16] In his letter to Nunn, McFarlane revealed the principal source of his interest in the project. His sharp Scotch businessman's eye had spotted what appeared to be an opportunity for an enormous profit. "Why can't you come in with me on a contract to put through the Moffat Tunnel," he wrote. "I am sure it can be taken for much less than the Tunnel Commission figures it is worth, namely, $4,200,000. There is a million dollars in it at a $4,000,000 job."

Neither Nunn nor Brown was interested, but Peter never deviated from his view that the estimates for completing the tunnel were too high. Writing to Representative Benjamin Hilliard, who was trying to obtain support for a federal appropriation for the project, McFarlane expressed the view that the tunnel should not cost more than $2,500,000, and that it ought to be completed in twenty-seven months.[17] He was, of course, considerably off in these estimates. But when the final cost of the tunnel, $15,470,000, is taken into consideration, his margin of error was not much greater than that of the Moffat Tunnel Commission in its original estimates.[18]

During the second decade of the century, McFarlane's business gradually changed from that of manufacturing and distributing mine and milling machinery and equipment to that of selling scrap metal. His correspondence for 1917, for instance, records over eleven tons of scrap metal shipped to Denver, much of it to McFarlane and Eggers.

There is reason for believing that this activity, with its small profits, was not an entirely unhappy one for McFarlane. Although he had some pressing financial problems, which will be dealt with later, they were not of a nature to force him to drive himself on the job. He could work more or less at his own pace, and his work was not at all unpleasant. During the long Colorado summers and falls, he traveled around the country in his buggy, visiting all of the familiar mines and mills of a bygone day in search of scrap metal, enjoying all the while the "purest of air," and what he considered to be some of the best natural scenery in America.

Despite the fact that he was approaching seventy years of age, McFarlane often traveled more than forty miles a day,[19] a fact which testifies to his robust health. On his trips, he occasionally encountered a situation which showed that his sense of humor had not been impaired by the passing years. Driving through Rollinsville one day on his way home, he spotted an air compressor which had been damaged

by fire. In a letter to its owner, he recounted his unsuccessful attempt
to get close enough to appraise it.

> I stopped the team and got partly unbuggied when I spied coming
> at me 10 feet at a jump a big, white, short-tailed vicious looking
> bulldog. The seat of my pants were already badly demoralized,
> and knowing that further loss and I would freeze to death, I
> quickly got in again, thus saving my miserable life.[20]

McFarlane's semiretirement, however, was not entirely idyllic, for he
still was faced with a large part of the debt he had incurred in order to
establish Fred and George in business in Denver. In order to reduce
this debt, he took out of the business for himself only what was
necessary to provide a modest standard of living. For instance, he paid
himself wages of only $2,013.46 in 1917, and $1,335.50 in 1918.[21]
During these two years, the income and expenses of the business just
about balanced. The collection of old debts, however, which amounted
to $6,500 in 1917, enabled him to make some progress in liquidating
his own indebtedness. By the end of March 1918, he had retired one of
the notes held by the Rocky Mountain Bank in Central City, leaving a
balance owed of $3,000.[22] Late in May of the same year, he sold a 72
inch boring mill and a large lathe out of his Black Hawk shop to a San
Francisco company for $8,550.[23] Soon after receiving payment, he sent
John Ross $5,000 on the principal and $67.50 for interest on the note
which the latter held. This payment reduced what he owed Ross to
$4,000.[24]

At the time of this transaction, McFarlane was the chairman of the
Liberty Loan drive in Gilpin County. His campaign to raise the county's
quota of $24,000 reflected his deep love and pride of the area in which
he lived. Gilpin County might be faltering economically, but it would
pull its weight in the nation's war effort if Peter McFarlane had
anything to say about it. In a letter accompanying his $5,000 check to
Ross, McFarlane revealed just how seriously he took his position as
county chairman for the Liberty Loan campaign:

> Our county is in bad shape as you know. It has been asked
> by the government to raise $24,000 in W. S. S. [War Savings
> Stamps]. I am going to ask you to subscribe $1,000 to help
> out.... We are counting on your help. If you will take $2,000,
> we will pay you another $1,000 on what we owe you—*now*.[25]

In his drive to meet his quota, McFarlane was as willing to play upon sentiment as he was to use a gentle form of business pressure. Scattered across the state of Colorado were a number of former residents of Central City who had got their start toward wealth and position in Gilpin County. To several of these persons, McFarlane addressed appeals designed to invoke the memories of the past. To his cousin, D. R. C. Brown, then living in Denver, he wrote:

> As a county we would like to meet our quota, but as a county we are in bad financial shape. Undoubtedly you will subscribe, but Denver will get the benefit. We wonder if you could not be induced to so invest that this county might have the credit of some of the amount. We hate decidedly to fall down in our allotment.[26]

His appeal to another Denver man who had strong ties to Central City was even more eloquent.

> We want you to take $2,500 in [War Savings Stamps]. Of course, you know this is not a gift, but a safe, patriotic, interest bearing investment. [The] U. S. government assigned to Gilpin County (poor and old and feeble and poverty stricken) a [War Savings Stamps] loan of $24,000, and in our tottering state we thought in as much as the innocense and purity of your life was [spent] here, and the finest family that the community ever knew was produced in this section, and the Honorable Theodore H. Becker laid the foundation for his great wealth here, you would do something for the perpetuity of such a cause. I will see that the newspapers give the transaction all due credit.[27]

With former residents of Gilpin County responding to McFarlane's appeals, the county *exceeded* its quota in the third Liberty Loan campaign by $22,900.[28] He had never kissed the Blarney Stone, but it is clear that McFarlane was seldom at a loss for words. His ability to express himself with some eloquence led an old friend to remark: "I always had an idea that you were a pretty smooth talker, but if I heard you giving a public speech, and I didn't know you, I should certainly come to the conclusion that it was the silver tongued orator on his feet."[29]

McFarlane was unable to make another payment on the principal of the mortgage on the Capitol Hill house until March 1, 1920. On that date he paid $2,000, which reduced the balance to the same amount.[30] In the meantime, however, Ross had died and the executor of his estate was demanding a new note bearing 8% interest on the amount still due.[31] McFarlane's desire to liquidate the debts that he had accrued in order to set his sons up in business in Denver eventually precipitated a family situation which, while of short duration, could hardly have been pleasant.

In 1906, when he sold his interest in the Denver foundry and shop to his son Fred and to Henry Eggers, McFarlane had agreed to reimburse his son George for the one-quarter interest he held in the business. Following the demise of the Peter McFarlane & Sons Iron Works Company, George had returned to Central City to work for his father. As the years went by, there was less and less work for him to do. In addition, his father had been unable to pay him all that was rightfully his from the sale of the Denver business. As matters stood in the fall of 1921, McFarlane still owed George $4,000.[32]

This matter weighed heavily with him.[33] In addition, his creditors were pressing him for payment, and McFarlane was finally forced to remind his son Fred and Henry Eggers that they still owed him $4,000, and that payment was five years overdue.[34] He was thus in the uncomfortable position[35] of having to press one son for money in order to pay another.

There is no record of the outcome of this situation. However, on May 14, 1922, McFarlane paid off the last of what he owed to the John Ross estate.[36] The liquidation of this debt had required more than fourteen years, and it had cost McFarlane over $9,000 in interest.[37] Within just a few months, a new turn of events would free him of debts for the first time in almost a decade and a half.

In January 1919 McFarlane lost his wife of forty-two years. Marie died without leaving a will. In such cases, Colorado law stipulated that the surviving partner inherited one-half of the estate and that the other half be paid to any surviving children. It will be remembered that the house on Capitol Hill was held in Marie's name. Consequently, after her death, a half interest passed to her husband and the other half to their three children. This joint ownership of the house was hardly a satisfactory arrangement, and in November 1923 McFarlane and his three children agreed to sell it to Fred's wife Ida for $18,000. With the $9,000 he thus received, McFarlane immediately paid off the $3,000 note held by the Rocky Mountain National Bank and approximately $1,000 in back taxes he owed on a group of mining properties in Gilpin County.[38]

With his debts at last a thing of the past and cash on hand, McFarlane was able to give serious attention to a project he had been thinking about for some time. To a Denver correspondent he confided: "I am going to operate the Buell."[39] At this time McFarlane was almost seventy-four, and the gold fever he had contracted over fifty-five years before had not subsided at all. In fact, it may have become worse. With the enthusiasm of a neophyte he wrote to an old friend seeking backing for this project:

> Tennyson asks the question,
>
> > What is it that I should turn to
> > Lighting upon days like these.
> > Everyone bored with suitors
> > And open thus to golden keys.
>
> Here you are sick of coal mining, so you will be sick of tungsten mining, so you will be with all mining except gold mining. Gold is the only stuff worth going after.... Construct your banking house on a gold foundation and the gates of Hell shall not prevail against it. Build it on a tungsten foundation and a little dog galloping past is liable to wash it away. There is more gold in Gilpin County mines today than many people are willing to admit. Given a Gilpin County slow drop mill without feeder,... battery coppers, cast iron bumpers, electric motor powers, put Charles Cox in charge, give it Buell ore, and I'll gamble my life it will pay. I am moving in the matter of preparing 10 to 20 stamps of the east section of the Buell [mill].... If I don't get ore from the Buell, I will run it custom. I shall cut windows in the side of the building opposite the batteries and unload from wagons just the same as they did 50 or 60 years ago.[40]

True to his word, McFarlane had a section of the Buell mill operating in about four months. Apparently he was working it as a custom mill, as the 6⅓ cords of ore he processed in his first run were from the Americus mine, not the Gregory-Buell. The results were quite disappointing. A little over three ounces of gold were retrieved, which did not quite cover the cost of processing the ore.[41] McFarlane, nevertheless, persisted in his attempts to operate the mill on a paying basis. In a letter to a Nederland man in December he reported that he had "retorted 173 ounces of gold ... treated at the Buell from ten stamps for 30 days run."[42] It is impossible to tell whether or not this represented a profit, for McFarlane did not mention the number of cords of ore processed. But presumably there was no profit, for surely he would have mentioned it if there were—and there is no mention.

It seems possible that what McFarlane actually intended when he restarted the Buell mill was to revive, single-handedly, the mining industry in Gilpin County. In addition to the Buell, he had plans for restarting the U. P. R. mill, reopening the St. Louis Mine, and building and operating an ore sampling works in Black Hawk.[43] Apparently, he felt that if he could just demonstrate that it was still possible to extract gold from Gilpin County ores on a paying basis, investment capital could be attracted, and the mining industry of the county would, like the mythical Phoenix, rise once again.

Although McFarlane was correct in his opinion that there was more gold in Gilpin County than had been taken out, the low grade ores and the depth of the mines made mining uneconomical. None of his projects ever materialized. They were the nostalgic dreams of an old man, but a man who at seventy-six believed in them enough to borrow $1,000 on his life insurance in order to finance one more attempt to breathe a little bit of life into what had once been Colorado's most famous mining camp.[44] Ironically, the miracle he hoped for lay only a few years in the future, but Peter McFarlane, the "Little Kingdom's" most loyal citizen, would not live to see it.

....OPERA HOUSE....

F. J. ALTVATER, Manager.

ONE
PERFORMANCE

SATURDAY, MAY 20

GRANDER THAN EVER.

The New Production of that Gorgeous
Spectacular Extravaganza

~≈M. B. LEAVITT'S≈~

SPIDER AND FLY.

40—People—40   15—High Class Specialties—15   See the
magnificent scenery. the gorgeous costumes, the superb
ballets, the gold and silver march.

Matchless Chorus of Sixteen Beautiful Girls.

The new hits in follies and fancies—Yankee Doodle Boys; The
Widow Brown; Throw 'Em Down, Dewey; The Domestics
of the Palace; Sousa Vivandiere Band; The Mermaids'
Revels; The Chefs of the Occidental.

Prices as Usual.   **Seats Now on sale at Couch's.**

THE HIT

OF THE

SEASON.

Opera House.

F. J. ALTVATER, Manager.

Sunday & Monday.

MAY 21 & 22.

Georgia up to Date.

Farce Comedy, Comic Opera and Vaudeville,
and in fact everything that's New.

≋≋ A RIOT OF FUN. ≋≋

Lookout for Band.
50—People—50
Read Denver Criticisms this Week.

Prices 50 and 75 Cts.   **On Sale at Couch's.**

CHAPTER IX

The Central City Opera House 1878–1927

O N the morning of July 17, 1932, the *Rocky Mountain News* carried this banner headline:

CENTRAL CITY ROARS WIDE OPEN
IN REVIVAL OF OLD MINING DAYS

The occasion which brought an "uproarious throng estimated at more than 5,000" streaming up to Gregory Gulch the day and evening of July 16 was the opening night of the Central City Play Festival in the old Opera House on Eureka Street. The play was *Camille;* the star, Lillian Gish.

Only a few hundred of the thousands who came to Central City on this historic occasion actually viewed the play, and these were described as the flower of Denver society. For the rest, however, there was adequate compensation—free-flowing bootleg liquor, roulette, crap, and faro games in gambling establishments hastily set up in the "Golden Queen's" long-vacant buildings.

The festivities that night in the old mining camp offered an opportunity to forget for a moment the deepening depression that was settling over the nation, suffocating its industry, its will, and its intellect in a grey blanket of fear and uncertainty. And those who could

117

take advantage of this moment of forgetfulness—and memory—did so. As the *News* put it, a howling mob looking for a good time filled Central City's steep, crooked streets, and "tore off the lid and heaved it into Gregory Gulch."

For a fleeting moment that summer, the streets of Central City again pulsed with life, but many a summer festival would come and go before the people who came to mingle with the ghosts of a bygone day would retrieve the ebullient optimism and self-confidence of the pioneers who had created the mining camp. For the moment, a legacy of the western frontier had been regained—but briefly.

Lillian Gish's gala opening night in 1932 had its origins in an amateur performance of *The Bohemian Girl* in the old Belvedere Theatre, which was located on the second story of a brick building at the head of Main Street, on April 17, 1877. The success of this musical event resulted in the formation of the Gilpin County Opera House Association, which took as its immediate objective the raising of funds to build a structure in which grand opera could be properly staged. Less than a year later, on March 4, 1878, the Central City Opera House, a $32,000 tribute to the pride and spirit of the pioneer citizens of Gilpin County, raised its curtain for the first time.[1] A glittering audience composed of the local aristocrats and the leaders of Denver society filled its eight hundred chairs for an evening of music provided by local musicians, and the "Little Kingdom's" reign as the cultural as well as the mining capital of the state began.

This reign, however, was to be short-lived. Within a year, the dollar value of Lake County silver superseded the dollar value of Gilpin County gold, and in 1881 Leadville money built in Denver what quickly became the leading theatre of the state—the Tabor Grand Opera House on Fifteenth Street.

Just one year after the opening of the Tabor Grand, the stockholders of the Central City Opera House put their property up for sale. It was purchased by the county for $8,000 to be converted into a courthouse. This move to turn Gregory Gulch's cultural monument into a habitat for local politicians produced a strong wave of protest. A campaign to raise the funds necessary to buy the structure back from the county was launched. By December the campaign was successful, and the Opera House became the property of a combine of fifty-nine local citizens holding a total of 670 shares in a reorganized Gilpin County Opera House Association.[2]

Although never a moneymaker, the Opera House managed to survive year after year, largely due to the Tabor Grand's success in attracting to Colorado important touring theatrical troupes. Some of these troupes could afford to play Central City after finishing their Denver engagement, and it was by this means that professional entertainment continued to come to Gregory Gulch. Having to rely on the crumbs from Denver's entertainment table must have been galling for those who had participated in erecting the first opera house in the state.

It is not certain that Peter McFarlane was among the group that saved the Opera House from becoming a courthouse. It hardly seems possible, however, that he could have turned a deaf ear to the appeals emanating from the *Daily Citizen* in the fall of 1882. After all, he had not only been involved in its construction, but he had also been mayor of the city during the first exhilarating months after its completion.

Following its purchase from the county, the Opera House was managed for a number of years by Horace M. Hale, who had in the early days been Central City's school principal. Hale was an avid theatre goer and amateur actor. On the so-called "second opening night" of the Opera House on March 5, 1878, he had played one of the leading roles in that evening's amateur dramatic production. He also was the largest stockholder in the Gilpin County Opera House Association, having subscribed $2,000 of the $8,000 needed to purchase the building from the county.[3]

Hale was barely able to keep the Opera House operating for the next four years, and after that time, for reasons unknown, he moved to Denver. In the years following 1882, the building deteriorated rapidly due to lack of income for upkeep, and by the early 1890s rumors were abroad that it was unsafe for public performances. Hale, as the principal stockholder, was summoned from Denver, and he and McFarlane inspected the building. They found the basement filled with sand from floods, the foundation timbers rotten, and the whole building badly deteriorated. Following their inspection, Hale asked McFarlane to assume indirect management of the Opera House. McFarlane not only accepted Hale's proposition but proceeded immediately to carry out the necessary repairs at his own expense.[4]

Having been asked to assert himself in the management of the Opera House, McFarlane did just that. In February 1896 he sent Hale a plan for installing electric lights. Hale approved, and McFarlane proceeded with the installation. On June 15 the switch was thrown, ten incandescent lamps installed in the canopy of the original chandelier beamed down on the Opera House stage, and sixteen footlights winked back.[5]

McFarlane was not the kind of man who could manage anything indirectly for long. He felt strongly that under the proper management, the Opera House could be made to pay,[6] and by proper management, he meant Peter McFarlane. Consequently, sometime in the fall of 1898, he sought to acquire all the available stock of the Gilpin County Opera House Association.[7] Two years later, in the fall of 1900, Fritz Altvater, the official manager of the Opera House, resigned, and McFarlane formally took over. Altvater's resignation was due to the city fathers' refusal to renew a license permitting Sunday evening shows.[8]

Now in full command, McFarlane pressed ahead with his project to become the owner, as well as the manager, of the Opera House. In the spring of the following year, Hale offered to sell his stock for $900,[9] an offer McFarlane quickly accepted. Writing to H. M. Teller a year and a half later, he recalled his campaign to obtain a controlling interest in the Opera House. "I have only regretted it once," he said, "and that is all the time."[10] Interestingly, the purpose of his letter to Teller was to get him to sell or donate his fifty shares to McFarlane. Teller eventually sold these shares to him, but not until almost ten years later; with them, McFarlane had accumulated four-fifths of the 670 original shares.[11] Even then he did not rest content, but aggressively pursued the effort to purchase the few that remained in other hands.[12]

At the time he took over the Opera House, McFarlane estimated that it would cost at least $3,000 to repair the building.

> The roof is in bad shape, the ceiling plaster shaky from leaky roof and ready to drop, the walls and ceilings have on them the dust of 25 years, the floors are worn out, furnaces almost unfit for use, scenery in need of entire renewal, all the stage walls ought to be plastered, a new flume put in under the house, newly painted—and a lot of other things ought to be done.[13]

Early in 1903 he began the task of renovation. New scenery and a new curtain were ordered from a Kansas City company, and an inquiry was sent out regarding new chairs. By September the scenery, $576 worth of it, had arrived. So had the curtain, but McFarlane refused to accept it because he believed that it made the stage look like "a small boy wearing his father's overalls."[14]

Unfortunately, there is a gap in the *McFarlane Papers* at this point, and it is impossible to trace in detail all of the work that was done to get the Opera House ready to resume its role as Central City's only theatre. Those letters that have survived, however, provide one interesting fragment of the old building's history, and the hint of another.

McFarlane's correspondence with the Kansas City Scenery Company reveals the fact that the original stage was raked, that is, that the area of the footlights was at least one foot lower than the back. This slope, however, reduced the height of the scenery, and McFarlane objected to that fact. So, in order to expose as much scenery as possible, he leveled the stage, and although it is not certain, probably raised the roof over the stage at least a foot.[15]

His inquiry to a Chicago firm regarding new chairs casts light on the legend that the solid hickory memorial chairs now used in the Opera House are part of the original equipment.[16] Because of the hiatus in the *McFarlane Papers* covering the period when McFarlane was renovating the building, there is no record of new chairs having been purchased. Nevertheless, the fact that McFarlane considered replacing them indicates that the original chairs must have been in bad condition and possibly were replaced. And it raises some doubt about the authenticity of the legend.

Once in full control of the Opera House, McFarlane was in a position to test his belief that under proper management the old theatre could return a profit. Again there is the problem of gaps in the records, which make it difficult to evaluate the degree of his success. The *Opera House Account Book,* for instance, is blank from November 16, 1900, through January 1, 1912, but what evidence is available seems to indicate clearly that he was fortunate if at the end of a year he broke even; the profits from an occasional good attraction were absorbed by deficits from the half-empty houses for the second- and third-rate vaudeville troupes on which he had mainly to rely. For instance, one of McFarlane's most profitable bookings in the early days of his career as a theatrical promoter was *Uncle Tom's Cabin,* which played in the Opera House on the evening of November 11, 1902. The gross receipts for this performance were $468.75, and he realized a profit of $117.00, which he sadly noted "only helped me out of the hole that much."[17]

Sometime prior to 1906, McFarlane turned his considerable talents at persuasion on the city officials and got them to reverse their previous decision regarding Sunday performances in the Opera House. This was

..OPERA HOUSE..

F. J. ALTVATER, Manager.

Sunday, February 12, 1899.

John L. Sullivan's

BIG COMEDY COMPANY.

30 STAR PERFORMERS 30

MUSICAL FARCE.

"A Trip Across the Ocean."

A Farce Comedy Full of Fun.

PRETTY GIRLS   CLEVER COMEDIANS

A SHOW A LADY CAN ENJOY.

Scenes in a Gymnasium between

John L. Sullivan and Jake Kilrain.

Seats Now on Sale at Couch's.

✹ OPERA HOUSE

One Night Only.

TWO By GEO. R. EDESON.

⌐MARRIED

MEN.

TUESDAY,

SEPTEMBER

13th.....

The Laughing Success of the Season.

SPECIAL SCENERY.   NOVEL SPECIALTIES.
SPARKLING WIT.   PRETTY GIRLS.

✹ **A Grand Company of Comedians**

Popular
Prices

50 and 75c.

Reserved
Seats at

Couch's.

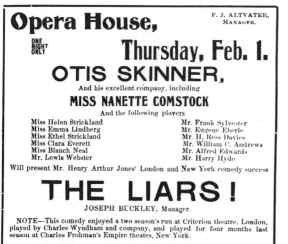

Central City newspaper ads, 1898, 1899, 1900.
Courtesy State Historical Society of Colorado.

an achievement of no little importance, for it meant that a theatrical company which had booked Denver for Friday and Saturday· night performances could afford to detour fifty miles into the Rocky Mountains for a Sunday evening performance in Central City before moving on to the next large town on its itinerary. As a matter of fact, had McFarlane not succeeded in getting a license for Sunday evening performances, it is unlikely that he could have kept the Opera House open.

Although the City Council was persuaded to overcome its objections to theatrical entertainment on Sunday, they stood adamant in their refusal to permit Sunday parades. This refusal was a source of no little irritation to McFarlane, as it made it almost impossible for him to book minstrel shows. In those days, a minstrel show without its street parade would have been like Barnum and Bailey coming to town without sending its menagerie, its clowns, its acrobats and other performers down the main street to advertise the show in the big tent. In the age of television, it is hard to recapture the excitement that was generated in a small town when someone spotted the posting of the first gaudy lithographs announcing the imminent arrival of a minstrel show. And what a day it was when the "silver or gold cornet band gorgeously attired in colorful coats and trousers, big brass buttons, and striking hats, led the procession through the streets of the town to the theatre, followed by the whole company, perhaps in long vests or colored lapels and high silk 'plug' hats"—everyone, performers and crowds alike, stepping along to such lively old tunes as "Dixie," "The Natchez and the Robert E. Lee," and "Hot Time in the Old Town Tonight!"[18] The City Council's refusal to permit an extravaganza such as a Sunday parade caused McFarlane to lament at the end of the 1905-06 theatrical season that he had had only "one colored show this season, [the] Georgia Minstrels."[19]

There is some evidence that it was pressure from the Methodists which prompted the city's ban on Sunday parades. The Opera House stood just across the street from the St. James Methodist Church, and its members, with their religious precepts regarding proper Sunday observance, could hardly be expected to condone these lavish parades which ended practically on the church doorstep, particularly when the minstrels concluded their parade with a short concert, often followed by a display of fireworks.

As noted, in the days when live entertainment was the only kind available, it was almost impossible to book anything for the Opera House on a Saturday night because of the competition of the Denver theatres. McFarlane, however, did everything he could to arrange at least two or three Saturday evening shows a season. In a slightly sarcastic letter to his Denver booking agent he noted that his diligence in this matter was due to the fact that "my Methodist friends contend that the exclusive Sunday night bookings give them no opportunity for amusement."[20]

McFarlane's attitude reflected the fact that he ran the Opera House for reasons which transcended any profits he might make. In a real sense, the Sunday evening vaudeville shows were his gift to the citizens of Gilpin County. For instance, for 1898-99, the first year recorded in the *Opera House Account Book,* entries note thirty three shows were booked during the September-June theatrical season. Twenty-seven made money; six went into the red. The house profits for the year were $192.93, or an average of $5.84 a show.[21] Presumably, whatever salary Fritz Altvater, who was the official manager at the time, received had to come out of the profits, and every indication points to the fact that for the year 1898-99, the Opera House just managed to break even. While this situation may not have repeated itself every year, it seems clear that McFarlane stood little chance of securing a profit from the Opera House. The time and effort which he devoted to it served for a pleasant hobby and contributed to the life of the community.

The Opera House served not only as a theatre but as a community center where all kinds of civic, religious, and political functions were held, and on many of these occasions, McFarlane donated the use of the building free of charge. For instance, during the 1898-99 season, he donated one night for a speech by a member of the Fusion Party, four nights to the Republican Party, five Sundays to the Methodist church, one night to an elocution contest sponsored by the Episcopal church, one night to the Central City schools, and one night to a "businessmen's carnival." His contribution was not inconsiderable, as it cost an average of $9.00 a night just for the janitor, light, and heat.[22]

McFarlane tried to get the best entertainment he could for the citizens of the "Little Kingdom," and he was not always happy with what his Denver booking agent was able to obtain. On such occasions,

Peter McCourt could expect a letter similar to the following:

> I want to say that some of the shows sent up here are pretty rotten, "Hearth and Home," and "Just Struck Town" were very poor. I notice you have booked for 14th Oct., "On the Bridge At Midnight." I am afraid I'll be mobbed if that appears here. It has been here many times, and never at its best was anything but a 10 cent show, and if it can be done, I wish you would cancel it, if you please. I would rather my house would stand idle entirely.[23]

Perhaps McFarlane was expressing his personal disapproval of *On the Bridge at Midnight*, rather than that of the theatre-going public in Gilpin County. That he was in little danger of being mobbed if he booked the show is revealed by the fact that his agent McCourt either could not or did not cancel its Central City appearance, and it played in the Opera House as scheduled to the third largest audience of that season's first ten shows.[24]

Prior to the motion picture era, McFarlane maintained a policy of generally putting on only one show a week. If, however, there was a chance to book a show in which he had a personal interest, this policy could be momentarily set aside. One such occasion occurred during the 1906–07 season. McFarlane was very interested in booking a touring Shakespearean company, but he had already filled all of the Sundays on which the troupe could possibly play Central City. In a letter to the company's agent, he reiterated his policy of only one show a week, but went on to say:

> I would like, however, to strain a point and give my patrons an opportunity to see "The Merchant of Venice," and have the date *on a week night,* and thus give my good religious friends an opportunity to be present if they desire.[25]

The sincerity of McFarlane's concern for his "good religious friends" is open to question. He wanted to see *The Merchant of Venice,* and that was reason enough for breaking his one-show-per-week rule. In all probability, if the show did come to Central City, it must have cost more than a few dollars out of his own pocket. As he himself had to admit sadly, there were not enough people left in Central City at this time "to give sufficient patronage to first class ... theatricals,"[26] and if he were lucky enough to schedule occasionally a first-class show, the chances were good that he also had to subsidize it.

Even with an old favorite and moneymaker like *Uncle Tom's Cabin,*
the troupe had to arrange to arrive in Central City on the morning train
so there would be time for a street parade, as without this attractive
publicity, he felt sure "they would not have a house."[27]

During the first decade of the century, McFarlane found it more and
more difficult to keep the Opera House open even on Sundays. In the
summer of 1907, he wrote McCourt that he seriously doubted the
"wisdom of opening the house" for the 1907-08 season "because of the
fact that it don't pay to run."[28]

He had second thoughts, however, and opened the season on
schedule in the fall. As it drew to a close in the spring of the following
year, his books revealed that he had lost $250.00 on the twenty-five
shows he had booked, and he was again considering closing the Opera
House.[29] To an Omaha agent seeking booking for an act, he felt
obliged to write the following letter:

> I write in regard to your contract which I have before me, and
> to say that I am afraid that you can't play to a paying house in
> this city. Times are so dull here and mining so depressed that
> nearly all our theatre patrons have moved away and I feel its
> a duty I owe you to say that I do not think you will take in
> enough to meet your expenses if you show here.[30]

For the same reason, McFarlane discouraged the "Kempton Komedy"
troupe from coming to Central City, even though its appearances in the
past had drawn good crowds there.[31]

The best evidence that McFarlane had serious problems keeping the
Opera House open is contained in an interesting letter he penned to an
official of the Colorado and Southern Railroad, in which he attempted
to blackmail the railroad out of a pass:

> I have instructed Mr. McCourt, who does my booking, that my
> house would not be open during the coming theatrical year,
> 1908-9.... Last year I had 25 travelling shows appear here, all of
> whom patronized your road, and each of the 25 paid you $27.50,
> or a total of $687.50 ... while I 'went into the hole' for $250.00.
> I enclose letter from Mr. McCourt that will convince you that my
> house is not to be opened coming season because it don't pay.
> I have thought the matter over again, however, and have con-
> cluded that if you will give me a pass on your road between
> Black Hawk and Denver good for one year and also good on

Sundays that I will write Mr. McCourt and instruct him to make bookings for my house as usual.[32]

There is, unfortunately, no record of Johnson's reply. Presumably he rejected McFarlane's maneuver. In any event, this time McFarlane meant what he said about closing the Opera House. In May 1908 the curtain came down on the last show of the final regularly scheduled vaudeville season. For the next two years, community events and an occasional traveling show which he personally arranged for seem to have been the only times the old building was in use. Just how little it was used can be seen in this letter McFarlane wrote to a Denver firm that was soliciting a renewal of his ticket order:

> Out of a consignment of a lot of 60 sets of Opera House tickets ordered by us in January last, we have used to date two sets only. This will give you an idea of how long you will have to live at the present rate of Opera House business before the tickets we now have would be used up—say 25 years. At the end of that time, you will be in Heaven and have wings at least 25 ft. long each way and will not be chasing after the dollars as you now are. Teller, whom your tickets advertise, will be hobnobbing with you, Penny will be shoveling coal, not in Boulder either. No Sir, we cannot use your tickets.[33]

In May 1910 McFarlane wrote to McCourt in Denver of his intention to install motion picture equipment in the Opera House.[34] This decision probably stemmed from the fact that earlier in the year someone had converted a storeroom in one of Central City's many vacant buildings into a makeshift movie theatre with 175 seats, and the citizens of Gilpin County were flocking to see the stars of the silent screen. The Opera House had been idle for two years, but its potential as a movie theatre was obvious. Consequently, McFarlane moved rapidly ahead with plans for a grand opening on the evening of June 29, 1910.[35] Delays in the arrival of his equipment, however, forced him to move the date up a week, but on July 4 the house lights dimmed, and George McFarlane, operating a hand-cranked #5 Powers Cameragraph, inaugurated a new chapter in the history of the Opera House.[36]

When the camera broke down on opening night, McFarlane probably discovered why the entertainment industry has traditionally insisted that the "show must go on": the paying customers tend to become quite angry if it does not. The fiasco with the camera was a harbinger of things to come. If McFarlane knew "nothing about motion picture shows," he was about to learn.[37]

A type of film popular with his patrons in the early days was the illustrated song. For musical accompaniment on these occasions, McFarlane hired a group of "Songsters" composed of local men to lead the singing. Getting the music the day before a reel of illustrated songs was to be shown, in order for his "Songsters" to be properly rehearsed, proved to be a problem, and on more than one occasion his singing group was in the position of the "blind attempting to lead the blind."[38]

Then there was the problem of the quality of the early films themselves, a subject to which McFarlane, as a self-educated literary critic, was quick to turn his pen. About a month after he opened the Opera House for movies on Wednesday, Saturday, and Sunday evenings, he sent off the following letter to a Denver distributor, clearly expressing his views regarding the content of the movies he had been sent:

> Generally speaking, the films are good—that is, they show clear and plain on the canvas, but the subjects are manufactured, dry and not interesting, are usually gotten up in the same studio or same town.... One film mfg. artist has an old spotted horse, and he appears ... in all these films, and is recognized by every man, woman and child in the county. What we want is something funny, something to laugh at.[39]

Although he wanted comedies above any other type of film, he wanted the kind he felt could be shown to children. He would not tolerate a film which, in his opinion, breached the standards of good taste, and if a film distributor was unfortunate enough to send something which conflicted with McFarlane's strong sense of morality, he was quick to hear about it.

> The "Billy Reeves" comedies that you sent us do not please the people. They are gross, vulgar, low, sensual and disgusting, and we ask that you do not send us any more pictures from that artist. It you can't ship anything but a "Reeves," please cut them [comedies] out entirely and send us a Selig animal or something of that type that will please the youngsters, and for that matter, the *oldsters* too. But "Billy Reeves," I drop my head in shame.... Please keep him home and put him in the barnyard among the cattle where he belongs.[40]

The kind of comedy that McFarlane had in mind was that produced by Charlie Chaplin a few years later. When the "Little Tramp" began to delight audiences, both young and old from coast to coast, McFarlane made a special effort to see that the citizens of the "Little Kingdom" did not miss the antics of the silent screen's most beloved comic. And he was not at all happy over the fact that most of the Chaplain films were more than six months old by the time he could get them to Central City. This delay, however, was in all probability of little concern to the residents of Gilpin County, for beginning in the summer of 1916, they could at least count on seeing a Charlie Chaplin film once a month in the old Opera House.[41]

Maintaining a regular series of Chaplin films for his patrons was a project to which McFarlane devoted considerable energy. Nothing was as sure to set off a blast of temper as the failure of a Chaplin film to arrive on schedule. When this happened, the Denver firm was sure to hear about it.

> What are you going to do about your mishap and failure to get to us your last Chaplin booking? Now that you got your money for your part of it in advance, please do not forget that we perhaps have some rights in the matter. You don't forget to send your films collect if by any means we forget to mail check to you as contracted to do. Are we to get anymore Chaplin's from you, and if so when, and also the name of the picture. We figure that you owe us $40.00 on the last exhibit. Are you going to fix it up, or shall we negotiate adjustment through your Chicago office?[42]

Although he made a special effort to provide the kind of films his patrons wanted to see, McFarlane was not above attempting on occasion to force his preferences on them. In one such instance, his exclusion of a particular type of film brought him into conflict with his female patrons and, as might be expected, resulted in an ignominious retreat on the part of the Opera House's manager. To put it mildly, McFarlane was not overly fond of the "love scene drama" that was the stock in trade of the early silent films. He clearly disapproved of the passionate romances which formed the plots of so many early films:

> Sometime we are going to write you and say that Biograph pictures N. G. The Lubin is no better. The manufacturers

will have to come up with something else besides *love* and *hugging* all the time. The public is getting tired of too much kissing.[43]

However, the public was *not* getting tired of too much kissing. In fact, when not enough "love" and "hugging" and "kissing" were projected on the Opera House screen, some patrons took their complaints directly to the film supplier in Denver. McFarlane's letter to his supplier about one such complaint is worth reading in full, because, running the gamut from defiance to capitulation, it reveals well Peter's frustration over this tricky problem:

> We have yours of yesterday in regard to the picture for our use on May 3rd enclosing Mrs. Evan's letter to you, and also your reply to Mrs. Evans. We don't want someone to butt into our business, especially when they know nothing about it, as in this case. Her first paragraph would seem to indicate dissatisfaction with the pictures you supply us. We assure you your pictures give good satisfaction, and our patrons are well pleased with them.
>
> Half a dozen women's clubs and if one eats too much mush they want the moving pictures to proclaim it. If reading clubs would use their hands more and their mugs less, they might do good. They make me tired. However, you may set aside "Salvation Nell," and substitute "Hearts of Men" for our use on May 3rd as Mrs. Evans wants.[44]

Although McFarlane never would have admitted it, Mrs. Evans sensed the public taste in movies better than he did. *Hearts of Men* grossed more at the box office than any film shown that year until July 14 when the first of the Chaplin films arrived. In fact, it outdrew every movie except a thriller entitled *The Iron Claw,* D. W. Griffith's *The Birth of a Nation,* and those starring Chaplin.[45]

Although McFarlane expended a great deal of effort and tried every trick in the trade, including give-away nights with prizes of furniture, jewelry, and samples of Gilpin County gold,[46] the Opera House was no more of a success as a motion picture theatre than it was as a vaudeville house. Complete figures are available for only nine years during the period 1912-26: in only two of these was McFarlane able to show any profit at all; losses for the other seven years averaged $350.00 a year. As with the vaudeville shows, McFarlane must have had motives other than the hope of profits during the sixteen years he kept the Opera House open as a movie theatre. These statistics clearly reflect that:[47]

Year	Gross Receipts	Expenses	Profit or Loss
1912	$3,966.35	$3,900.00	+$ 66.35
1913	3,665.70	3,675.00	— 9.30
1914	3,629.15	3,198.00	+ 431.15
1915	3,997.00	4,147.00	— 150.00
1916	5,104.70		
1917	4,647.20	4,792.30	— 145.10
1918	2,535.40	3,463.30	— 927.90
1919	1,752.48	1,841.28	— 88.80
1920	1,443.68	1,796.72	— 353.04
1921	2,021.88		
1922	1,731.81		
1923	1,035.15	1,868.40	— 815.25
1924	1,033.47		
1925	1,154.40		
1926	1,534.55		

Almost from the time he installed his first movie projector, McFarlane's plan to show movies on a regular three-night-a-week schedule was as precarious as the heroine's life in an episode of the *Perils of Pauline*. In January 1912, just a year and a half after his venture into the motion picture business, the Wednesday evening shows were discontinued, not to be resumed until May. This schedule was repeated the following year,[48] and was apparently due to the fact that few people were inclined to brave the elements during the winter months for the luxury of a mid-week movie.[49] The three-evenings-a-week schedule was resumed in the spring of 1915, however, and McFarlane stuck to it until the first week of October 1918, when the flu epidemic of that year forced him to close down altogether.

When the quarantine was lifted about four months later, McFarlane had serious doubts about the wisdom or the possibility of reopening the Opera House. In a letter to L. A. Kempton, who had written requesting a booking for his "Kempton Komedy" troupe, McFarlane stated that he had been "going in the hole from $5.00 to $15.00 every night he opened," and that if he "could not make it before the 'flu' he could only expect even larger losses" since the flu epidemic had ravaged the county. He continued, "15% of our people died, 10% are in mourning, 25% have moved away, 35% are penniless, 15% out of employment, leaving only 10% to support amusements."[50]

McFarlane presumably thought it over and decided that Gilpin

66

Page from McFarlane's Central City Opera House Account Book. See that in addition to his money and movie entries, Peter noted the weather for each evening.

County, above all else, needed some form of entertainment after its ordeal, for on March 16, 1919, five months after the Opera House had been closed by the flu epidemic, he reopened it for Saturday night movies.[51] And he continued to provide a movie almost every Saturday night from then until January 1, 1927, when Tom Mix in *No Man's Gold* rang down the curtain for the last time.[52]

The Opera House was then forty-eight years old, a dilapidated but proud reminder of the pioneers' urge to recreate in the mining camps a semblance of the kind of life some of them had known before they packed up stakes and headed westward. For twenty-eight years it had been preserved from almost certain destruction by the man who built it—Peter McFarlane, who at considerable expense had seen that the damage inflicted by the rains and floods of spring and summer and the snows and winds of the harsh Rocky Mountain winter had not resulted in total destruction. In the pursuit of this labor of love, and out of his affection for his community, he had given three generations of men, women, and children who clung to its granite peaks and gulches with a quiet desperation their only professional entertainment—the dying days of vaudeville and the epics of the era of silent films.

In a sense, it was he who made possible Lillian Gish's triumphant portrayal of *Camille* on the night of July 16, 1932; it was the only kind of revival possible for the region he had served so faithfully for over sixty years. Its once prosperous mining industry could not be revived as he hoped and believed to his dying day. But through the summer opera and drama festival, made possible in the second instance when his children presented the old Opera House to the University of Denver in May 1931, another kind of gold flows into the pockets and cash registers of the citizens of Gilpin County each summer. Tourists who flock to Gregory Gulch spend thousands of dollars each year to see the remains of a mining camp once known as "the richest square mile on earth."

CHAPTER X

"Grown Gold"

FOR more than six decades Peter McFarlane lived amidst the excitement, the monotony, the frustration, the success, and the heartache of the mining camp. In most respects his career as a mining engineer and a businessman was neither remarkable nor unique. With thousands of others—prospectors, capitalists, miners, mechanics, speculators, business entrepreneurs, adventurers, saints, and sinners— he migrated to the mining frontier, drawn by the glory that was gold. Of this mass of men who rushed to the West following the first gold strikes in California's Sacramento Valley, one of its distinguished members has written:

> On the mesas of the Southland, on the tundras of the North,
> You will find us, changed in face but still the same;
> And it isn't need, it isn't greed that sends us faring forth—
> It's the fever, it's the glory of the game.[1]

In common with all of the others, McFarlane gloried in the game, but in addition he possessed two attributes which raised him considerably above the mass of men who moiled for gold on the mining frontier. These attributes were the soul of a poet and the instincts of a historian. Because of these, his interest in gold transcended the excitement of the search, the exultation of the finding, and the material benefits of possession. Gold has played an important role in man's life almost from the dawn of history to the present day, and McFarlane sought to understand it. For fifty years he pondered the historical relationship between man and gold, and in 1921 he published as a vanity press item the results of his labors, a remarkable but little known pamphlet entitled *Grown Gold.*

In this essay McFarlane advanced two related theses, one geological, the other historical. On the basis of over fifty years of mining experience, he concluded that under certain conditions gold actually grows.

> While the enormous all-sides pressure of the earth, due to gravitation, is gradually forcing the fissure material up to the apex where it is seen as a "cropping;" nature with its equipment of pulverization and its use of chemicals, is busy on the surface, transforming it into a decomposed quartz where grown gold is fostered and flourishes; where oxidized vein gold is prepared and where all alluvial gold has its origin.
>
> The forthcoming or upheaving of the crevice supply is just equal to nature's reduction apparatus; or, in another way, nature's mill and nature's supply of ore are in capacity the same, are in equal synchronization, as there is not any surplus accumulation visible or known at either works. Thus, the constant supply is as constantly milled and taken care of, and the process of continuous surface growth becomes perpetual, and will remain so, as long as gravity and pressure are natural forces....
>
> The statement, "crop of gold," here used is not a technical one, nor is it intended to befog or mislead. It means literally and exactly what it appears to mean; to-wit, a genuine crop or harvest of gold, determinable by assay after its growth and indeterminable by any assay or by anyway prior to its growth. In this respect it is in contradistinction to decomposed quartz or to any other and all other gold which is always amenable to the fire assay test.[2]

McFarlane's thesis that gold will grow on the exposed surface of an abandoned vein makes him sound like a medieval alchemist. Recognizing this, he noted in the preface to *Grown Gold:*

> Much of [what I have to say] will produce surprise and criticism and much of the criticism will be in the nature of ridicule, for the idea that gold is grown either as a primary or even secondary product, or in fact grows at all, appears at superficial glance to be so preposterously absurd as to place the thought outside the domain of serious attention and quite unworthy of sober consideration.

Behind his advocacy of a theory he knew would tarnish his reputation among mining men was McFarlane's need to explain a recurring phenomenon which had baffled him for many years. This was the repeated discovery of rich gold-bearing ores on the surface of veins which had been abandoned as unproductive many years previously. Two mining ventures undertaken by the original partners of Barclay & Company shortly after McFarlane arrived in Central City, both of which ended in bankruptcy, apparently started the speculations that eventually resulted in the publication of *Grown Gold.*

McFarlane's first experience in mining was with the Wautauga Mine in Russell Gulch which he and his partners leased in the fall of 1869. The story of this venture is best told in his own words.

> It [the Wautauga Mine] had been idle some years when we took hold of it. On the one hand we had youth, muscle and vigor to aid in producing results. On the other, little sense, less money, and no experience; surely a trinity of worthless assets.... Our first shipment of ore went to the smelter ... in November, 1869. For this consignment we received a check ... for $96.00, on a basis of $33.00 per ton in gold.... The second shipment a few weeks later showed very little gold.... The third and final smelter consignment only a "trace." Four cords treated at a stamp mill ran us in debt for hauling and crushing.... So the pool got together, and talked over the matter of our mining chances,... [and] we shut down and quit ... [and the] ... mine remained undeveloped for 31 years.... The curtain was run down on our Wautoga venture leaving only its memories of hard work, disappointment and mystery.
>
> Twenty-seven years after our lease expired another company operated the Wautoga property, resuming where we had abandoned it. The first shipment gave gold in paying quantities, but each succeeding consignment showed smaller and smaller values until they too were forced to surrender.[3]

Still smarting from the Wautauga experience, McFarlane and his partners approached their next mining venture with an eye toward obtaining the best possible assays before any investment was made.

> With our previous experience in mining we imagined that we were mistake proof and could avoid former pitfalls. We had graduated at nature's college and had our degree in gold mining.... Armed thus we sampled and sampled again and again, for we felt as though imperfect sampling may have been the cause of our previous disaster.... We fooled the assayer by

dividing the samples and checking the results of one test by others. They all agreed very closely. Barring the possibility of collusion, which was very improbable, on the part of the assayer, there was no room for suspicion or mistake. The assays showed the presence of a gold value that would easily yield a profit.... The only thing of importance that had escaped attention in making our calculations proved to be the weakest link in the chain, namely, the original sample values were richer than the ore mined in subsequent actual mining operations, and "there was the rub." Beyond the original samples, the mine output carried no gold value.[4]

Thus, despite all of their careful precautions, McFarlane and his partners failed at mining for the second time.

According to McFarlane, his experiences were repeated by others many times in Gilpin County. As evidence, he cited the history of the War Dance Lode. Discovered and worked for the first time in 1874, the mine shut down three years later when the ore played out. In 1893 rich gold-bearing ore was discovered on the exposed surfaces of the veins. Development was resumed, but each successive shipment of ore yielded less gold, and the mine was closed for the second time. In 1914 the cycle was repeated again. This time some of the samples off the mine faces assayed at as much as $15,000 of gold to the ton, but the third group of operators nevertheless suffered the same fate as the first two.[5] From these and other similar experiences, McFarlane drew his conclusion that "grown gold on the face of the workings and taken in the original samples was the factor that played havoc" with many a Gilpin County mining venture.[6]

McFarlane noted in his essay that critics of his grown gold theory might retort that what actually took place was the oxidation through the years of mineral on the exposed mine faces. His answer was as follows:

There is not any known or recognized limit to the fullness and completeness of a skillfully made fire assay test. If the fire test does not show gold the conclusion is surely a safe one ... there is not any gold present to be shown.... If at the shut down of a mine the unaltered sample shows no gold, ... rest assured ... there was not any gold in the sample for the assay to show.[7]

It is unfortunate that a search of the mining industry journals and the local newspapers uncovered no reviews of *Grown Gold*. Perhaps

McFarlane's colleagues and the professional geologists felt that his thesis was too preposterous to be dignified by a formal rebuttal. Common sense would tend to reject the idea that a "genuine crop of gold, determinable by assay after its growth and indeterminable by assay or by anyway prior to its growth" could appear on the exposed faces of abandoned gold-bearing veins. Yet, if McFarlane's facts regarding his own personal mining experiences and those such as have been extracted out of the history of the War Dance Lode are true, the phenomenon he described called for an explanation. To McFarlane's credit, he attempted to provide a theory which would explain an observable and documented phenomenon. This theory, furthermore, was based on the standard and indisputable fire assay test for gold.

In order to obtain a scientific opinion on McFarlane's theory of grown gold, I sent the pamphlet to M. H. Bergendahl, geologist with the U. S. Geological Survey in Denver, who kindly agreed to provide a review. Mr. Bergendahl's opening paragraph confirmed McFarlane's prediction regarding the reaction of the scientific community:

> I have just finished reading the pamphlet *Grown Gold* by Peter McFarlane and have found it to be a truly amazing product of an imagination that was completely unfettered by any rational concepts of fact, reason, or evidence. His ideas were so fantastic, his style so allegorical for a mining man, and his conclusions so biased and unscientific that I wonder if he was really serious. He must have been an interesting person, indeed. [8]

Although he totally rejected McFarlane's thesis regarding the enrichment-with-time phenomenon, Mr. Bergendahl did concede that if McFarlane's account of his own mining experiences and the histories of various well-known mines are correct, the phenomenon did require an explanation. In his opinion, this was to be found in the fact that Gilpin County ores are rich in pyrites. Through several simple reactions with oxygen and water, these dissolve into ferric sulphate and sulfuric acid, both strong solvents. These solvents, in turn, could percolate downward, dissolving more pyrite and other sulfides. Gold, being generally resistant to such solvents, would remain in the oxidized zone. The net result would be "an apparent enrichment of gold due to the reduction in volume of the original mass of sulfides." [9] Mr. Bergendahl concluded his review with the following remarks:

> Despite the tenor of the above comments, I think that

McFarlane's pamphlet shows that he had potential for some worthwhile contributions to ore genesis had he been subjected to some scientific training and discipline early in his career.

In light of the above, it is interesting to note that in November 1920, when McFarlane had completed the manuscript for *Grown Gold* and was making arrangements to publish it, the American Institute of Mining Engineers asked him to submit an application for membership in recognition of his contributions to the mining industry. Characteristically, he refused the honor, saying:

> [I]n regard to my application in the American Institute of Mining Engineers,... I will say I have not the slightest qualification that would entitle me to such a distinction. Have neither education, experience, brains nor association by which I would hope to qualify. Would be ashamed in fact to have people know that I were ambitious in that line. Much as I would appreciate the honor, I could not suppress the blush of conscious [sic] shown in the endeavor to align myself with such a noteworthy institution. [10]

The primary purpose of this chapter is not to refute McFarlane's theory of grown gold, but rather to use his little pamphlet to illustrate the fact that, in addition to his business acumen, he had a lively curiosity and more than a dash of poetic imagination. The best example of this latter quality is to be found in that section of *Grown Gold* where he presented an allegorical version of John H. Gregory's discovery of the rich vein of ore that came to be known as the Gregory Lode. A fragment of the section is reproduced below:

> The golden goddess had established her domicile in the vicinity of what was afterward known as the "Gregory-Bobtail" mines. Had made it her home and dwelling place and as such, occupied it for many centuries, secure and undisputed in its possession, holding therefore a title from Almighty God, she reigned majestic and alone....
> Not content though with being beautiful and continuing hidden, she had to advertise her natural charms. Emissaries of her household in golden bouquets were thrown into the stream ... and she soon saw Gregory a-panning, slowly and cautiously but surely to the very portal of her home....
> In vain she pleaded and reasoned. In vain she begged and beseeched. In vain she asked him to forever seal his lips and take his mysterious departure.... In vain she asked and implored

permission to live the remainder of her days in that quiescent solitude wherein she could continue to practice the good work of charity in which she had always been occupied.

Gregory, authoritative and importunate ... enraged and unforgiving, deaf to her entreaties; ill-tempered and revengeful, unmindful of the consequences, ordered the work of destruction; and as ruthless a piece of slaughter as was ever known was thereupon enacted. Without the usual opportunity for preparation she was ushered, unfortunately pure and undefiled, into the presence of her Creator. Beautiful in her ascension robes her soul wafted its way to an eternal reward; but the ghost of her departed spirit still lingers and may be occasionally seen hovering around the battle field of her untimely death. A mist sometimes arises over the ground and people in the neighborhood imagine they can yet hear the voice of the goddess's heartrending cry, as on that memorable day so long ago she made her piteous appeal to her assassin to spare her life. Children passing to and from school, in nervous expectancy, pause and look and listen. The cross that now marks the place of the original discovery of the Gregory lode may some day be used to designate the locality of a foul and unwarranted murder, or to indicate a warning of folly to those who place their trust in vanishing gold.[11]

It is possible to measure the extent of McFarlane's self education by tracing the quotations which are sprinkled liberally throughout *Grown Gold.* The text is heavily larded with references to such writers as William Shakespeare, Francis Bacon, Thomas Gray, Alexander Pope, Alfred Lord Tennyson, Rudyard Kipling, and Karl Marx, and with quotations from the Bible. When he began his project, McFarlane may have had in mind a strictly technical paper. But in the course of his writing he was led into flights of allegory and romanticism which give the pamphlet its peculiar charm and flavor. The overall result was a publication whose primary importance lies in the manner in which it reflected the catholic nature of McFarlane's mind and his wide reading interests.

Although his major interest was to explain the phenomenon he called "grown gold," McFarlane also added his views on the gold versus silver question to the worldwide library of literature already produced on this controversial and emotional subject. As might be expected, McFarlane was a gold man, an unequivocal believer—if only his views as expressed in *Grown Gold* are taken into consideration—in the proposition that any monetary policy other than a gold-backed currency would be an irretrievable disaster not only for the United States but ultimately for the whole human race.

> It seems that the presence of gold and the development of humanity are one and indissoluble and mournful as it may appear, if gold ceases to be a part of our life, there will be no life for gold to be a part of, for as one dies so does the other.[12]

McFarlane was seriously concerned about the dwindling supply of gold in the world. The decline in production, the failure to discover any really significant new sources, and the irretrievable loss of gold due to the wearing away of circulating gold coins led him to the unpleasant conclusion that the ultimate prospect for man was a world without sufficient gold to sustain civilization. Hence, his use of the word "mournful" to describe the indissoluble association of "gold and the development of humanity."

> The day is fast approaching when this segment of the earth's orbit will be referred to and known in history as the GOLDEN AGE. The created gold all mined and brought to the earth's surface, as far as man's ability to produce it is concerned; alluvial gold placered and exhausted beyond the point of profitable recovery; the material basis of grown gold likewise dissipated and its re-appearance forever made impossible; the world's gold accumulation wearing away, diminishing, vanishing —getting less and less; the emasculated globe itself spinning through space on its annual journey at the rate of 90,000 feet per second, without money or friends, destitute, bankrupt.... This is the knell our old earth is singing as it rushes onward to its destructive end.[13]

On the basis of his belief that civilization and gold are synonymous, and that the world's supply of gold was diminishing to a dangerous point, McFarlane offered what he considered to be two practical suggestions which, if adopted by the United States, could postpone the final disaster:

1. Retire all gold coins in circulation and refuse either to mint or to circulate gold coins at any time in the future.
2. Move to government ownership of that section of the mining industry involved in the production of gold and silver.[14]

The first proposal would serve to conserve the gold then held by the United States,[15] while the second would produce a temporary revival of the gold mining industry. The United States would consider gold a strategic resource and would mine it even though the cost of producing an ounce of gold was more than twice the market value. The revival of gold mining, in McFarlane's view, would, unfortunately, have to be temporary, as there was a point beyond which even government-subsidized mining was impractical.

McFarlane's advocacy of government ownership of the gold and silver mines of the United States was indicative of the desperate straits of the mining industry of Gilpin County by 1920. For more than a decade, he had helplessly watched the deterioration of the industry and the town which he loved. "O, God, how sick I get thinking about it," he wrote some years earlier to an old friend with whom he had shared Central City's days as a great mining camp.[16] With the cost of producing an ounce of gold more than twice the market price, the last hope for a mining revival, as McFarlane saw it, was government action of some kind.

At the time he was writing *Grown Gold,* a bill was placed before Congress to provide a bonus of $10.00 for each ounce of gold produced. McFarlane had little hope of its passage. Congress, he felt, would correctly mirror the feelings of a majority of the American people and conclude, in Shakespeare's words, that "it's better to bear the ills we have than to fly to others we know not of." The nation, McFarlane believed, would accept neither a government subsidy of the mining industry nor government ownership of the gold and silver mines until the disastrous effects of "the almost total abatement of gold production" were clearly understood.

> When the federal government sees and realizes the diminution . . . of its federal gold reserve, when it sees and realizes that the fatuity of the miner on which it depends can no longer be relied on as a national asset; then will the nation see and realize for the first time, that in order to obtain gold it will be required to go into the mining business itself.[17]

To his credit, McFarlane realized that there might be an alternative to the gold standard. But having admitted that, he just as quickly dismissed the idea by saying, "the problem of our national treasury existing without gold is so intricate as to be unworthy of considera-tion."[18] Elsewhere in his writings, however, McFarlane left a line or two that indicates that he never succeeded in totally convincing himself of the indissoluble bond between gold and civilization. For instance, in a long letter in which he recounted the history of silver coinage in the United States, he noted that the "country is prosperous in the discovery and knowledge of the fact that it requires neither gold nor silver, but can get along without either."[19]

***

Peter McFarlane died on May 1, 1929, in Denver at the home of his daughter on the eve of his eightieth year. At long last, he joined the silent majority who had created in the area surrounding Gregory Gulch the "Little Kingdom of Gilpin," whose mines had poured over $84,000,000 in gold into the coffers of the nation. He went to his grave still hoping that by some miracle the Gilpin County mining industry could be revived and that Eureka Street would once again be the center of a great mining camp. Perhaps as his life drained away he heard once again the "clang of the signal bell; the rumble of the ore cars; the buzz of the air drill; the detonation of the giant; the rattling of the falling rock and the echo of distant thunder" and saw "the sturdy miners going [to] or coming off shift . . . or the mutilated remains of some unfortunate fellow placed in a bucket and raised to the top"[20]—sensed once again, and for the last time, all of the sights, sounds, and smells, all of the excitement and heartache of the glory that was gold.

McFarlane left for posterity the Central City Opera House, which serves as the focus for a nationally recognized opera and drama festival, and the Cold Springs Camp Ground located in the Roosevelt National Forest at the junction of Highway 119 and the Golden Gate Canyon Road. His role in preserving the Opera House has been recognized, but his contribution to an ever growing army of campers has gone unnoticed.

McFarlane loved the rugged natural beauty of the Colorado mountains. Fully aware of the ugliness created by mining or logging operations, he launched, in the summer of 1919, a campaign to preserve the area surrounding Cold Spring, which had been a favorite spot for picnickers and campers for many years. The land was in the public domain, but McFarlane and his small band of supporters felt that the creation of a public park was the only way to ensure preservation in its natural state. In the summer of 1919, he addressed the following appeal to the U. S. Forest Service office in Boulder:

On the automobile road between Missouri Lake and the top of Dory Hill is a little place called "Cold Spring." It's nice for picnics or camping or out-of-doors romp or outing. People from here and Denver and other places pilgrimage there. It is our intention next year to equip it with shelters, etc. We understand it's public domain, but we are afraid someone might homestead or in some way acquire private ownership and write to you to find out whether the ground is in your jurisdiction, or whether you can aid us in the matter . . . of preserving the place as a public playground. It's well forested now but if it were denuded the spring would probably dry up. We ask you to kindly advise, and if you can, direct us so that steps may be taken to preserve the place intact.[21]

Mr. Clark replied on August 22 that the land in question was in fact under the jurisdiction of the U. S. Forest Service. He also agreed to the proposal for creating a camp ground if the Gilpin County group that McFarlane headed would underwrite the entire cost of construction. This arrangement was acceptable to McFarlane, who replied: "We will do our best to bear [the] expense . . . and not ask the government to pay any of the cost."[22]

Construction on the camp ground, however, did not begin until the summer of 1922. The site had to be surveyed and plans drawn up by the U. S. Forest Service, and this was delayed until the summer of 1920 by the flu epidemic and bad weather.[23]

In June 1920 McFarlane received the plans for the Cold Spring recreation grounds from the Denver office of the U. S. Forest Service,[24] but further delays developed. According to the agreement with the U. S. Forest Service, the construction of the camp ground was to be carried out by volunteer labor under McFarlane's supervision. In addition, he had agreed to finance the entire project. Business affairs prevented his starting construction in 1920, but the project was begun and apparently completed two years later.[25]

Peter McFarlane was not one of the giant figures in the exploration, exploitation, and settlement of the West. By the same token, neither was he part of that anonymous army of men and women whose contributions to this movement must be measured in the aggregate. He stood somewhere between the men whose deeds and accomplishments captured the imagination of future generations and those whose individual roles cannot be measured. He was, perhaps, more representative of the typical pioneer than either. His contributions to the Colorado mining industry, particularly in Gilpin County, were considerable. In addition, because of his efforts, thousands of people each summer are able to enjoy the cultural events which take place in the Central City Opera House and the outdoor pleasures offered by the Cold Spring Camp Ground. The Opera House and the camp ground are his legacy to the living. And it can be truly said of him by way of an epitaph that his last services were worthily performed.

APPENDIX A

Barclay & Company Contracts 1870

Name and Occupation	Location	Contract*
Chatfield	Nevadaville	stamp mill
Morse		store
W. B. Rockwell	Chase Gulch	stamp mill
Hall	Nevadaville	house
Mack & Schonecker	Central City	saloon and billiard parlor
	Central City	Post Office
Catherine Rice	Central City	house
George W. Currier capitalist	Black Hawk	building
Clinton Reed lawyer	Central City	house
Peter Thompson		table and bedstand
Henry Rogers miner	Nevadaville	house
Henry Blewitt miner	Nevadaville	house

*Barclay & Company may have had only a portion of the job.

145

Daniel Knodle miner	Nevadaville	house
Gardiner		house
Jo Harper		stamp mill
	Central City	brick store on Main Street
	Central City	St. James Methodist Church
Stokes		stairs
Gott		shop
Hall		windows
		water tank
		picture frame
		wagon
Wallace Wightman agent, Eureka St. Foundry	Black Hawk	box
Berger		house
Billy Cozen		house
	Central City	school
Charley Nickolls miner	Nevadaville	house
J. N. McCarg miner	Nevadaville	house

1871

Richard Martin miner	Nevadaville	house
W. B. Rockell	Chase Gulch	house
Robert and James Cash owners, reduction works	Central City	water tank
John Gray miner	Central City	house
Thomas and Frank Bates	Mountain City	house and stamp mill

Ben Wisebart
  merchant
	Central City	drawers, roof,
		  and new gutter

Solomon Rowe miner	Nevadaville	house
Hitzer	Clear Creek	stamp mill
Henry Bolthof machinist	Central City	house
Jake Lasher		axeltree
Richare Harvery carpenter	Central City	whim
	Caribou	house
	Gunnel Lode	whim
Lounby		house
Meaney	Mountain City	sash
A. Van Camp butcher	Central City	slaughterhouse
Sam Brown		house
A. J. Van Deren mining operator	Central City	privy
Thomas Pollock miner	Central City	house
G. B. Reed lawyer	Central City	house
Oscar Servis	Mountain City	steps
Charles Webber	Central City	
Charles Weston furniture dealers		
Henry Teller lawyer	Central City	moving office
W. W. Tiffany miner	Central City	house
A. N. Rogers mining agent	Central City	house
O. S. Buell stationer	Central City	fireproof mail house
John Gray miner	Central City	barn
Moses		water tank
Robert Gray and W. H. Root contractors	Central City	water tank

D. D. Lake	Central City	house
grocer		
Horace Aitkins		fence
Steve S. Martin	Black Hawk	store front
S. J. Lorah	Central City	house
clerk		
Steve Hale		house
Tom Morgan		shop
W. M. and F. M.	Central City	barn moving
Roworth, merchants		
	Central City	St. James Methodist Church
		axeltree
Carrie Burnett	Dry Gulch	partition
Nettie Cunningham		railing
Wood		vehicle repair
Morris		house
W. L. Newell		bob slays [*sic*]
Steve S. Martin	Black Hawk	house
Mrs. Rory		hanging curtains
Jake Bensal		filed saw
Hurst	Mountain City	house
	Mountain City	house
Schaffener		door
		Cornish wheel barrow
Sam Brown	Mountain City	signboard
Rogers	Mountain City	signboard
Thomas Pollock	Central City	office
miner		
Jake Bensal		house
G. B. Reed	Central City	ironing board
lawyer		

APPENDIX B

McFarlane's Sunday Diary Entries, Illustrating His Leisure Activities 1870-1871

Sunday, March 6, 1870
>Wrote to George[1] today. Heard the Rev. Vincent[2] preach from no text. Insulted England. Showed his ignorance by so doing.

Sunday March 13, 1870
>Did not write a letter to anyone today for the first Sunday since I came to Colorado. Cooked apple dumplings for dinner. Baked a short cake for supper.

Sunday, March 20, 1870
>Wrote to the boys today. Went to Sunday School, and to a concert after supper. Peter Barclay complains of a bad cold, but doctor thinks him not dangerous. Baked pies today and had apple dumplings for dinner. Have not got any letters from anyone for three weeks.

Sunday, April 17, 1870
>Wrote to Jim Mc[3] and J. Barclay[4] and sent some papers to Jim. Heard Mr. Wallace lecture on temperance.

Sunday, June 19, 1870
>Did not write to any person today. Something strange. Cooked all day and heard a Presbyterian preach in the I.O.O.F. Hall. The first of the kind I heard since Stuart Patterson.[5]

SUNDAY, JULY 9, 1871.

This is the first
day in our own house
I done all the cooking
today, got roast Beef
for dinner had
James McKay with
W. J. Newel was here a
short part of the day

MONDAY 10

This morning P. K.
and myself begin
work on Greggs house
we were putting up
a prop day amyst th
building to shove it
over when a stone drop
out of the wall and on
my big toe and mad
it feel kind of queer
for a spell

TUESDAY 11

Tuesday
my foot aint quite
so sour as I thought
it was feel quite
smart today in
every other respect
got a letter from
Miss Foly in last ma

Pages from Peter McFarlane's 1871 diary.

Worked 3/4 of this day
at Greys house
Harvey all day
got my Hamlet
tonight 100 people
killed and 400 wounded
in New York City today
in the Orange accident

worked 3/4 of this
day for Grey and
Harvey all day
got the papers tonight
one sheet
My toe is getting
better fast

Peter McC

worked all day
at Greys house
Harvey all day
our Boys finished
moving Dillers
house today

Sunday, July 3, 1870

Cooked today & wrote to Father. Went to Black Hawk with Currier[6] & looked at a building. Figured on a new one to work 160 ft. Gave a figure tonight. Heard a speaker [undecipherable] on the text, "Who shall roll away the stone from the sepulchre."

Sunday, August 7, 1870

W. J. Barclay, Eugene Lackey, William Price and myself went out to Bald Mountain to pick raspberries. I got enough for Will McFarlane and Peter B. and myself, and the rest did not get any. So much for this day's work.

Sunday, November 20, 1870

Walked up to Quartz Hill today just for greens.

Sunday, January 8, 1871

Will Price, Will Mc & myself went down to church in the morning, Sunday School afternoon. Peter B. cooked turkey for dinner.

Sunday, February 5, 1871

Let me see what I was doing today. Darned my socks in the afternoon. Made out my report for the lodge [in the] afternoon, and heard Vincent preach after night.

Sunday, February 19, 1871

Got up, washed, cooked breakfast. Sewed my pants and vest. Wrote a letter to Will Price after dinner. Read a part of the history of Burns. Talked to our Captain Bates.[7] Did not read the Bible today. Wound my watch and went to bed.

Sunday, March 5, 1871

Did not go to Church today. Laid around the house most of the time. Reading some of the day. I guess I'll have a chaw of terbacker.

Sunday, April 9, 1871

Cooked dinner tonight. Barley soup from pork ham bone. Baked four pies today. Stafford is playing the fiddle.[8] I am going to church.

Sunday, April 30, 1871

Went to the Congregational Church this morning and heard Dickinson preach his farewell sermon.[9] Then went to Harvey's for dinner. Same to Sunday School with his [undecipherable] and went to the Baptist Church in the evening with Mrs. Murray.[10]

Sunday, May 7, 1871

Skulled around all day. Went to Sunday School. Joined Stanton's class. Went around by the Winnebago to the Cash lode. Had quite a nice time stoning squirrels in Chase Gulch.

Sunday, May 14, 1871

Skulled around all day. Went to church tonight at the Baptist. Heard Bowker preach.

Sunday, July 16, 1871

Jim and Will B and I went up to the slaughterhouse today and saw them kill and dress 3 sheep in 27 minutes.

Sunday, July 23, 1871

Got up washed and went to bed. Cooked breakfast. Went up to the slaughterhouse in the forenoon. Went down to the shop and tried to pan out some gold but could not. I guess that will be the end of my mining in this country.

Sunday, July 30, 1871

W. J. B., J. B. Mc and myself went out to pick berries today. Got our dishes full and came home by the slaughterhouse and saw them kill an ox. While in the house I thought I was going to faint from the smell of blood. Got quite sick in an instant.

Sunday, October 1, 1871

Went downtown last night. Played two games of cards. Lost 50 cents. The last I shall play for some time. Picked out a ring for Kate[11] a ten dollar moss agate ring. Will Barclay and Ed Lindsay are in the kitchen playing cards and the two McFarlanes are downtown at the O.K.[12] I have been eating maple syrup all day.

Sunday, October 15, 1871

This morning I went down to Moses's tank and looked around some. Then went to the shop and made a clock shelf for Jake Bensal. Came home and eat dinner. Laid around for a spell. Went with Moses to break in his lanky mare. Came home. Washed my feet. God forgive me.

Sunday, November 26, 1871

The sun rose cheerful. But blackened up and showed a little after which it shown out bright and was very fine. W. B. and I are going to hear Chase[13] preach tonight. Will Mc put down his foot and stopped the card playing on Sundays.

Central City. *From* Harper's Monthly, *June 1867.*

Notes

Chapter I   The Early Years

1 McFarlane's obituaries carried by the *Rocky Mountain News,* May 3, 1929, and the Central City *Weekly Register-Call,* May 3, 1929, both give his date of birth as May 9, 1849. The fact that he was one year older than commonly thought is established by the following entry in his diary for May 9, 1870: "This day 22 years ago, I was born." In all his correspondence McFarlane used only his first and last names. In his diaries, he often added the middle initial "B." Confirmation of his middle name is contained in a letter to the author, August 17, 1965, from a cousin, Frank McFarlane, who was then still living in Bedeque.
2 For a good description of Prince Edward Island, particularly its geography, see Lawrence J. Burpee, "Prince Edward Island," *Canadian Geographical Journal,* XXXIII (November 1946), 193–214.
3 For an excellent and probably somewhat romanticized account, see Neil MacNeil, *The Highland Heart in Nova Scotia.*
4 Ibid., 120.
5 Mrs. R. R. Demeter recalls how her childhood visits to her Uncle George McFarlane's farm on Prince Edward Island were highlighted by culinary delights from both the land and the sea.

Her uncle had planted a bed of the famous Malpeque oysters in a bay near the farm, and often she and her cousins would shuck them on the front porch of the farmhouse. The McFarlanes had prospered on Prince Edward Island, and Uncle George had in his employ several French maids. In the summer time, these young ladies would pick buckets of wild raspberries which were served with unlimited amounts of thick, fresh cream. The cousins would also meet the lobster fishermen as they came in with their catches and purchase baskets of this ocean delicacy. The French maids would have huge pots of boiling water ready in George McFarlane's great kitchen, and when the lobsters were cooked, twenty to thirty of the McFarlane clan would gather there for a feast. Author's interview with Mrs. R. R. Demeter, March 15, 1965.

6 MacNeil, *Highland Heart,* 113.
7 Ibid., 119–20.
8 Ibid., 118–19.
9 Ibid., 28.
10 Peter McFarlane, *Diary,* February 23, 1871. Peter's grammar, spellings, and sentence completion were not always perfect, but I have transcribed his writings the way he wrote them. A few times only throughout this book have I added a reminder of these habits, when I thought it helpful to distinguish clearly from what might be considered a printing error.
11 Ibid., December 30, 1871.
12 Author's interview with Mrs. R. R. Demeter, March 15, 1964. From the very early days to its years of decline, music was a conspicuous aspect of life in Central City. As Frank R. Young put it, "Central is nothing if not musical. . . . Musical? It might almost be necessary to say that Central is a mining community; if there is any one thing that the colony prides itself upon a little more than another, among its many artistic accomplishments, it is, and always has been, its general musical proficiency, its critical appreciation, and its creative or interpretive abilities. . . ." Frank R. Young, *Echoes from Arcadia,* 178.
13 A. B. Warburton, *A History of Prince Edward Island,* 399–400.
14 Ibid., 400.
15 The Reverend Robert Stuart Patterson served as the Presbyterian minister of Bedeque and Richmond Bay for fifty-seven years, 1825-1882. Ibid.
16 Author's interview with Mrs. R. R. Demeter, November 11, 1964.
17 Ibid.
18 W. L. Cotton, *Chapters in Our Island History,* 87.

19 Ibid., 86.
20 Warburton, *Prince Edward Island,* 378.
21 Cotton, *Chapters in Our Island History,* 86-87.
22 Ibid., 87.
23 Ernest Hurst Cherrington, *The Standard Encyclopedia of the Alcohol Problem,* III, 335. By 1867, the Good Templars were well enough established in Colorado to take the lead in the temperance movement there. In that year they joined with other groups in publishing a temperance tabloid called *The Pledge.* The first issue was published in Golden City on May 1, 1867. It carried under its masthead the admonition: "Look not upon the wine when it is red. . . . At the last it biteth like a serpent and stingeth like an adder." Proverbs 23:31-33.
24 Author's interview with Mrs. R. R. Demeter, September 6, 1965.
25 Peter McFarlane, *Diary,* October 25, 1871.
26 Cotton, *Chapters in Our Island History,* 54.
27 Peter McFarlane, *Diary,* December 31, 1871. Author's interview with Mrs. R. R. Demeter, March 15, 1964. Letter to the author from Frank R. McFarlane, May 15, 1965.
28 Peter McFarlane, *Diary,* December 31, 1871.
29 On the fifth anniversary of the beginning of his apprenticeship McFarlane noted: "Five years ago today I went with John McCallum to learn my trade for which I have never been sorry but once." Peter McFarlane, *Diary,* June 4, 1871. In the remnants of McFarlane's library there is the textbook on carpentry which he used in learning his trade in McCallum's shop, William E. Bell, *Carpentry Made Easy; Or the Science and Art of Framing, on a New and Improved System* (Philadelphia, 1857). Inside the front cover is the notation, "John McCallum, Bedeque, Prince Edward Island."
30 Author's interview with Mrs. R. R. Demeter, September 12, 1965. Frank R. McFarlane, a cousin still living in Bedeque, gives his destination as Boston. Letter to the author dated May 15, 1965. Two diary entries, however, support Mrs. Demeter's side of the story. Peter McFarlane, *Diary,* August 26 and 27, 1871.
31 MacNeil, *Highland Heart,* 23.
32 Quoted in A. M. Pope, "The Catholic Scotch Settlement of Prince Edward Island," *The Catholic World* (July 1882), 556.
33 Peter McFarlane, *Diary,* December 31, 1871.
34 Ibid., October 15, 1870.
35 Letter from Frank R. McFarlane to the author, May 15, 1965.
36 Stories were rife among the Maritime Provinces about Captain Kidd's treasure and other buried treasures. John MacKinnon, *A*

Sketch Book Comprising Historical Incidents, Traditional Tales, and Translations, 75, 94. The most famous and most credible treasure tale from this area involves Oak Island, where an elaborate underground shaft-and-tunnel structure was discovered 180 years ago. Enterprising and frustrated individuals and corporations have probed this Oak Island "money pit" ever since but without success. Whether buried treasure exists there or whether it was Captain Kidd's, we may never know; we do know that someone, sometime went to a lot of trouble and effort on Oak Island. Reginald V. Harris, *The Oak Island Mystery;* Ron Rosenbaum, "The Mystery of Oak Island," *Esquire,* LXXIX (February 1973), 77.

37 Letter from Frank R. McFarlane to the author, May 15, 1965.

38 Peter McFarlane, *Diary,* October 16, 1871.

39 Ibid., October 19, 1871.

40 Peter McFarlane's obituary in the *Rocky Mountain News,* May 3, 1929, gave the year as 1868. In a followup story two days later, the paper erroneously reported that he and his brother William arrived in Central City together. Frank R. Hollenback, *Central City and Black Hawk, Then and Now,* sets the year as 1867. This is also the date given in *The Glory That Was Gold,* published by the Central City Opera House Association, 98. Caroline Bancroft, *Gulch of Gold,* 208, does not state a definite date, but implies that the year was 1870, while LeRoy R. Hafen (ed.), *Colorado and Its People,* II, 596, sets his arrival as early as 1865. Of the best known authors, only James Burrell notes the correct year: "History of Gilpin County," in *The History of Clear Creek and Boulder Valleys,* 446.

41 On May 5, 1870, McFarlane noted in his diary that "12 months ago, I was home. . . ." An advertisement in the "New Today" column of the Central City *Daily Register* on September 1, 1869, listed McFarlane as a partner in a newly formed construction company.

Chapter II   An Immigrant Arrives in the "Little Kingdom of Gilpin"

1 In the late 1860s the stages from Golden City to Gregory Gulch took one of two routes. From Golden City they went up the Golden Gate Road over Guy Hill. A short distance after descending the west slope of Guy Hill, the route divided, one branch going to Dory Hill, the other over Smith Hill. The Smith Hill Road joined North Clear Creek Canyon about four miles

south of Black Hawk. C. H. Hanington, "Early Days of Central City and Black Hawk," *Colorado Magazine,* XIX (January 1942), 3-14, recalls a trip over the Guy Hill-Dory Hill route in 1869, the same year that McFarlane made the journey. Bayard Taylor, *Colorado: A Summer Trip,* 52-53, has a vivid description of his trip over the Guy Hill-Smith Hill route in 1866. The roads were primitive and the stage drivers in a hurry, and more than one traveller breathed a sigh of relief when the journey was safely over. Barham Zincke, after arriving in Central City, asked the landlord of the hotel in which he was staying if anyone had been killed lately on the road over Guy Hill. " 'No,' he replied, 'no one killed,' he was glad to say, 'for two or three years, but every year several persons had died of accidents on the hill.' " F. Barham Zincke, *Last Winter in the United States,* 246.

2 The basic facts of McFarlane's trip from Denver to Central City were supplied by Mrs. R. R. Demeter in an interview with the author on May 5, 1965. The story of Peter's arriving in Central City with his pockets stuffed with "fool's gold" is a cherished family anecdote.

3 Letter from Frank R. McFarlane to the author, May 15, 1965.

4 New York *Times,* September 10, 1882, 4/4. In this dispatch from the newspaper's Colorado correspondent who was writing from a prospector's tent in the San Juan mountains, the author recalled that he had once met two youths from Baltimore who "were provided with about forty of the small sacks in which smoking tobacco is retailed." The sacks were "intended to hold the gold dust which the lads were to accumulate out of the irrigation ditches of Denver . . ." Josiah Royce, *California,* 231-34, has an interesting analysis of the impact of the false accounts of the leisurely life of gold gleaning available to all in California in 1848-49.

5 Henry Villard, *The Past and Present of the Pike's Peak Gold Regions,* 77.

6 Hiram A. Johnson, "A Letter from a Colorado Mining Camp," *Colorado Magazine,* VII (January 1930), 194.

7 New York *Times,* September 10, 1882, 4/4.

8 Ibid.

9 Ovando J. Hollister, *The Mines of Colorado,* 133.

10 Quoted in Carlyle Channing Davis, *Olden Times in Colorado,* 448. Henry Villard wrote in much the same vein: "Of the three or four thousand men that made the Eastern and Western slope of the Rocky mountains the scene of untiring and, in numerous instances, successful search for gold, not many would have over-

come the discouraging effect of the disappointments in which the first attempts at digging resulted almost uniformly, had it not been for the peculiar enchantment under which they labored. The constant excitement produced by daily and hourly circulated rumors and reports, conveying intelligence of new rich strikes; the consequent migration from place to place; the continued succession of hopefulness by despondency, luck by misfortune, success by failure; . . . united formed a charm whose hold upon the gold hunters was deep and strong." *Pike's Peak Gold Regions,* 78–79.

11 New York *Times,* September 10, 1882, 4/4.

12 Ibid.

13 "Miners are always superstitious about luck. No matter how it goes with them, everything is attributed to luck. . . . I have known men for years who no matter what enterprise they enlisted in, were sure to triumph; and then possibly luck would forsake them and leave them in poverty. . . . Nevertheless, you can't make an old timer believe but that there is something to luck." Charles D. Ferguson, *A Third of a Century in the Gold Fields,* 169.

14 "The shine of hope and faith in the old fellow's eyes followed me long after he had disappeared from sight. And it came to me as it had once long ago, that it wasn't the gold he wanted. It would likely slip through his fingers in no time, or be given away for the asking. It was the enticing hunt that led him on, the elusive chase, the everlasting love of the game." Mabel Barbee Lee, *Cripple Creek Days,* 270.

15 By an act of the Territorial Legislature, the Golden Gate and Gregory Road Company was granted the right to construct a toll road from the town of Golden Gate over Guy Hill and into Black Hawk via Dory Gulch. The Company was authorized to construct one toll gate and to collect tolls on "all wagons, vehicles, horses, mules, asses, cattle and sheep." Vehicles or individuals on horse or muleback going to or from places of worship or funerals were exempt from paying tolls. This provision was of considerable importance as the cemetery serving the city of Black Hawk was located at the top of Dory Hill. *General Laws and Joint Resolutions, Memorials and Private Acts* passed at the Second and Third Sessions of the Legislative Assembly of Colorado, 1862 and 1864. The *Tri-Weekly Mining Life,* December 27, 1862, 4/2, carried a story about a pen and ink sketch of the city of Black Hawk by the Colorado artist John E. Dillingham. According to the newspaper, Dillingham had set his easel at a vantage point "above the Gregory Toll Gate." An examination of a copy of Dillingham's

panoramic view makes it certain that the Gregory Toll Gate was located at the bottom of Dory Gulch where it joins North Clear Creek.

16 Taylor, *Colorado,* 57.
17 Young, *Echoes from Arcadia,* 57.

Chapter III Barclay & Company

1 The causes of the depression were simple. As the surface veins of oxidized ores played out and deep, hard rock mining began, the central problem which plagued the Gilpin County mining industry throughout its history began to manifest itself. The New York *Times* correspondent, or "stringer", in Central City summed it up very succinctly: "The great consideration of the Coloradian is the development of a process by which gold may be extracted from the ore without the expenditure of more funds than the extracted gold" is worth. New York *Times,* February 22, 1866, 6/4. Deep, hard rock mining required heavy equipment of all kinds such as steam hoists and pumps. Costly to begin with, this equipment had to be dragged across the plains and up into the mountains by a very primitive transportation system which added 10 to 20 cents a pound to its original price. When added to other costs such as fuel, the over-all effect was to escalate the cost of getting the ore out of the ground almost to the critical point. Ibid., February 18, 1866, 3/6.

Although Peter McFarlane could not have known it when he stepped off the stagecoach in Central City on that summer day in 1869, the difficulties of processing Gilpin County ores were to be his major interest for over fifty years. His role in the development of such specialized pieces of ore treating equipment as the Gilpin County slow drop stamp mill and the Gilpin County Gilt Edge Concentrator will be discussed in later chapters.

It is interesting to note that two of the best known authorities on the history of Gilpin County date the years of the depression in the mining industry as 1864-65. Charles W. Henderson, whose work is the definitive source for historical mining statistics, flatly states that in 1864 "mining came to a standstill." *Mining in Colorado: A History of Discovery, Development, and Production,* 30. Bancroft, while not quite as explicit, echoes this view, noting that "by the fall of 1864 . . . the gulch's gold production [was] in a bad way." *Gulch of Gold,* 158. The statistics of gold production, however, tell an entirely different story. Far from being a year of depression, 1864 was actually the best year the county had had to date. Production was up $193,534 from the previous year to $1,741,806. On the other hand, production dropped drastically in 1866 and 1867 to $725,753 and $967,670 respectively. Henderson's carefully compiled statistics and his statement that mining came to a standstill in 1864 cannot be reconciled. The only possible explanation is that in writing his narrative account he relied on secondary authorities rather than the results of his own statistical research.

2 New York *Times,* February 18, 1866, 3/6. Writing in 1867, Bayard Taylor noted that labor in Gilpin County was very "scarce and very dear. Mechanics demand from six to ten dollars and the commonest miners five dollars." *Colorado,* 63.

3 Peter McFarlane, *Grown Gold,* 9. See chapter X infra for discussion of McFarlane's booklet.

4 *Rocky Mountain Directory and Colorado Gazetteer for 1871.* The advertisement is to be found on the fourth page of advertising following the Central City business directory.

5 For a partial list of contracts for 1870 and 1871, see Appendix A.

6 Hollenback, *Central City and Black Hawk,* 82.

7 Peter McFarlane, *Diary,* October 21, 22, 24, and 25, 1870.

8 Ibid., August 15, 1871.

9 Ibid., August 30, 1871.

10 Ibid., October 23, 1871.

11 Ibid., October 27, 1871.

12 Ibid., November 30 and December 2, 1871.

13 Ibid., December 19 and 23, 1871.

14 Ibid., December 25, 1871. Peter's estimate of the size of the crowd was exaggerated. The present oak pews, installed in 1899, seat 400 people. It is possible that another hundred, or maybe only fifty, could have found space there.

15 Hollenback, *Central City and Black Hawk,* 82.

16 *Gilpin County Records,* Book 48, 198. The location on Eureka Street is confirmed by the fact that both Hall, a laborer, and Washington, a miner, were listed as living on Eureka Street in 1871. *Rocky Mountain Directory, 1871,* 348, 354.

17 Peter McFarlane, *Diary,* October 15, 1870

18 Ibid., December 18 and 23, 1870.

19 Ibid., December 23, 1870.

20 Peter McFarlane, *Diary,* March 3, 1871. See also January 6, 8, 12, and 14, 1871.

21 Ibid., March 16, 1871.

22 Ibid., February 6, 1871.

St. James Methodist Church, Eureka St. (1974 photo). Note steep pitch of the roof which gave Peter so much trouble when he shingled it in 1871.

FRED S. COOPER,
Business Manager

O. B GRIGGS, M. D.
Medical Director.

THE KEELEY INSTITUTE,

423 EAST HOPKINS AVENUE.   - - For the Treatment of the - -   OF ASPEN, COLORADO.

Liquor, Opium, Chloral and Cocaine Habits, Nervous Diseases and Tobacco Habit,

BY DR. LESLIE E. KEELEY'S CHLORIDE OF GOLD REMEDIES.

The Authorized Branch Institute for the State.
Treatment Identical with that Employed
by Dr. Leslie E. Keeley.

COLORADO SPRINGS INSTITUTE, 219 North Nevada St.

The Keeley Treatment for the Liquor, Opium, Morphine and Tobacco
Habits has received the endorsement of the United States, and is now used in
all of the State and Military Homes for disabled volunteer soldiers and sailors.

DENVER INSTITUTE, Club Building

Aspen, Colorado, June 27 1892

W. O. McFarland
Central

Dear Bro yours
rec today it has been my in—
tentions for some time to try
+ get Will B. to take the Keeley
Cure I think as soon as I can
get my business in shape I
will go + try him I think I can
talk him into it.

I think by the Muddle July
I can go we are working the
Bertha again drifting on the
Contact I dont look bad may
strike on any day

They shut it down while I was
away Alex Sutherland is going
over to central I think he said on
Sunday I have a notion to
Start a saw mill on Rock Creek

Letter from Andrew McFarlane to Will McFarlane about the Keeley Cure for Will
Barclay. (See Chap III, note 38.)

23 Ibid., September 20, 1871. Emphasis added.

24 Ibid., December 31, 1871.

25 Eugene Lackey ceases to be mentioned in the work assignments recorded in Peter's diary immediately after the completion of the "Barclay-McFarlane house" in the middle of October 1870. William Price left Central City for Hydes Hills, Wisconsin, approximately three months later. Peter McFarlane, *Diary,* January 12, 1871. The only hint as to the reasons for their leaving is in Peter's remark that "forced circumstances compelled them to move to different spheres of labor." Ibid., December 31, 1871.

26 Ibid., April 17, 1871.

27 Ibid., April 18 and 19, 1871.

28 Central City *Daily Register,* March 27, 1872.

29 Peter McFarlane, *Diary*, April 26, 1871.

30 Ibid., June 7, 1871. Mrs. Moses Hall was a next-door neighbor. Bob Hood was a Barclay & Co. employee. Mrs. Murray, wife of Robert Murray, a Barclay & Co. employee, was housekeeper at the Barclay-McFarlane home.

31 Ibid., June 8, 1871.

32 Ibid., June 16, 1871.

33 Ibid., June 19, 1871.

34 Ibid., June 20, 1871.

35 Ibid., June 22, 1871.

36 The new home was set on a lot 80 x 100 feet and was purchased on July 3, 1871, from Catharine E. and Dywer W. Gardiner of Jefferson County for $500. *The Gilpin County Deed Record Books and Tax Record Books,* July 3, 1871. On July 27, Peter wrote in his diary: "We brothers sit on the steps of our new cottage . . . . Who would have thought 10 years ago we would be 3,000 miles from our native land."

37 This is a typographical error; it should read P. F. Barclay.

38 Peter McFarlane, *Diary,* December 31, 1871. Just when Will Barclay left Central City cannot be definitely determined. He was, however, "trying to collect money to carry him home" in the latter part of December 1871. Ibid., December 23, 1871. Peter McFarlane's fears that his cousin would become "a confirmed sot" seem to have been realized. Many years later another of the McFarlane brothers, Andrew A. McFarlane, himself an alcoholic, apparently attempted to persuade Will Barclay to take the "Keeley Cure." Letter from Andrew A. McFarlane to William O. McFarlane, June 27, 1892. With the dissolution of Barclay & Company on August 1, 1871, Peter Barclay ended his business association with his brother and his cousins. What he did for a

living immediately after is not clear. It is known that he and Lizzie continued to live in the old Barclay-McFarlane house until December 13, 1871, when they moved to Russell Gulch. Peter McFarlane, *Diary,* December 13, 1871. Shortly thereafter they were reported to be "enjoying the blessedness of married life," and "with a fair prospect of one day being richer than Croesus dreamed of." Ibid., December 31, 1871.

Chapter IV   A Bachelor's Life

1 Peter McFarlane, *Diary.* This is part of an entry made after the last notation for the year 1870.
2 In May 1889 Peter had been erecting stamp mills in the Aspen, Breckenridge, Leadville areas for ten months. It must have been with a very heavy heart that he sent the following plea to Will in Central City. "If it ain't too late when you get this, be sure and hear Booth in Hamlet. Get a lower front seat, and have good opera glasses, and don't allow anything to prevent." Peter to William McFarlane, May 1, 1889. *McFarlane Papers.*
3 Royce, *California,* 272.
4 Young, *Echoes from Arcadia,* vii.
5 *Daily Register,* December 19, 1871.
6 Albert D. Richardson, *Beyond the Mississippi: 1857–1867,* 177.
7 Ibid., 182.
8 Peter McFarlane, *Diary,* August 1, 1871.
9 Ibid., September 26, 1871. McFarlane was probably referring to the following lines from "Tree of Liberty," a poem generally attributed to Robert Burns, one of McFarlane's favorite authors:
> We labor soon, we labor late,
>   To feed the titled knave man,
> And a' the comfort we're to get,
>   Is that ayont the grave man.
10 Ibid., October 7, 1871.
11 Ibid., October 8, 1871.
12 Ibid., October 15, 1871.
13 Ibid., October 22, 1871.
14 Ibid., October 23, 1871.
15 Ibid., October 29, 1871.
16 Ibid., November 19, 1871.
17 Ibid., December 25, 1871.
18 McFarlane, *Grown Gold,* 9–10.
19 Letter from Peter McFarlane to Howard L. Winchester, Boston, Massachusetts. July 26, 1917. *McFarlane Papers.*

20 "Took it into my head to study the history of America. Got along very well for the first day." Peter McFarlane, *Diary,* November 5, 1871. In this and other self-study reading, Peter got along very well *after* the first day also. His cousin recalled: "I was astounded at his intellectual stature, the power of his personality. With no education on Prince Edward Island save the three R's he had become conversant with the best dialogues of the time, and his company was not only a joy but an inspiration." Letter to the author from Frank McFarlane, May 15, 1965.

21 Ibid., November 3, 1871.

22 Ibid., November 20, 1871.

23 Ibid., October 26, 1870

24 It was a very disappointing turn of events when the stagecoach brought no mail from home. Peter was a good correspondent, apparently operating under the assumption that in order to receive letters one must write letters. "Will got two letters last night, and not one of us got any. I think that I will give up this act of letter writing." Ibid., January 1, 1870.

25 See Appendix B for a large sample of McFarlane's Sunday diary entries. These illustrate what he did when not working.

26 On one occasion he went to town, sat in on a game of cards, and lost 50 cents. He concluded: "It will be the last I shall play for some time." Peter McFarlane, *Diary,* October 1, 1871. Whether Peter ever played cards again for money at all, certainly gambling halls, saloons, and whore houses were not his haunts. On the contrary, during his first years in Central City, the bright institutional spot in McFarlane's life seems to have been the Good Templars Lodge, an organization dedicated to the cause of temperance. Here he could relax in fraternal conviviality among men who shared his views. As he wrote: "Went to lodge tonight. Any amount of fun. Always is." Ibid., December 27, 1970.

27 Ibid., March 24, 1870.

28 Ibid., April 14 and 15 1870. In 1921 McFarlane penciled in a notation on the April 15 page of his diary that he remembered seeing Helen Nash and Alf Burnett that evening when he first ventured into a theatre fifty-one years earlier. (In 1870 Alfred Burnett was acknowledged as "America's favorite humorist." One theatre historian at that time said Burnett "has appeared as actor, lecturer and humorist in every State in this country. As a mimic and ventriloquist, he stands pre-eminent." Burnett gave comic lectures, performed farces with his colleague, Helen Nash, and did musical renditions "on the mouth-organ, teapot, and bellows." T. A. Brown, *History of the American Stage,* 57; M. Schoberlin, *From Candles to Footlights,* 255.)

29 Peter McFarlane, *Diary*, April 16, 1870.
30 Ibid., June 15, 1871.
31 Central City *Daily Register*, April 15, 1871.
32 Peter McFarlane, *Diary*, April 21, 1870.
33 Ibid., November 30, 1871,
34 Central City *Weekly Register*, November 29, 1871.
35 *McFarlane Papers.*
36 The twenty-three candy jars probably reflect McFarlane's fondness for sweets. Maple sugar was his favorite treat. His daughter recalled how each young man who came to call on her had to endure listening to her father while waiting for her to finish last-minute primping for a date. McFarlane always told the same story and began by relating how his family home on Prince Edward Island had a cellar in which the maple syrup was stored each fall. One day, when he was a young boy, he went to the cellar with his mother to get a pitcher of syrup. The pitcher was filled, but before the lid could be put back on the barrel, a mouse fell into it. He grabbed the mouse and held it up in the air and drank the syrup as it ran off the sticky little animal. Author's interview with Mrs. R. R. Demeter, August 20, 1965.
37 Peter McFarlane, *Diary*, October 5, 1871.
38 Ibid., April 17 and 26, and May 4, 1871,
39 Ibid., April 23, 1871.
40 Ibid., July 9, 1871.
41 Ibid., July 16, 1871.
42 Ibid., August 7, 1871.
43 Ibid., August 11, 1871.
44 Ibid., August 14, 1871.
45 At the beginning of the year and at the end of the summer McFarlane had recorded with satisfaction the good wages and the ample work available. "Plenty of work this summer at $5.00 per day. . . .We all worked on Martin's house today, four of us at the rate of $5.00 per day per man. Soon runs up a snug bill of $20.00 per day, $120.00 per wek, $480.00 per month, $5760.00 per year." Ibid., September 2 and January 28, 1871. The company consisted of the partners (four in January and three in September) and four employees. During 1870 the partners had been paying $2.00–$3.00 per day for carpenters, so the margin of profit appears to have been good. Ibid., March 21 and 30, 1870. It is obvious from this that the influx of men to Gilpin County in 1869 and 1870 had resulted in a large labor pool and a reduction in the daily wage rate.
46 Ibid., January 1, 1871.

47 Ibid., February 22, 1871.
48 The recipe for McFarlane's home remedy was as follows: "One pint of whiskey, 4 oz. of ground mustard. Mix and rub three times a day." Ibid., March 27, 1871.
49 Ibid., April 24, 1871.
50 On Christmas Day, 1870, he noted that on December 25, 1869, he was in bed with rheumatism. Ibid., December 25, 1870.
51 The nature of the work is not made entirely clear, but it seems that they were building a house for a man named J. Lurchen or J. Lerchen; Peter spelled the name both ways and sometimes in the same entry.
52 *Rocky Mountain News,* June 23, 1871. the Fountaine-qui-Bouille consisted of four springs located "about 3 miles above Colorado City in the valley of Fountain Creek." The temperature of the water was about 65 degrees and the main spring "contained about 1 ounce of medicated matter for every 4 gallons of water."
53 Peter McFarlane, *Diary,* May 3, 1870. The House was located at Fourth near Front Street.
54 Ibid., May 4 and 5, 1870.
55 Ibid., May 9, 1870.
56 Ibid., June 1, 1870.
57 Peter McFarlane to Ren Manhire, Kendall, Montana, August 22, 1906. *McFarlane Papers.*
58 Peter McFarlane, *Diary,* June 1, 1870.
59 Ibid., June 2, 1870.
60 Ibid., June 3, 1870. The Tremont House was located on Front Street between Third and Fourth.
61 Ibid., June 4, 1870.
62 Ibid., December 31, 1870.
63 Ibid., December 31, 1871.
64 William Warren Sweet, "The Frontier in American Christianity," in *Environmental Factors in Christian History,* edited by John T. McNeill, *et al.,* 396.
65 Central City *Daily Register,* July 8, 1875. Later in the same month, the paper noted that Pueblo had passed a bond issue for a $30,000 school. "If that fails," the editors wrote, "the place will be fenced in and given up to the devil and his smelting works." Ibid., July 24, 1875.
66 There were one Congregational, three Episcopal, two Methodist, one Presbyterian, and one Catholic church. U.S. Census Bureau. 9th Census, 1870. *Statistics of the Population of the United States,* I, 531.
67 Letter from the Reverend William Crawford to the American

Home Missionary Society, September 18, 1863. Quoted in Virginia Greene Millikin, *et al.*, *The Bible and the Gold Rush,* 25.

68 Peter McFarlane, *Diary,* January 30 and March 6, 1870.

69 Ibid., June 19, 1870.

70 Ibid., January 1, April 30, and May 14, 1871.

71 On January 1, 1871 the Methodist and Congregational churches began a series of nightly union prayer meetings under the leadership of the Reverend William Chase (Methodist) and the Reverend S. F. Dickinson (Congregationalist). Central City *Daily Register,* January 1, 1871.

72 Balcom arrived in Central City on November 15, 1871. During the following months he held nine revival meetings in Nevadaville, thirteen in the Presbyterian Church in Black Hawk, two in Black Hawk saloons, fourteen each in the Methodist and Baptist churches in Central City, and one each in Jone's Concert Saloon, Schmitz's Saloon, and Pitt's Saloon. He collected a total of $180 for the churches and brought twenty souls back into the fold. Ibid., November 12 and 26, and December 5, 14, 15, and 19, 1871, and January 9, 1872.

73 Ibid., June 15, 1871.

74 Peter McFarlane, *Diary,* June 17, 1871.

75 Ibid., September 17, 1871.

76 Ibid., November 19, 1871.

77 Central City *Daily Register,* January 1, 1872. A similar comment was made by the editors of the paper regarding the preaching of the Reverend George Barnes of Kentucky, who carried on the revival after the Reverend Balcom left town: "His style of oratory savors a little too much of the sensational, appealing to the emotions of his audiences rather than their reason." Ibid., February 1, 1872.

78 This was a first edition copy, published in 1879. McFarlane also owned a first edition of another of Ingersoll's works, *The Gods and Other Lectures,* published in 1874.

79 Robert Ingersoll, *The Ghosts and other Lectures,* 85-86.

80 Ibid., 122.

81 Ingersoll, *The Ghosts,* 91. "Religionist" is Ingersoll's terminology.

82 This is a quotation from Alfred, Lord Tennyson's *In Memoriam,* Part 96, lines 11 and 12.

83 Ingersoll, *The Ghosts,* 91.

84 Letter from Peter McFarlane to Sam Newell, Bonsal, California, July 30, 1916. *McFarlane Papers.*

LIBERAL AND SCIENTIFIC PUBLISHING HOUSE.

THE TRUTH SEEKER COMPANY.

PUBLISHERS, BOO SELLERS, AND IMPORTERS OF FREETHO HT WORKS.

Office of **The Truth Seeker.**

E. M. MACDONALD, EDITOR
AND BUSINESS MANAGER.

A Journal of Freethought and Reform.

PUBLISHED WEEKLY AT $3.00 PER YEAR.   SAMPLE COPIES SENT FREE UPON APPLICATION.

28 Lafayette Place,

New York, June 25 1894

Peter McFarlane Esq
Central City.

Dear Sir

Replying to yours
of 17th.

We find by our Cash book that
we did receive the Dft of 5⁰⁰
March 10th but the letter some
way is lost and did not
get to your credit on Ledger
first. However, we now place
same to your act, paying to
1 Mch 94 and trust this may
be satisfactory to you.
Regret the trouble caused you.

Very Truly Yours. Truth Seeker Co

Chapter V   McFarlane & Company

1 *Gilpin County Record Books,* Book 48, 366. On the deed recording the transaction, William Barclay is shown as partner in the company.

2 There is evidence that two decades later Will Barclay was back in Colorado and once again associated with his cousins, the McFarlanes, most probably as an employee. In 1895 Will McFarlane, who was then managing the Denver branch of McFarlane & Company at 1734 Fifteenth Street, wrote to Peter in Central City stating that he and "W. J. B." had started working on a pattern that he had ordered. It is hard to escape the conclusion that "W. J. B." referred to William J. Barclay. William to Peter McFarlane, June 6, 1895. *McFarlane Papers.*

3 This volunteer fire fighting company was organized on March 30, 1875, about ten months after the great fire had destroyed most of the central business district of the town. Its first foreman, whom Andrew McFarlane succeeded, was M. H. Root, who had also been foreman of the earlier Central City Fire Company No. 1, organized on December 6, 1869. Frank Hall, *History of the State of Colorado,* III, 422. A business transaction places Andrew in Central City in June. In the *Gilpin County Record Books,* Book 52, 251 records a trust deed, dated June 29, 1875 made out to Robert A. Campbell securing $2,500 owed to Hanington and Mellor, bankers, Central City, by William O., Peter B., and A. A. McFarlane.

4 Andrew McFarlane became a popular citizen in the community. In 1878 he was elected Undersheriff of Gilpin County and in 1879 was the Republican nominee for Sheriff. Central City *Daily Register,* October 10, 1878, and July 23, 1879. Will McFarlane also served in the Rough and Ready Company for at least twelve years. In the *McFarlane Papers* there is a certificate dated December 24, 1890, showing that he became a member of the company on February 6, 1878, and was still active on the date the certificate was issued.

5 *Gilpin County Record Books,* Book 48, 366. The McFarlane brothers paid $200 for the lot.

6 *Records of Taxes Collected in Gilpin County, 1873,* 76-77.

7 The production of precious metals for this three-year period was $2,224,679 in 1872, $1,498,002 in 1873, and $1,634,274 in 1874. Henderson, *Mining in Colorado,* 88.

8 A custom stamp mill was one designed to handle the ore from a specific mine.

9 Peter McFarlane to A. H. Potter, Idaho Springs, December 5, 1909. *McFarlane Papers.*

10 Central City *Daily Register,* May 7, 1871.

11 Henderson, *Mining in Colorado,* 88. Apron plates are plates of amalgamated copper over which the pulverized ore is allowed to flow from the stamp battery and upon which the gold is caught as amalgam. A bumping table is a mechanical device designed to catch gold which the apron plates or the plates inside the battery of the stamp mill miss. The pulverized ore flows across the bumping table. As it does, a series of regular jars separates the lighter and less valuable portions of the ore from the heavier. Bumping tables are also known as concentrators. Rossiter W. Raymond, "A Glossary of Mining and Metallurgical Terms," American Institute of Mining Engineers *Transactions,* IX (1880-81), 122.

12 Letter from Peter McFarlane to A. H. Potter, Idaho Springs, December 5, 1909. *McFarlane Papers.*

13 Letter from Peter McFarlane to Robert L. Martin, Central City, April 2, 1903. *McFarlane Papers.* For discussion of the Gilpin County Gilt Edged Concentrator, infra, 79-82.

14 C. A. Stetefeldt, "Russell's Improved Process for the Lixiviation of Silver Ores," American Institute of Mining Engineers *Transactions,* XIII (1883-84), 115.

15 Frank Fossett, *Colorado, Its Gold and Silver Mines* (1879), 219; ibid. (1880), 586.

16 Letter from Peter McFarlane to John Beattie, Denver, December 29, 1907. *McFarlane Papers.*

17 It is difficult to determine precisely how long it took McFarlane & Company to get Colonel Randolph's mill into operation, but judging from later contracts of similar proportions for which the details are available, six months would not appear to be an exaggerated figure. For instance, in April 1903 Peter McFarlane submitted a bid to Robert L. Martin for a forty-five stamp battery in the Gregory-Buell mill building in Central City. In the bid, McFarlane agreed to have the stamp battery running in three months. (There is a handwritten chart of the bid and a typed copy of the specifications in the *McFarlane Papers.*) In contrast to the provision of the Randolph contract, no building was involved this time, and McFarlane & Company could call on thirty years of experience and the resources of three foundries and machine shops in Central City, Black Hawk, and Denver, which employed about 125 men. Letter from Peter McFarlane to Montana Iron Works, Butte City, December 1, 1894. *McFarlane Papers.* A fifty

stamp mill, even if the mill building was not included, probably took almost twice as long to complete in 1872 when the company was in its infancy.

18 For the early history of the Gilpin County mining industry, I relied primarily on Edson S. Bastin and James W. Hill, *Economic Geology of Gilpin County and Parts of Clear Creek and Boulder Counties,* 53-56.

19 Rossiter W. Raymond, *Statistics of Mines and Mining in the States and Territories West of the Rocky Montains,* U.S. 41st Congress, 2nd Session, House Executive Document No. 207, 345.

20 Andrews N. Rogers, "The Mines and Mills of Gilpin County, Colorado," American Institute of Mining Engineers *Transactions,* XI (1882-83), 33.

21 Raymond, *Statistics of Mines and Mining,* op. cit., 346.

22 Ibid.

23 Ibid., 729.

24 The specifications for the slow and fast drop stamp mills and their rates of efficiency are taken from T. A. Rickard, "The Limitations of the Gold Stamp Mill," American Institute of Mining Engineers *Transactions,* XXIII (1893), 37-47.

25 Central City *Daily Register,* December 2, 1875.

26 Raymond, *Statistics of Mines and Mining,* op. cit., 347. See also William P. Blake, "The Mechanical Appliances of Mining," ibid., 657; H. S. Munroe, "On the Weight, Fall and Speed of Stamps," American Institute of Mining Engineers *Transactions,* IX (1881-82), 84-99; Albert Reichenecker, *The Treatment of Aufiferous Ores in Colorado,* U.S. 42nd Congress, 1st Session, House Executive Document No. 10, 339-63.

27 Raymond, *Statistics of Mines and Mining,* op. cit., 349-50. Emphasis added.

28 Ibid., 365-66.

29 Rossiter W. Raymond, "On the Relation between the Speed and Effectiveness of Stamps," American Institute of Mining Engineers *Transactions,* I (1871-73), 52.

30 Ibid., 54.

31 William M. Thayer, *Marvels of the New West,* 436.

32 Rogers, "The Mines and Mills of Gilpin County," 10, 13. Andrews Rogers' paper was read for him by his brother E. M. Rogers.

33 Ibid., 33.

34 Ibid., 36.

35 Ibid., 36. Rogers here cited an article by Melville Atwood that appeared in the *Mining and Scientific Press* on June 24, 1882, just

prior to the Denver meeting. In this article Atwood reported that fine crushing (a fineness of approximately 400,000 particles to the cubic inch) attempted on ore from two California mines, the Grass Valley and the Bodie, produced battered and laminated grains of gold.

36 Rogers, op. cit., 36-37.
37 Ibid., 49-50.
38 Rossiter W. Raymond, "Discussion," American Institute of Mining Engineers *Transactions,* XI (1882-82), 53.
39 Ibid.
40 Ibid.
41 Ibid. Emphasis added. In the printed proceedings of the meeting Dr. Raymond noted that he had checked an earlier article of his and had had to modify his remarks—that he *had* been critical of a rate of fall of 30 drops per minute. He went on to state that he still was.
42 Robertson Gray [pseudonym], *Brave Hearts,* 78.
43 Ibid., 218-19.
44 Rossiter W. Raymond, *Statistics of Mines and Mining in the States and Territories West of the Rocky Mountains,* U.S. 42nd Congress, 1st Session, House Executive Document No. 10, 295.
45 Letter from Peter McFarlane to Philip Mixsell, Idaho Springs, February 7, 1893. *McFarlane Papers.*
46 Letter from Peter McFarlane to S. A. Tarbet, Milford, Utah, April 2, 1906. *McFarlane Papers.*
47 Letter from Peter McFarlane to George E. Collins, Denver, November 21, 1909. *McFarlane Papers.*
48 McFarlane's views on the medium-rapid drop mill are discussed at length in his letter to Collins noted above and in another to George M. W. Mabee, Central City, November 3, 1909. *McFarlane Papers.*
49 I Thess. 1:21. McFarlane used this quotation to describe his feelings on the slow drop mill in his letter to Philip Mixsell on February 7, 1893. *McFarlane Papers.* For more on McFarlane's belief about stamps and battery amalgamation, and about the criticism he sustained, see interview with A. B. Sanford, March 16, 1924. MSS XV-14e. Colorado State Historical Society Library.
50 Chase Withrow, *The Charter and Ordinances of the City of Central, Colorado,* 8-13.
51 Also, after the great fire of May 21, 1874, W. O. McFarlane, George Randolph, and five others served as the relief committee to distribute food and clothing. Central City *Daily Register,* May 23, 1874.

52 Bancroft, *Gulch of Gold,* 164–65, 201, 219.
53 James Burrell, "Gilpin County Biographies," in *The History of Clear Creek and Boulder Valleys, Colorado,* 435.
54 See the detailed list of losses published in the *Daily Register* on May 25, 1874. Bancroft gives the figure as $500,000, which is obviously incorrect. Total insurance paid on adjusted claims was $114,533. Central City *Daily Register,* June 8, 1874.
55 Central City *Daily Register,* May 23, 1874.
56 *The Colorado Business Directory* (1875), 83.
57 *The Colorado Business Directory* (1876), 81.
58 Central City *Daily Register,* July 8, 1875.
59 Ibid., November 2, 1875.
60 Ibid., June 1, 1875. The newspaper misspelled Hanington's name.
61 Hanington, "Early Days of Central City and Black Hawk,"3.
62 Hall, *Colorado,* III, 417. Bancroft gives the year as 1876. *Gulch of Gold,* 268. Hanington and Mellor, however, were advertising in the *Daily Register* on January 4, 1875, giving their business location as the Wells Fargo building on Lawrence Street.
63 Central City *Daily Register,* May 25, 1874.
64 Ibid., June 1, 1875.
65 Ibid., June 16, 1875. Hollenback erroneously labels two buildings at the junction of Spring and Gregory Streets as the Mellor-Mc-Farlane buildings. *Central City and Black Hawk,* 30.
66 Central City *Daily Register,* July 16, 1875.
67 Ibid., July 31, 1875.
68 Ibid., November 17, 1875.
69 *The Colorado Business Directory* (1876), 88. Eighty-eight buildings with a total value of $125,000 were completed in Central City in 1875.
70 *Gilpin County Record Books,* Book 52, 251, and marginal note on the recording of the original transaction.
71 Ibid., 272–73.
72 Central City *Daily Register,* January 3, 1876.
73 Ibid., March 26, 1878.
74 Ibid., March 21, 1878.
75 Ibid., March 28, 1878,
76 Ibid., March 29, 1878.
77 Ibid.
78 Ibid.
79 By the end of 1879, the population of Leadville was 12,000. Hall, *Colorado,* II, 452.
80 Ibid., II, 66,
81 Ibid., II, 66–67.

Remains of McFarlane & Co. foundry on Eureka St., Central City (1974 photo, from rear).

82 James H. Baker and LeRoy R. Hafen, *History of Colorado,* IV, 127.
83 The sale was reported in the *Rocky Mountain News* on August 15, 1882.
84 Supra, 32–33.
85 Peter McFarlane, *Diary,* August 15, 1871.
86 Burrell, "Gilpin County Biographies," 435.

Chapter VI   Men to Match The Mineral Mountains

1 Central City *Weekly Register-Call,* January 7, 1881.
2 *Frank Leslie's Illustrated Newspaper,* May, 1879.
3 Fossett, *Colorado* (1880), 365.
4 Central City *Weekly Register-Call,* January 21, 1881.
5 Fossett, *Colorado* (1879), 348.
6 Ibid. (1880), 296.
7 Ellsworth C. Mittick, "The Development of the Mining Machinery Manufacture in Colorado" (M.A. thesis), 3–10.
8 Letter from Pelton Water Wheel Company to McFarlane & Company, September 29, 1892. *McFarlane Papers.*
9 Undated ledger sheet recapitulating the details of the contract. Ibid.
10 "We mail to you today the blue print drawings of your buildings and machinery. . . . We will send by tomorrow the agreement and the specifications complete." Letter from McFarlane & Company to L. L. Nunn, April 1, 1892. Ibid.
11 Undated letter from Peter to Will McFarlane, September 1892. Ibid.
12 Letter from Peter McFarlane to Eugene Teats, Telluride, April 9, 1892. Ibid. The letter contains his proposed travel schedule from Central City to Telluride. Teats (1847–1929) was a Colorado pioneer and mine owner.
13 Letter from Peter to Will McFarlane, September 15, 1892. Ibid. In this letter Peter estimated the mill would be running in approximately three months.
14 Ibid.
15 Hendrie and Bolthoff in Denver.
16 Letter from Peter to Will McFarlane, September 10, 1892. *McFarlane Papers.*
17 Letter from Peter to Will McFarlane, September 5, 1892. Ibid.
18 Letter from Peter to Will McFarlane, August 1, 1892. Ibid.
19 William Story was Lieutenant Governor of Colorado, 1891–92.

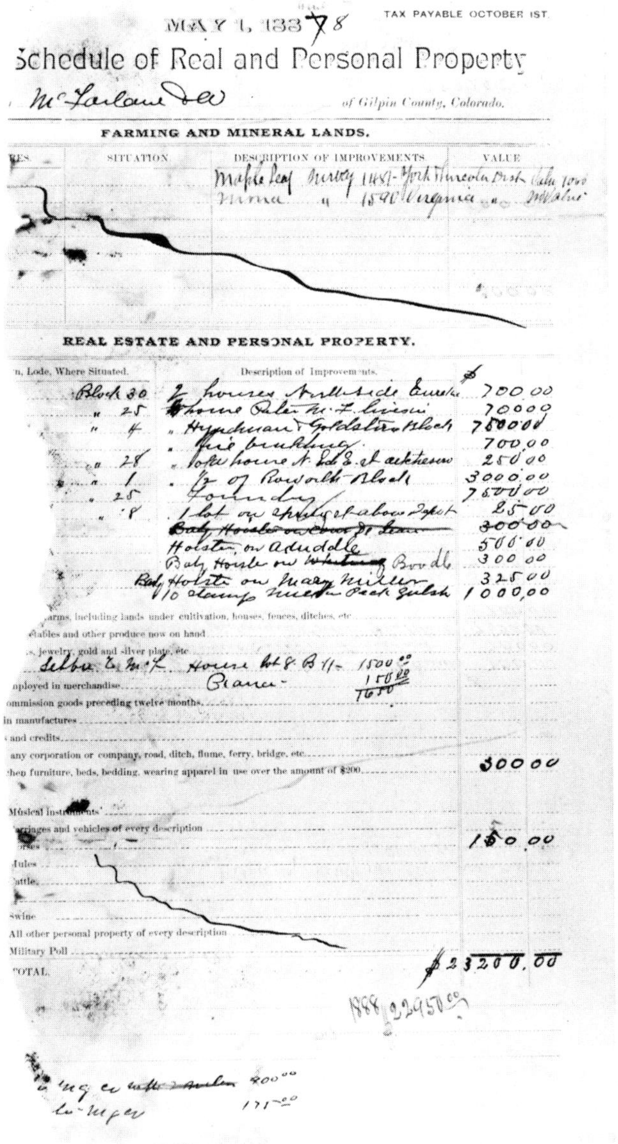
MAY 1, 1887 8 TAX PAYABLE OCTOBER 1ST.

Schedule of Real and Personal Property

McFarlane & Co of Gilpin County, Colorado.

FARMING AND MINERAL LANDS.

SITUATION	DESCRIPTION OF IMPROVEMENTS	VALUE
	Maple Leaf survey 1481 - York - Lincoln Dist.	Value 1000
	Mima " 1590 Virginia "	no value

REAL ESTATE AND PERSONAL PROPERTY.

Lode, Where Situated.	Description of Improvements.	$
Block 30	2 houses Northside Eureka	700.00
" 25	house Peter McF. living	700.00
" 4	" Hyndman & Goldstein Block	7500.00
	" Fire brick ...	700.00
" 28	" Ice house N. Side ...	250.00
" 1	" 1/2 of Roworth Block	3000.00
" 25	Foundry	7500.00
" 8	1 lot on Spring St above Depot	25.00
	~~Baby Hoist on ...~~	~~300.00~~
	Hoister on Adudelle	500.00
	Baby Hoist on ~~Whiting~~ Boodle	300.00
	Baby Hoister on Mary Miller	325.00
	10 stamps mill ... Peck Gulch	1000.00

Farms, including lands under cultivation, houses, fences, ditches, etc.

Vegetables and other produce now on hand

..., jewelry, gold and silver plate, etc.

Silbie E. McF. House lot 8 B 11 — 1500.00 Piano — 150.00 1650

...ployed in merchandise

...ommission goods preceding twelve months

...in manufactures

... and credits

... any corporation or company, road, ditch, flume, ferry, bridge, etc.

...chen furniture, beds, bedding, wearing apparel in use over the amount of $200 — 300.00

Musical instruments

Carriages and vehicles of every description

Horses — 150.00

Mules

Cattle

Swine

All other personal property of every description

Military Poll

TOTAL — $23200.00

1888 $22950.00

McFarlane & Co. tax schedule, May 1, 1888.

The Markham

B. M. SLACK, MANAGER.

WELCH & SLACK,
PROPRIETORS.

Cor. Seventeenth and Lawrence Sts.

Denver, Colo. *Oct 8"* 1889.

McFarland Bros
Central City Colo

Gents

You will please send by Ex C.O.D. one of your concentrators as per agreement. Send it soon as possible by Pac, Ex. Send full particulars how to set it up. You had better number the pieces so I will know where they go.

Truly

Address box to Charlotte North Carolina

John C. Blake

This order for one of the McFarlanes' concentrators to be shipped to North Carolina illustrates the wide geographic market the brothers found for their machines. In addition to supplying many mines in Colorado, McFarlane & Co. shipped the concentrators or bumping tables to Arizona, California, Georgia, Idaho, Montana, Nevada, New Mexico, Oregon, etc., not to mention Mexico and overseas countries.

20 The widely read *Solid Muldoon* was published in Ouray by David
   Day, one of Colorado's most famous pioneer newspapermen. "A
   man of keen and biting wit, he proved himself the ablest para-
   grapher the state ever produced." Baker and Hafen, *History of
   Colorado,* III, 1249.
21 Letter from Peter to Will McFarlane, July 19, 1892. *McFarlane
   Papers.*
22 Letter from William Story to McFarlane & Company, July 20,
   1892. Ibid.
23 Letter from William Story to W. O. McFarlane, August 25, 1892.
   Ibid.
24 Central City *Weekly Register-Call*, August 7, 1885.
25 Letter from Peter McFarlane to Minnie Frey, February 25, 1889.
   McFarlane Papers.
26 Letter from William McFarlane to Cora Bonner, Winona,
   Wisconsin, January 1, 1921. Ibid.
27 Gold production, which had been $1,054,065 in 1889, fell to
   $805,236 worth in 1890. It rose slightly the following year,
   reaching a figure of $938,016. Henderson, *Mining in Colorado,*
   122.
28 Letter from Will McFarlane to Eugene Teats, Telluride, September 29, 1890. *McFarlane Papers.*
29 Letter from Will McFarlane to Bela Buell, January 1, 1891. Ibid.
30 Letter from Peter to Will McFarlane, August 8, 1901. Ibid.
31 Letter from Will McFarlane to Bela Buell, January 24, 1891. Ibid.
   "Libbie" was Mary Elizabeth Hale McFarlane, Will's wife.
32 Letter from Peter to Will McFarlane, November 7, 1890. Ibid.
33 Letter from Peter to Will McFarlane, December 16, 1890. Ibid.
34 Patent issued January 27, 1891.
35 Letter from Peter to Will McFarlane, December 16, 1890. *Mc-
   Farlane Papers.*
36 Letter from McFarlane & Company to William Henderson,
   Washington, D. C., February 2, 1892. Ibid.
37 Letter from an Idaho Springs man to McFarlane & Company,
   September 6, 1887. The letter is legible; the signature is not. Ibid.
38 Letter from U.S. Patent Office to Peter McFarlane, June 3, 1887.
   Ibid.
39 Letter from Frue Vanning Company to McFarlane & Company,
   June 6, 1887. Ibid.
40 Text of the argument in the original patent.
41 Letter from Peter to Will McFarlane, June 1889. The date is almost illegible, but the letter was with a group written while Peter
   was in Breckenridge in the summer of 1889. *McFarlane Papers.*

42 In 1892 the tables were successfully used at Bendigo, Australia. Letter from T. A. Rickard to McFarlane & Company, September 28, 1892. Ibid.

43 The original agreement complete with the seal of the U.S. government. Ibid.

44 Letter from McFarlane & Company to Lemke Mining and Milling Company, Salmon City, Idaho, November 17, 1891. Ibid.

45 Letter from Silas Bertenshaw to McFarlane & Company, June 29, 1892. Ibid.

46 Mittick, "Development of Mining Machinery Manufacture in Colorado," 8.

47 Letter from Will to Peter McFarlane, October 2, 1889. *McFarlane Papers.*

48 D. R. C. Brown, McFarlane's cousin.

49 The Hawley Merchandise Company in Central City.

50 Letter from Will to Peter McFarlane, October 3, 1889. *McFarlane Papers.*

51 Ibid.

52 Mittick, "Development of Mining Machinery Manufacture in Colorado," 6.

53 Letter from Will to Peter McFarlane, October 3, 1889. *McFarlane Papers.*

54 In a letter from Will to Peter McFarlane, October 13, 1889, reference is made to the offer from the Denver group as a one-quarter interest instead of one-third. Ibid.

55 Letter from J. H. Hale to Will McFarlane, August 12, 1892. Ibid.

56 Letter from Will McFarlane to James W. Jackson. The date is very difficult to read, but appears to be September 1, 1892. Ibid.

57 Letter from Peter to Will McFarlane, September 5, 1892. Ibid.

58 Letter from McFarlane & Company to M. M. Barnett, Fort Worth, Texas, September 29, 1892. Ibid.

59 Letter from Peter to Will McFarlane, September 5, 1892. Ibid.

60 Letter from Will to Peter McFarlane, June 6, 1895. Ibid.

Chapter VII   The Prosperous Years

1 Davis R. Dewey, quoted in Elmer Ellis, *Henry Moore Teller,* 213.

2 The naivete of the widespread belief in the cure-all effect of the repeal of the Sherman Act was similar to that portrayed in the popular film of the late 1930s, *Mr. Deeds Goes to Town,* in which "forty acres and a mule" was seriously proposed as a solution to widespread industrial unemployment.

A. RICKARD,
MINING ENGINEER.

207 McPHEE BUILDING,
DENVER, COLORADO

Sept 28 1892

Messrs McFarlane & Co

I learn fr Mr Lansell. to whom you shipped Gilpin County bumper at Bendigo. Australia that the machine is giving good satisfaction and that he is thinking of either making or ordering several more. He says that he has not received the invoice. I would advise you to communicate with him & offer to make a reduction in quantity if he takes a number of yr machines.

Yrs faithfully

T. A. Rickard

The letter above (See Chap. VI, note 42.) and
the letter on the following page illustrate the
foreign market potential for the McFarlane bumping table
(the Gilpin County Gilt Edge Concentrator).
The Fraser & Chalmers letter (following page)
also illustrates the lack of concern
the McFarlanes had at that time about patents.
Their own manufacture of the machines and their
relationship to other firms wanting to manufacture
this Gilpin County device for retrieving gold concentrates
from pulps and slimes seems to have been, legally speaking,
very loose and informal.

DAVID R. FRASER. WILLIAM J. CHALMERS. THOS. CHALMERS. NORMAN D. FRASER.

ALL AGREEMENTS MADE CONTINGENT UPON STRIKES, FIRES, ACCIDENTS OR CAUSES BEYOND OUR CONTROL.
QUOTATIONS SUBJECT TO CHANGE WITHOUT NOTICE.

CABLE ADDRESS
VANNER, CHICAGO.
USE A B C CODE, FOURTH EDITION.

OFFICE OF

FRASER & CHALMERS,

→→→→→→ Manufacturers of ←←←←←←

MINING MACHINERY ✸ Steam Engines, Boilers,

AND MACHINERY FOR SYSTEMATIC
MILLING, SMELTING & CONCENTRATION OF ORES.

Corner
UNION & FULTON STS
Chicago, SEPT. 27TH, 1889.

GENERAL OFFICE & WORKS, CHICAGO, ILL. U.S.A.
BRANCH OFFICES:

NEW YORK.   SALT LAKE CITY, UTAH.   DENVER, COLORADO.
Room 43 Nº2 Wall St.   7 West Second South St.   1316 Eighteenth St.
LONDON, ENGLAND.   LIMA, PERU.   CHIHUAHUA CITY, MEXICO.
23 Bucklersbury, E.C.   SOUTH AMERICA.   Nº 11 Calle de Juarez.
            JOHANNESBURG.   TOKIO,
        TRANSVAAL, SOUTH AFRICA.   JAPAN.

MESSRS. MC FARLANE & CO.,

CENTRAL CITY, COLORADO.

GENTLEMEN:-

WE BEG TO ACKNOWLEDGE RECEIPT OF YOUR ESTEEMED FAVOR OF
SEPT. THE 2ND AND HAVE CAREFULLY NOTED THE CONTENTS OF SAME AND
WISH TO THANK YOU FOR THE OFFER THAT YOU MAKE TO US AND THE INFOR-
MATION THAT YOU GIVE US, THAT THERE IS NO PATENT UPON THE MACHINE
AND THAT YOU WOULD SELL US A MACHINE AT REDUCED PRICE SO THAT
SHOULD WE DESIRE MAKING THEM OURSELVES WE COULD GET ALL THE PARTIC-
ULARS. WE WISH TO SAY THAT WE ARE FIGURING WITH PARTIES NOW FOR A
NUMBER OF THESE MACHINES AND WE THINK WE WILL SECURE THEIR ORDER.
IF SO, WE WILL ORDER SAME FROM YOU AND HAVE ONE SHIPPED TO US HERE
SO THAT FOR SHIPMENTS TO FOREIGN COUNTRIES WE COULD SAVE THE
FREIGHT THAT WOULD BE NECESSARY TO BRING THE MACHINE FROM CENTRAL
CITY TO CHICAGO. WE APPRECIATE YOUR KINDNESS IN OFFERING US THE
MACHINE AT THIS PRICE WITH THE OBJECT OF ENABLING US TO MANUFACTURE
THEM OURSELVES, AND WOULD SAY THAT WE WILL BE PLEASED AT ANY TIME
TO RETURN THE FAVOR.

RESPECTFULLY,

FRASER & CHALMERS,

PER

3 *Letters of John Hay and Extracts from Diary,* II, 264. In supervising the publication of her husband's letters in 1908, Mrs. Hay deleted many names, such that the printed version of the excerpt quoted reads: ". . .the ills of life,—scarcity of money, baldness, the comma bacillus, Home Rule, J—— —— ——, and the Potato Bug,—are due to the S—— Bill'', but I have restored the deletions and clarified a spelling. (See original manuscript used in preparation of *Letters and Diary,* Illinois State Historical Library, Springfield.) "Jimmy Van Alen" perhaps deserves additional clarification. James J. Van Alen was appointed ambassador to Italy in 1893 by President Grover Cleveland, and the Senate confirmed the appointment; however, it was then revealed that Van Alen had contributed $50,000 to Cleveland's campaign, and the public outcry was so great that Van Alen withdrew his acceptance of the post. All of this happened in 1893 just prior to Hay's writing his letter of October 2 to Adams. Therefore, the Van Alen reference seems to be a kind of barb between friends— Hay joshing Adams who was a "silver" man and a supporter of Cleveland.

4 Henry Moore Teller, quoted in Ellis, *Teller,* 186.

5 Colorado, Bureau of Labor Statistics. *Fourth Biennial Report* (1894), 44–46.

6 Ellis, *Teller,* 255.

7 Wilbur Fiske Stone (ed.), *History of Colorado,* I, 437. The discovery of gold in the United States and Australia greatly increased the world's supply during the last half of the 19th century. During the same period, the world's supply of silver increased rapidly. As the supply of gold increased, the value of silver in relation to gold steadily declined largely due to the leading commercial nations of the West adopting the gold standard and substituting gold for silver coins, a development which released large amounts of silver to the open market. France was the first to substitute gold for silver in 1852, followed closely by the Scandinavian countries. In 1871 Germany followed suit. Between 1872 and 1876, the price of silver on the open market fell by more than 20%. Most of the silver released in the West was absorbed in the Far East, particularly by the government of India which purchased over $1,300,000,000 worth between 1852 and 1875. As the price of silver continued its downward trend, India found itself in an increasingly difficult financial situation. Its only revenues were in silver, but goods purchased abroad had to be paid for in gold. In addition, India had floated a number of large loans in England. Both the loans and the services had to be paid in gold.

On June 1, 1893, the price of silver dropped to 83 cents an ounce on the open market. This meant that during the period following the end of the U.S. Civil War, the Indian rupee had depreciated approximately 39%; on June 26 the Indian government closed its mints to the free coinage of silver. See George Chesney, "The Depreciation of Silver and the Indian Finances," in Joshua T. Smith (ed.), *Silver and the Indian Exchanges;* Louis R. Ehrich, *The Question of Silver;* and W. Jett Lauck, *The Causes of the Panic of 1893.*

8 Henderson, *Mining in Colorado,* 93–95.

9 Jesse B. Grant, owner of the largest smelter in Colorado, quoted in the New York *Times,* January 8, 1894, 1/5. Another expert noted that "this region [Colorado] contains a greater assortment of metals . . . than almost any other in America." George D. Hubbard, "Gold and Silver Mining and Reduction Processes as Responses to Geographic Conditions," *Scottish Geographical Magazine,* August 1911.

10 U.S. Census Bureau. 11th Census, 1890. *Report on the Mineral Industries of the U.S.,* 59-60. The procedure followed by the Census Bureau stated that "in cases in which the mine as reported produces chiefly gold or silver, or both, the mine is taken as a precious metal mine, and its complete returns of labor, expenditures, evaluation etc., are taken as belonging *entirely to gold and silver.*"(emphasis added) Since all of the mines in Colorado, except coal, fell into this category, it is necessary to add the dollar value of the by-products to that of gold and silver in order to achieve a true picture of the cost of producing a dollar's worth of metal. In 1890, Colorado produced $5,489,507 worth of lead, copper, and zinc. This was added to the $27,641,610 worth of gold and silver reported by the U.S. Census Bureau to give the total figure for all metals of $33,131,117. For the industry as a whole, the U.S. Census Bureau reported the following additional statistics (ibid., 61):

Capital invested per dollar of bullion produced	$5.08
Amount of bullion produced per dollar of capital	.20
Value of bullion per dollar of expenses	2.00
Amount of expense per dollar of bullion	.50
Profit on total capital	9.84%

An idea of the importance of the by-products of gold and silver mining can be seen in the production statistics for the Leadville District from 1879 to 1892. During this period, the district produced $179,710,209 worth of metals of which $69,788,268, or more than 40%, represented by-products. Colorado, Bureau of Labor Statistics. *Fourth Biennial Report* (1894), 41–42. The New

York *Times,* January 13, 1893, carried an article which estimated the cost of producing an ounce of silver in Colorado at just over 30 cents, and in the five states and territories (including Colorado) which produced 4/5 of the U.S. total, at just over 40 cents.

11 Ibid. Even more profitable than the Mollie Gibson was the Granite Mountain Mine in Montana, which between 1881 and 1893 paid dividends of $12,120,000 on an original investment of $70,000. For the year ending July 1, 1886, the company produced silver which sold for $1,334,686 of which $940,000 was distributed in dividends and $127,319 was deposited in undivided profits. The cost to produce an ounce of silver was less than 12.5 cents. In the same year, the company increased the monthly rent in one of its boarding houses from $10.00 to $25.00, and in another from $30.00 to $75.00, using as its justification the fact that a fall in the price of silver from $1.06 to 91.5 cents an ounce had reduced profits to an unacceptable level. Ibid., January 30, 1893.

12 U.S. Census Bureau. 11th Census, 1890. *Report on the Mineral Industries of the U.S.,* 59-60.

13 Forest Lowell White, "The Panic of 1893 in Colorado" (M.A. thesis), 62–63. Wages in the Colorado mining industry in 1890 were as follows: foremen, mechanics, and laborers working above ground, $4.33, $3.80, and $2.91 a day respectively. For men in the same categories working underground, the figures were $4.22, $3.08, and $2.88 a day respectively. U.S. Census Bureau. 11th Census, 1890. *Report on the Mineral Industries of the U.S.,* 35. The dollar-a-day reduction in the Leadville District was particularly severe in view of the fact that during the summer the price of lead rose $10.00 to $12.00 a ton. New York *Times,* September 30, 1893, 1/4.

14 Ibid., July 24, 1893, 9/7. The Colorado miners and smelter men were the most highly paid in the mining industry taken as a whole. On the other hand, they were the most productive. The average annual earning was $729.00. Average annual productivity was $1,732.00. U.S. Census Bureau. 11th Census, 1890. *Report on the Mineral Industries of the U.S.,* 35. The smelters survived the closing of the mines without hardship, because they had approximately a three month's supply of ores at the time of the closing. When the mines reopened, they discontinued the old practice of paying the market price for ores which would be smelted 30 to 90 days later and went instead to a system whereby payment was made within 30 days at the market price then prevailing. New York *Times,* September 30, 1893, 1/4, and July 24, 1893, 9/7.

15 Creede was a good example of a camp that suffered. Silver

production which reached almost 4,900,000 ounces in 1893 dipped to 1,866,000 ounces in 1894. Nevertheless, production rose again to over 3,000,000 ounces in 1897 and over 4,000,000 ounces in 1898. Hafen's position, which is generally accepted, that the "Panic of 1893, the repeal of the Sherman Silver Purchase Act, and the precipitous fall in the price of silver combined . . ." to produce a disaster from which the camp never recovered simply does not fit the facts. Hafen, *Colorado and Its People,* 460.

16 U.S. Census Bureau. 11th Census, 1890. *Report on the Mineral Industries of the U.S.,* 35.

17 Henderson, *Mining in Colorado,* 93-95.

18 Letter from Peter to Will McFarlane, September 23, 1892. *McFarlane Papers.* "Walter" was Walter McLeod, bookkeeper for McFarlane & Company.

19 Letter from Will McFarlane to Ed Mayhew, Fulton, Colorado, December 19, 1892, and letter from Will McFarlane to Joseph Hanbrick, Prescott, Arizona, December 14, 1892. Ibid. The asking price for the Eureka Street foundry was $9,000, and that for the Black Hawk foundry $7,000. Mayhew was a millwright for the McFarlane company.

20 Letter from Will to Peter McFarlane, March 24, 1894, and letter from the Pelton Water Wheel Company to McFarlane & Company, April 30, 1894. Ibid.

21 Letter from Will to Peter McFarlane, April 28, 1894. Ibid.

22 Letter from Will to Peter McFarlane, April 24, 1894. Ibid.

23 Letter from Will to Peter McFarlane, May 5, 1894. Ibid.

24 Letter from Peter to Will McFarlane, September 2, 1894. Ibid. This company was owned by Louis R. O'Neill of Chicago.

25 Letter from Peter to Will McFarlane, March 27, 1894, and a bill for lumber for the Silver Creek Mill, April 25, 1894. Ibid.

26 Letter from California Milling and Mining Company to McFarlane & Company, March 30, 1894. Ibid.

27 Henderson, *Mining in Colorado,* 93-96.

28 Letter from Peter McFarlane to Adam Hazelwood, Oconomowas, Wisconsin, October 13, 1895. *McFarlane Papers.*

29 Arthur L. Pearse of London was the principal backer. The original contract was for $14,835, but the final bill for the mill was over $30,000. Letter from Peter McFarlane to W. C. Lawler, October 28, 1895, and copy of the Lawler Gold Mines Limited Account, May 26, 1896. Ibid.

30 The contract was for a rapid drop mill on Ute Creek for W. D. Cameron of Raton. Letter from Peter McFarlane to W. D. Cameron, November 10, 1895. Ibid.

31 Letter from Peter McFarlane to Edward Mayhew, November 25, 1895. Ibid.

32 Letter from Peter McFarlane to E. E. Hill, March 23, 1895. Ibid.

33 Letter from McFarlane & Company to E. E. Hill, December 5, 1898. Ibid.

34 Letter from Peter McFarlane to W. E. Renshaw, August 24, 1921. Ibid.

35 Letter from Peter McFarlane to L. J. Williams, Denver, January 13, 1925. Ibid.

36 Letter from Peter McFarlane to an unidentified friend in Denver, April 1, 1922. Ibid.

37 Letter from Walter McLeod to Will McFarlane, October 21, 1896. Ibid. McFarlane's daughter told me the story of the old prospector who, the day he heard of McFarlane's death, walked fifteen miles into Central City from his cabin; with tears streaming down his cheeks, he told her he wanted to pay his last respects to the man who had paid all his grocery bills for the past fifteen years. Author's interview with Mrs. R. R. Demeter, November 11, 1964.

38 *Cash Account Book, 1895-97.* Ibid.

39 Ibid.

40 Monthly tally of equipment sold in 1899. Ibid.

41 Letter from Peter McFarlane to Stroehle and Sons, Black Hawk, March 20, 1900. *McFarlane Papers.*

42 Letter from Peter McFarlane to J. D. Westover, September 8, 1899. Ibid.

43 His daughter recalled that her father took particular delight in his honorary title, as did one of Central City's famous characters, Irish Annie, who would never have won anybody's beauty prize. Whenever they met on the street, Annie would say, "Good day, Lord McFarlane." He would greet her with a sweeping bow worthy of a queen and say, "Annie, you're as pretty as you were twenty years ago." And Annie, with a regal curtsy, would reply, "Aw, go on, ya Irish pup." (She always thought McFarlane was of Irish descent.) Author's interview with Mrs. R. R. Demeter, March 15, 1964.

44 George D. Hubbard, "The Influence of Gold and Silver Mining on the Characters of Men," Geological Society of Philadelphia *Bulletin,* X (January 1892). McFarlane was constantly in the business of leasing claims in partnership with other men and working them in accordance with the system developed in Colorado. His *Cash Account Book* for 1895-97 shows that during this period he was working leases on the Enterprise, Ohio,

Missouri, and Compromise Lodes in Gilpin County, the Mona and Maple Leaf Lodes in Clear Creek County, and what was probably the largest venture of all, a lease on the Rialto Lode in Gilpin County in partnership with J. E. Lightbourne, a venture into which he poured $5,000 between June 1896, and May 1897, with apparently no return.

45 Hubbard, "Influence of Gold and Silver Mining on the Characters of Men," 37.

46 One of Peter McFarlane's daughter's favorite remembrances is how much her father's men enjoyed having him in the foundry when a heat of cast iron was being poured. They would gather around and as the molten metal flowed into the mold, Peter would pass a finger rapidly back and forth through the red hot stream without getting burned. Author's interview with Mrs. R. R. Demeter, March 15, 1964. Peter McFarlane often brought several of his cronies home for an appetizer of a dozen fresh oysters on the half shell before dinner. When I asked his daughter about the hogshead of live oysters he ordered once or twice a year, she related the following story. "Every February Daddy would send to Long Island for a hogshead of live oysters. Mother would put the oysters on the damp floor of the cellar and sprinkle them with cornmeal and salt and water. The oysters would live, eat the cornmeal, and actually grow fat. Daddy would bring four or five men home with him and they would sit in the cellar with oyster shucking knives and each eat about a dozen live oysters before dinner. Mother would have Daddy take the empty shell to the shop and grind them up for fertilizer for her flower beds." Author's interview with Mrs. R. R. Demeter, November 11, 1964. Lingering doubts about the truth of this story were dispelled by the following recipe dating to about 1787:

To Fatten Oysters

Mix one pint of salt with thirty pints of water. Put the oysters in a tub that will not leak, with their mouths upwards and feed them with the above, by dipping in a broom and frequently passing over their mouths. It is said that they will fatten still more by fine meal with the water.

[*American Heritage Cookbook and Illustrated History of American Eating and Drinking,* 469.)

47 Letter from Marie McFarlane to C. I. Hunn, March 10, 1900. *McFarlane Papers.*

48 Denver *Times,* January 11, 1900.

49 Letter from Peter McFarlane to D. R. C. Brown, May 25, 1902. *McFarlane Papers.* Brown was Peter's cousin.

50 Letter from Will to Peter McFarlane, February, 1899. Ibid.

51 Letter from Peter to Will McFarlane, March 1, 1899. Ibid.

52 Letter from Peter McFarlane to Stroehle and Sons, March 12, 1900, offering to sell for $20,000. Stroehle, however, could not raise the money. Letter from Peter to Will McFarlane, June 3, 1900. Ibid.

53 Letter from Peter to Will McFarlane, August 8, 1901. *McFarlane Papers.* This letter makes it clear that in 1901 the lots were still vacant. Mittick states that in 1898 McFarlane & Company built a group of buildings there. "Development of Mining Machinery Manufacture in Colorado." The land comprised twelve lots at Thirty-third and Blake Streets which the McFarlane brothers purchased for $10,000 in 1892. Letters from Will McFarlane to James R. Cowan, New York, February 2, 1892, and April 23, 1892. *McFarlane Papers.*

54 Letter from Peter to Will McFarlane, September 23, 1892. Ibid.

55 Letter from Peter to Will McFarlane, December 17, 1902, Ibid.

56 Letter from Peter to Will McFarlane, August 4 or 5, 1901. Ibid.

57 Letter from Peter to Will McFarlane, January 1, 1906. Ibid.

58 Letter from Peter to Will McFarlane, February 28, 1906. Ibid.

59 Letter from Peter to Will McFarlane, March 4, 1906. Ibid.

60 Original architects plans for the building on file in the archives of the Silver Engineering Company, Denver.

61 Letter from Peter McFarlane to Lyons Johnson, January 1, 1906, and letter from Peter to Will McFarlane, January 1, 1906. *McFarlane Papers.*

62 Letter from Peter McFarlane to Bartels Brothers, Denver, July 3, 1906. Ibid.

63 The name of the new company first appears in the correspondence on July 15, 1906, Peter McFarlane & Sons to the American Woodworking Manufacturing Company. Ibid.

64 Letter from Peter McFarlane to John Rassmussen, June 1, 1906. Ibid.

65 Letter from Peter McFarlane to Ren Manhire, Kendall, Montana, August 22, 1906. Ibid. McFarlane's spelling.

66 Letter from Peter McFarlane to H. M. Teller, September 25, 1906. Ibid.

Chapter VIII The "Little Kingdom's" Most Loyal Citizen

1 It is hard not to regret the destruction of the Tramway, as its retention would have made a magnificent scenic railway for the

thousand of tourists who later swarmed into Central City each summer.

2 Joseph Thatcher, president of the First National Bank in Denver.

3 Letter from Peter McFarlane to Philip Mixsell, Idaho Springs, Februaury 7, 1908. *McFarlane Papers.*

4 Letter from Peter McFarlane to Frank Augustus, Rollinsville, December 24, 1908. Ibid.

5 Letters from John M. Ross to Peter McFarlane, October 3, 1908, and November 18, 1911. Ibid.

6 Letter from Peter to Fred McFarlane, April 29, 1916. Ibid.

7 Copy of the agreement signed by Peter and Fred McFarland and Henry Eggers. Ibid.

8 Copy of the receipt signed by John Rassmussen. Ibid.

9 In the old days the Teller House bar was called "the Elevator."

10 Letter from Peter McFarlane to H. M. Teller, February 11, 1914. *McFarlane Papers.* Misspellings in original.

11 Letter from H. M. Teller to Peter McFarlane, February 13, 1914. *McFarlane Papers.* The original cost of the hotel including furnishings was $107,000. Bancroft, *Gulch of Gold,* 218

12 Letter from Peter McFarlane to the Denver Dry Goods Company, March 16, 1914. *McFarlane Papers.*

13 Letter from Peter McFarlane to D. W. Brunton, November 26, 1913. Ibid.

14 Letter from D. W. Brunton to Peter McFarlane, November 28, 1913. Ibid.

15 Letter from Peter McFarlane to the Scientific American Publishing Company, December 13, 1913, and letter from Peter McFarlane to the Ingersoll Rand Company, December 6, 1913. Ibid.

16 Letter from Peter McFarlane to L. L. Nunn, December 8, 1913, and letter from Peter McFarlane to D. R. C. Brown, December 14, 1913. Ibid.

17 Letter from Peter McFarlane to Benjamin Hilliard, January 1, 1915. Ibid.

18 Between 1913 and 1927 general construction costs rose approximately 95%. From this it is obvious that both McFarlane and the Moffat Tunnel Commissioners were badly off in their estimates. *The Statistical History of the United States from Colonial Times to the Present,* 193.

19 Letter from Peter McFarlane to *Motor Field Magazine,* April 29, 1912. In this letter Peter inquired about a speedometer for his buggy so he could accurately measure his travels. *McFarlane Papers.* Over a decade later McFarlane was still driving his buggy.

I talked with one man who grew up in Central City during the 1920s and remembered McFarlane well — how many of the town's children liked the delightful old man and how he himself sometimes got to drive McFarlane in the buggy. Author's interview, February 27, 1964.

20 Letter from Peter McFarlane to George Ashmore, September 21, 1913. Ibid.

21 Letters from Peter McFarlane to Mark A. Skinner, U.S. Internal Revenue Service, Denver, January 1, 1918, and March 14, 1919. Ibid.

22 Letter from Peter McFarlane to H. A. Hicks, Denver, March 31, 1918, and letter from Peter McFarlane to Mark A. Skinner, U.S. Internal Revenue Service, March 14, 1919. Ibid.

23 Copy of the bill of sale dated May 24, 1918. Ibid.

24 Letter from Peter McFarlane to John Ross, June 23, 1918. Ibid.

25 Letter from Peter McFarlane to John Ross, June 23, 1918. *McFarlane Papers.*

26 Letter from Peter McFarlane to D. R. C. Brown, June 23, 1918. Ibid.

27 Letter from Peter McFarlane to Henry Becker, June 23, 1918. Ibid.

28 Denver *Post,* December 29, 1918.

29 Letter from Charles Manhire to Peter McFarlane, June 8, 1926. *McFarlane Papers.*

30 Letter from Peter McFarlane to E. P. Perry, Torrington, Wyoming, March 1, 1920. Ibid.

31 Ibid.

32 Letter from Peter McFarlane to Henry Eggers, September 27, 1921. Ibid.

33 "George has had no pay day for nearly a year, and he is making life hard for me, and I must do something for his relief." Letter from Peter McFarlane to C. L. Gage, Chicago, December 19, 1921. Ibid.

34 Letter from Peter McFarlane to Henry Eggers, September 27, 1921. Ibid.

35 "Fred and Ida are making life sick for me. Money tied up and no hope of getting it back anywhere in sight, and I only to blame."Letter from Peter McFarlane to C. L. Gage, Chicago, March 13, 1922. Ibid.

36 Letter from Peter McFarlane to E. P. Perry, Torrington, Wyoming, May 14, 1922. Ibid.

37 Letter from Peter McFarlane to E. P. Perry, Torrington, March 1, 1920. Ibid.

38 Letter from Peter to Fred McFarlane, November 11, 1923. Ibid.
39 McFarlane was a large stockholder in the Gregory-Buell mine, along with Robert L. Martin of Denver and W. H. Davis of Philadelphia, by virtue of approximately $24,000 which the company owed him. This large unpaid bill, mostly for mill supplies, had accumulated over a number of years. In 1911 the Gregory-Buell Consolidated Mining Company was reorganized and at this time Peter was brought in as a trustee, and the money owed to him secured by stock in the company. Letters from Peter McFarlane to Robert L. Martin, November 11, 1909, and to John Ross, November 21, 1911. Ibid.
40 Letter from Peter McFarlane to George Bowdery, Gorham, Colorado, February 24, 1924. *McFarlane Papers.* McFarlane's memory failed him slightly on Tennyson; he mixed two stanzas from *Locksley Hall*:

> What is that which I should turn to,
>   lighting upon days like these?
> Every door is barred with gold,
>   and opens but to golden keys.
>
> Every gate is thronged with suitors,
>   all the markets overflow.
> I have but an angry fancy;
>   what is that which I should do?

41 Letter from Peter McFarlane to Hal Sayre, June 18, 1924. Ibid.
42 Letter from Peter McFarlane to Cliff Gilbert, Nederland, December 4, 1924. Ibid.
43 Letters from Peter McFarlane to William Knight, Denver, February 17, 1924; to Charles Cox, Gorham, Colorado, February 10, 1924; and to the A. S. & R. Company, Denver, August 24, 1924. Ibid.
44 Letter from Peter McFarlane to his daughter, Yetta McFarlane Schroeder, February 10, 1925. Ibid.

Chapter IX   The Central City Opera House

1 Figures for the cost of the Opera House vary. Since Peter McFarlane was one of the original contractors, the figure he consistently used is given here. Letter from Peter McFarlane to W. H. Osborn, Clarinda, Iowa, March 30, 1913. *McFarlane Papers.*
2 Lynn I. Perrigo, "A Social History of Central City, Colorado, 1859–1900" (Ph.D. dissertation), 552.

3 Bancroft, *Gulch of Gold,* 207, 302, 320.
4 These details of the early history of the Opera House are revealed in a letter from Peter McFarlane to H. M. Teller, November 16, 1902. *McFarlane Papers.*
5 Letters from Peter McFarlane to Horace M. Hale, February 2, 1896, and June 15, 1896. Ibid.
6 Letter from Peter McFarlane to H. M. Teller, November 16, 1902. Ibid.
7 Letters from Peter McFarlane to J. M. D. Livesay, Denver, November 20, 1898, and to Julius Marx, Denver, December 16, 1898. Ibid.
8 Letter from Peter McFarlane to Peter McCourt, Denver, September 2, 1900. Ibid.
9 Letter from Peter McFarlane to Horace M. Hale, Denver, April 24, 1901. Ibid.
10 Letter from Peter McFarlane to H. M. Teller, November 16, 1902. Ibid.
11 Letter from Peter McFarlane to F. H. Messenger, February 2, 1912. The price was $75.00. Ibid.
12 Letters from Peter McFarlane to John Trezise, Boulder, February 20, 1912, and to Dr. and Mrs. Harry Paul, Englewood, February 21, 1912. Ibid. Historians of Central City have generally confused the facts about McFarlane's ownership of the Opera House and its use, especially during the twentieth century. For instance, Bancroft concludes:

> The Opera House . . . was opened . . . in March , 1878. But it fell into financial straits only a few years later because of the general exodus of the 1880's. The theatre weathered along until World War I when it failed, even as a movie house. The building was closed and stood desolate until 1931 when it was restored. [*Gulch of Gold,* 240]

Donald C. Kemp is even less correct in his summary of the Opera House and its ownership:

> With the shutdown of mining, the doors were locked and the historic old building fell to ruin . . . Peter McFarlane acquired ownership in 1931, and after his death a short time later [McFarlane actually died in 1929] his heirs presented it to the University of Denver. [*Colorado's Little Kingdom,* 149]

See also Perrigo, "Social History of Central City," 603. Th remainder of this Chapter IX should clarify that McFarla acquired ownership of the Opera House at the turn of the centu and with the exception of a couple of years kept it active until N Year's Day 1927.

13 Letter from Peter McFarlane to H. M. Teller, November 16, 1902. *McFarlane Papers.*
14 Letters from Peter McFarlane to the Kansas City Scenery Company, January 1, March 8, September 16, and September 27, 1903. Letter from Peter McFarlane to the Grand Rapids School Furniture Works, Chicago, July 3, 1903. Ibid.
15 Letters from Peter McFarlane to the Kansas City Scenery Company, January 1, 1903, and March 8, 1903. Ibid.
16 Charles Bayly, Jr., "The Opera House at Central City," *Theatre Arts Monthly,* March 1932.
17 Letter from Peter McFarlane to H. M. Teller, November 16, 1902. *McFarlane Papers.*
18 Carl Wittke, *Tambo and Bones,* 145–46.
19 Letter from Peter McFarlane to Harry Sanger, March 30, 1906. *McFarlane Papers.*
20 Letter from Peter McFarlane to Peter McCourt, May 1, 1906. Ibid.
21 *Central City Opera House Account Book,* 1898–99.
22 Ibid.
23 Letter from Peter McFarlane to Peter McCourt, September 30, 1906. *McFarlane Papers.*
24 Letter from Peter McFarlane to Peter McCourt, October 29, 1906. Ibid.
25 Letter from Peter McFarlane to George H. Davis, Los Angeles, September 15, 1906. *McFarlane Papers.* Emphasis is McFarlane's.
26 Letter from Peter McFarlane to Frederick Holland, Denver, February 2, 1907. Ibid.
27 Letter from Peter McFarlane to Peter McCourt, May 27, 1908. Ibid.
28 Letter from Peter McFarlane to Peter McCourt, July 7, 1907. Ibid.
29 Letter from Peter McFarlane to H. A. Johnson, Denver, May 14, 1908. Ibid.
30 Letter from Peter McFarlane to H. Harding, Omaha, May 23, 1908. Ibid.
31 Letter from Peter McFarlane to L. A. Kempton, Denver, July 4, 1908. Ibid.
32 Letter from Peter McFarlane to H. A. Johnson, Denver, May 14, 1908. Ibid.
33 Letter from Peter McFarlane to Curran Brothers, Denver, April 10, 1910. Ibid.
34 Letter from Peter McFarlane to Peter McCourt, May 5, 1910. Ibid.

35 Letters from Peter McFarlane to the Chicago Film Exchange Company, May 12 and June 19, 1910. Ibid.

36 Letter from Peter McFarlane to the Kline Optical Company, Denver, July 4, 1910. Ibid.

37 Letter from Peter McFarlane to the Chicago Film Exchange Company, June 19 and July 4, 1910. Ibid.

38 Letter from Peter McFarlane to the Denver Film Company, July 11, 1910. Ibid.

39 Letter from Peter McFarlane to the W. H. Swanson Company, Denver, August 11, 1910. Ibid.

40 Letter from Peter McFarlane to the General Film Company, Denver, January 9, 1916. Ibid.

41 Letters from Peter McFarlane to the Mutual Film Exchange Company, Denver, July 13 and 16, 1916, and February 2 and March 29, 1917. Ibid.

42 Letter from Peter McFarlane to the Mutual Film Exchange Company, July 13, 1917. Ibid.

43 Letter from Peter McFarlane to the General Film Company, December 3, 1913. Ibid.

44 Letter from Peter McFarlane to the World Film Corporation, Denver, April 23, 1916. Ibid.

45 *Central City Opera House Account Book,* 1916.

46 Letter from Peter McFarlane to Walter Harrington, Scottsbluff, Nebraska, March 20, 1912. *McFarlane Papers.*

47 For this table the following figures were taken from McFarlane's *Opera House Account Book:* gross receipts for 1912-16, 1921-22, 1924-26; expenses for 1912-14. The following figures were taken from letters from Peter McFarlane to the U.S. Department of Internal Revenue, August 10, 1919, March 8, 1919, February 1, 1920, January 6, 1921 (date uncertain), January 17, 1924: gross receipts for 1917, 1918, 1919, 1920, 1923 respectively; November 10, 1917 and February 18, 1918: expenses for 1915 and 1917 respectively. *McFarlane Papers.*

48 *The Opera House Account Book,* 1912, 1913.

49 Letter from Peter McFarlane to the General Film Company, Denver, January 1, 1913. *McFarlane Papers.*

50 Letter from Peter McFarlane to L. A. Kempton, January 5, 1919. Ibid.

51 *The Opera House Account Book,* 1918, 1919.

52 *The Opera House Account Book,* 1927,

Chapter X   "Grown Gold"

1 Robert Service, "The Prospector," *Collected Poems,* 129.
2 Peter McFarlane, *Grown Gold,* 29-30. The idea that metals can grow organically dates from classical antiquity and was current among miners and prospectors in the South before the days of the western gold rushes. Abandoned mine tailings were believed to produce "grown gold" over long periods of time. See T. A. Rickard, *History of American Mining,* 261-62. McFarlane's contribution to this subject was, as we shall see in this chapter, a unique and quasi-scientific attempt to account for what many men believed to be an established fact.
3 McFarlane, *Grown Gold,* 9-11.
4 Ibid., 11.
5 Ibid., 13-14.
6 Ibid., 12.
7 Ibid., 12.
8 Letter to the author from M. H. Bergendahl, U.S. Geological Survey, Denver, December 13, 1966.
9 Bergendahl's explanation would, of course, account also for the "apparent enrichment" of old mine tailings.
10 Letter from Peter McFarlane to L. A. Higgins, New York City, November 20, 1920. *McFarlane Papers.*
11 McFarlane, *Grown Gold,* 22-25.
12 Ibid., 40. That he was familiar with the labor theory of value is evident from the following passage: "A few of us may endeavor to persuade ourselves that labor and not gold constitutes the nation's greatness . . . and it has to be admitted that it comes nearly the truth. But as matters are, all people, of every race and tongue, agree that gold is the *sine qua non* of all real importance . . . " Ibid., 34.
13 Ibid., 28.
14 Ibid., 47, 40. McFarlane also held that government ownership could just as well be extended to lead, tungsten, copper, and zinc mining. This, however, appeared to be more of an afterthought than a serious proposal.
15 It was because of his belief that it was important to conserve a diminishing supply of gold that McFarlane, in retrospect, condemned the resumption of specie payments in 1872. Ibid., 33.
16 Letter from Peter McFarlane to Bela S. Buell, January 27, 1904. *McFarlane Papers.*
17 McFarlane, *Grown Gold,* 39.
18 Ibid.

19 Letter from Peter McFarlane to M. A. Dunbar, Jamestown, Colorado, August 24, 1919. *McFarlane Papers.*
20 McFarlane, *Grown Gold,* 26. McFarlane's word "giant" refers to dynamite, which Gilpin County miners called giant powder.
21 Letter from Peter McFarlane to Ray Clark, U.S. Forest Service, Boulder, August 14, 1919. *McFarlane Papers.* McFarlane had apparently been interested in this project for quite some time and had been active in organizing local support. In an earlier letter to Clark he said: "Since Mr. Agee and yourself were here I saw and talked with Mr. Seymour, Mr. Patterson, Mr. Caldwell, Mr. J. C. Jenkins, [and] Mr. George Fitz in regard to the matter we had under consideration. These men were all enthusiastic and willing to do whatever they could." Letter from Peter McFarlane to Ray Clark, April 27, 1917. Ibid.
22 Letter from Peter McFarlane to Ray Clark, August 27, 1919. Ibid.
23 Letters from Peter McFarlane to District Forest, U.S. Forest Service, Denver, February 27 and March 30, 1920. Ibid.
24 Letter from Peter McFarlane to Mr. Carhardt, U.S. Forest Service, Denver, June 23, 1920. Ibid.
25 Letter from Peter McFarlane to H. W. Wheeler, Fort Collins, November 14, 1920. Ibid. This letter is the last in the *McFarlane Papers* on the subject of the Cold Spring camp ground. Presumably, the construction was carried out as agreed, and no further correspondence was necessary.

Appendix B   McFarlane's Sunday Diary Entries

1 Peter's brother George McFarlane on Prince Edward Isalnd.
2 Rev. B. T. Vincent, St. James Methodist Church.
3 Peter's brother James McFarlane on Prince Edward Island.
4 Peter's cousin James Barclay.
5 See Chapter I, note 15.
6 George Currier of Central City.
7 Captain Thomas Bates.
8 A McFarlane & Company employee who came to the house quite often for an evening of fiddle playing with Peter.
9 Rev. S. F. Dickinson, Congregational clergyman of Central City. Cf. Chapter IV, note 71.
10 See Chapter III, note 30.
11 Peter's sister Kate McFarlane on Prince Edward Island.
12 Ben Wisebart's O.K. store in Central City.
13 Rev. W. D. Chase, St. James Methodist Church. Cf. Chapter IV, note 71.

Peter McFarlane's dedication page for his booklet *Grown Gold.*

Bibliography

Primary Sources

The McFarlane Papers. This collection consists of:

Peter McFarlane's *Diary* covering the years 1870-71.

Letterpress copies of the private and business correspondence of Peter and William McFarlane, August 8, 1890-July 19, 1925. 16 vols.

A collection of incoming correspondence, 1885-1920. Approximately three linear feet of documents.

The Central City Opera House Account Book, September 13, 1896-January 1, 1927.

A small collection of mine deeds and business contracts.

The Gilpin County Deed Record Books and Tax Record Books. Gilpin County Courthouse, Central City, Colorado.

COLORADO NEWSPAPERS:

Central City *Daily Register,* July 30, 1868-June 15, 1878.
Central City *Daily Register-Call,* May 27, 1878-November 3, 1890.
Central City *Weekly Register,* July 30, 1868-June 15, 1878.
Central City *Weekly Register-Call,* November 3, 1890, to date.
Denver *Rocky Mountain News,* August 27, 1860, to date.

Secondary Sources

DIRECTORIES:

The Colorado Business Directory. Denver: J. A. Blake, 1875.
The Colorado Business Directory. Denver: J. A. Blake, 1876.
Rocky Mountain Directory and Colorado Gazetteer for 1871. Denver: S. S. Wallihan and Co., 1871.

BOOKS:

American Heritage Cookbook and Illustrated History of American Eating and Drinking. 2 vols. New York: American Heritage Publ. Co., 1964.
Baker, James H., and LeRoy R. Hafen. *History of Colorado.* Denver: Linderman Co., 1927.
Bancroft, Caroline. *Gulch of Gold: A History of Central City, Colorado.* Denver: Swallow Press, 1958.
Bastin, Edson S., and James W. Hill. *Economic Geology of Gilpin County and Parts of Clear Creek and Boulder Counties.* U.S. Geological Survey, Professional Paper No. 94. Washington: U.S. Government Printing Office, 1917.
Bollinger, Edward T., and Frederick Bauer. *The Moffat Road.* 2nd edition. Chicago: Swallow Press, 1967.
Brown, T. Allston. *History of the American Stage.* New York: Dick & Fitzgerald, 1870.
Bruyn, Kathleen. *Aunt Clara Brown.* Boulder: Pruett Publ. Co., 1970.
Central City Opera House Association. *The Glory That Was Gold.* 3rd edition. Denver: 1936.
Cherrington, Ernest Hurst. ·*The Standard Encyclopedia of the Alcohol Problem.* Westerville, Ohio: American Issue Publ. Co., 1926.
Cotton, W. L. *Chapters in Our Island History.* Charlottetown, Prince Edward Island: Irwin Printing Co., Ltd., 1927.
Cushman, Samuel, and J. P. Waterman. *The Gold Mines of Gilpin County.* Central City, Colorado: Register Steam Printing House, 1876.
Davis, Carlyle Channing. *Olden Times in Colorado.* Los Angeles: The Phillips Publ. Co., 1916.
Ehrich, Louis R. *The Question of Silver.* New York: G. P. Putnam's Sons, 1896.
Ellis, Elmer. *Henry Moore Teller, Defender of the West.* Caldwell, Idaho: Caxton Printers, Ltd., 1941.
Ferguson, Charles D. *A Third of a Century in the Gold Fields.* Cleveland: Williams Publ. Co., 1888.
Fossett, Frank. *Colorado: A Statistical Work on the Rocky Mountain Gold and Silver Mining Region.* Denver: Daily Tribune Steam Printing House, 1876.
————. *Colorado, Its Gold and Silver Mines, Farms and Stock Ranges, and Health and Pleasure Resorts.* New York: C. G. Crawford, 1879.
————. *Colorado, Its Gold and Silver Mines.* New York: C. G. Crawford, 1880.
Hafen, LeRoy R. (ed.). *Colorado and Its People: A Narrative and Topic History*

of the Centennial State. 4 vols. New York: Lewis Historical Publ. Co., 1948.

Hall, Frank. *History of the State of Colorado.* 4 vols. Chicago: Blakely Printing Co., 1889-1895.

Henderson, Charles W. *Mining in Colorado: A History of Discovery, Development, and Production.* U.S. Geological Survey, Professional Paper No. 138. Washington: Government Printing Office, 1926.

Hollenback, Frank R. *Central City and Black Hawk, Colorado, Then and Now.* Denver: Swallow Press, 1961.

Hollister, Ovando J. *The Mines of Colorado.* Springfield, Massachusetts: Samuel Bowles and Co., 1867.

Ingersoll, Robert. *The Ghosts and Other Lectures.* Washington, D.C., 1879.
————. *The Gods and Other Lectures.* Peoria, Illinois, 1874.

Kemp, Donald C. *Colorado's Little Kingdom.* Denver: Swallow Press, 1949.

Kanpp, Martin Wells. *Revival Kindlings.* Albion, Michigan: The Revivalist Publ. Co., 1890.

Lauck, W. Jett. *The Causes of the Panic of 1893.* Boston: Houghton Mifflin, 1907.

Lee, Mabel Barbee. *Cripple Creek Days.* Garden City: Doubleday, 1958.

MacKinnon, John. *A Sketch Book Comprising Historical Incidents, Traditional Tales, and Translations.* St. John, New Brunswick: Barnes and Co., Ltd., 1915.

MacNeil, Neil. *The Highland Heart in Nova Scotia.* Toronto: S. J. R. Saunders, 1958.

McFarlane, Peter. *Grown Gold.* Central City, Colorado: Privately published, 1921.

McMechen, Edgar C. *The Moffat Tunnel of Colorado: An Epic of Empire.* 2 vols. Denver: Wahlgreen Publ. Co., 1927.

Millikin, Virginia Greene, *et al. The Bible and the Gold Rush.* Denver: Big Mountain Press, 1962.

Paul, Rodman W. *Mining Frontiers of the Far West.* New York: Holt, Rinehart and Winston, 1963.

Raymond, Rossiter W. *Mining Statistics West of the Rocky Mountains.* U.S. 42nd Congress, 1st Session, House Executive Document No. 10, Serial No. 1470. Washington: Government Printing Office, 1871.
————. *Statistics of Mines and Mining in the States and Territories West of the Rocky Mountains.* U.S. 41st Congress. 2nd and 3rd Sessions, House Executive Document No. 207, Serial No. 1424. Washington: Government Printing Office, 1870. 43rd Congress, 2nd Session, House Executive Document No. 177. Washington: Government Printing Office, 1875.

Richardson, Albert D. *Beyond the Mississippi: From the Great River to the Great Ocean.* Hartford: American Publ. Co., 1867.

Royce, Josiah. *California.* Boston: Houghton Mifflin, 1886.

Rickard, T. A. *History of American Mining.* New York: McGraw-Hill, 1932.

Schoberlin, Melvin. *From Candles to Footlights: A Biography of the Pike's Peak Theatre, 1859-1876.* Denver: Old West Publ. Co., 1941.

Smith, Joshua T. (ed.) *Silver and the Indian Exchanges.* London: E. Wilson, 1879.

The Statistical History of the United States from Colonial Times to the Present.
     Stamford, Connecticut: Fairfield Publishers, 1965.
Stone, Wilbur Fiske (ed.). *History of Colorado.* 4 vols. Chicago: S. J. Clarke
     Publ. Co., 1918-1919.
Sweet, William Warren. *Revivalism in America.* New York: Scribners, 1945.
Taylor, Bayard. *Colorado: A Summer Trip.* New York: G. P. Putnam and Son,
     1867.
Thayer, William M. *Marvels of the New West.* Norwich, Connecticut: Henry
     Bill Publ. Co., 1892.
U.S. Census Bureau. *Statistics of the Population of the United States.* Ninth
     Census, Vol. I, 1872.
Villard, Henry. *The Past and Present of the Pike's Peak Gold Regions.* Edited by
     LeRoy R. Hafen. Princeton: Princeton Univ. Press, 1932.
Warburton, A. B. *A History of Prince Edward Island from Its Discovery in 1534
     until the Departure of Lieutenant-Governor Reavy in A.D. 1831.* St. John,
     New Brunswick: N. B. Barnes and Co., 1923.
Willison, George F. *Here They Dug the Gold.* London: Eyre and Spottiswoode,
     1950.
Withrow, Chase. *The Charter and Ordinances of the City of Central, Colorado.*
     Central City, Colorado: Register Call Printing Office, 1904.
Wittke, Carl F. *Tambo and Bones.* Durham: Duke Univ. Press, 1930.
Young, Frank R. *Echoes from Arcadia.* Denver: Privately published, 1903.
Zincke, F. Barham. *Last Winter in the United States.* London: J. Murray, 1886.

ARTICLES:

Bayly, Charles, Jr. "The Opera House at Central City." *Theatre Arts Monthly*
     (March 1932).
Blake, William P. "The Mechanical Appliances of Mining." U.S. 41st Congress,
     2nd Session, House Executive Document No. 207, Part IV, 471-724.
     Washington: Government Printing Office, 1870.
Burpee, Lawrence J. "Prince Edward Island." *Canadian Geographical Journal,*
     XXXIII (November, 1946), 192-214.
Burrell, James. "History of Gilpin County" and "Gilpin County Biographies."
     The History of Clear Creek and Boulder Valleys, Colorado. Chicago: O. L.
     Baskin and Company, 1880.
Hanington, C. H. "Early Days of Central City and Black Hawk." *Colorado
     Magazine,* XIX (January, 1942), 3-14.
Hubbard, George D. "Gold and Silver Mining and Reduction Processes as
     Responses to Geographic Conditions." *Scottish Geographical Magazine*
     (August 1911).
————. "The Influence of Gold and Silver Mining on the Characters of Men."
     Geological Society of Philadelphia *Bulletin,* X (January 1892).
Johnson, Hiram A. "A Letter from a Colorado Mining Camp." *Colorado
     Magazine,* VII (January 1930), 194.
Munroe, H. S. "On the Weight, Fall, and Speed of Stamps." American Institute
     of Mining Engineers *Transactions,* IX (1881-82), 84-89.

Pope, A. M. "The Catholic Scotch Settlement of Prince Edward Island." *The Catholic World* (July 1882).

Raymond, Rossiter W. "A Glossary of Mining and Metallurgical Terms." American Institute of Mining Engineers *Transactions,* IX (1880-81), 99-192.

_____ . "On the Relation between the Speed and Effectiveness of Stamps." American Institute of Mining Engineers *Transactions,* I (1871-73), 40-54.

Reichenecker, Albert. "The Treatment of Aufiferous Ores in Colorado." U.S. 42nd Congress, 1st Session, House Executive Document No. 10. Washington: Government Printing Office, 1871.

Rickard, T. A. "The Limitations of the Gold Stamp Mill." American Institute of Mining Engineers *Transactions,* XXIII (1893), 137-147.

Rogers, Andrews N. "The Mines and Mills of Gilpin County, Colorado." American Institute of Mining Engineers *Transactions,* XI (1882-83), 29-49.

Stetefeldt, C.A. "Russell's Improved Process for the Lixiviation of Silver Ores." American Institute of Mining Engineers *Transactions,* XIII (1883-84), 115.

Sweet, William Warren. "The Frontier in American Christianity." *Environmental Factors in Christian History.* Edited by John Thomas McNeill, *et al.* Chicago: Univ. of Chicago Press, 1939.

UNPUBLISHED MATERIALS:

Fuller, Leon Webber. "The Populist Regime in Colorado." Ph.D. dissertation, Univ. of Wisconsin, 1933.

Mittick, Ellsworth C. "The Development of Mining Machinery Manufacture in Colorado." Master's thesis, Univ. of Denver, 1947.

Perrigo, Lynn I. "A Social History of Central City, Colorado, 1859-1900." Ph.D. dissertation, Univ. of Colorado, 1936.

Sanford, A. B. "Interview with Peter McFarlane." Colorado State Historical Society. MSS. XV-14e.

White, Forest Lowell. "The Panic of 1893 in Colorado." Master's thesis, Univ. of Colorado, 1932.

George McFarlane.

Yetta McFarlane Demeter
and Frederick McFarlane.

Acknowledgments

I am greatly indebted to Mrs. R. R. Demeter of Denver without whose help this biography could not have been written. In 1963 Mrs. Demeter gave me the extensive personal and business papers of her father, Peter B. McFarlane, a collection amounting to over 10,300 pages, including diaries covering his first two years in Central City. She graciously consented to interviews and went out of her way to arrange numerous visits to the McFarlane Foundry in Central City. Finally, I was privileged on many occasions to be a guest in her father's house on Eureka Street, a lovely victorian style home which at one time housed the carpenter shop run by Peter and William McFarlane and which now is the center of social activities during the annual Central City Opera and Drama Festival.

I also wish to thank the staff of the Western History Department of the Denver Public Library for its cooperation in making available the early Central City newspapers.

H. W. A.

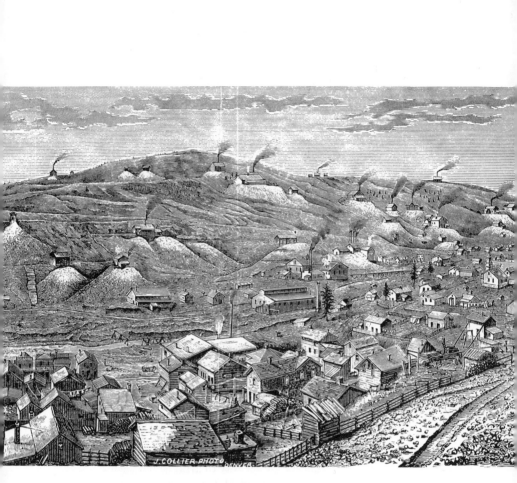

Nevadaville, 1870s. *From Fossett (1879).*

Index